A Witch in the Family

An Award-Winning Author Investigates
His Ancestor's Trial and Execution

D0913596

Also by the Author

In My Father's House
(a prizewinning metaphysical thriller)

The Color of Demons
(a metaphysical thriller written
with David Nathan Martin)

Death in Advertising
(a prizewinning whodunit)

*Keys to the Kingdom
and the Life You Want*
(an explanation of how and why life
works and how it can work for you)

A Witch in the Family

An Award-Winning Author Investigates
His Ancestor's Trial and Execution

by

Stephen Hawley Martin

RICHMOND, VIRGINIA

ISBN 1-892538-44-X

If your bookseller does not have this book in stock,
it can be ordered directly from the publisher.
Contact us for information about discounts
on quantity purchases.

The Oaklea Press
6912 Three Chopt Road, Suite B
Richmond, Virginia 23226

Voice: 1-800-295-4066
Facsimile: 1-804-281-5686
Email: Info@OakleaPress.com

This book can be purchased online at
http://www.OakleaPress.com

Dedication

For Evelyn Stadelman Martin.
Thanks, Mom. Here's the book.

CONTENTS

Author's Note

Often, I have quoted directly from seventeenth century texts and documents in order to illustrate or to make points. At the time they were written, no standard way existed to spell particular words or to determine what should be capitalized and what should not. Also, the actual words employed in the documents often are infrequently used nowadays and some may even have had different meanings or connotations than they do today. To aid the reader, in the majority of cases I have modernized spelling and changed capitalization to fit today's standards. In some cases where I thought the meaning an author had intended to convey was unclear, I have updated the language itself. In a few cases I have left direct quotes in their original form because I felt they would have more impact than if translated into modern English. For those who wish to read a particular text in its original form, some of the documents referred to can be found in the appendix of this book. Others may be found online. A University of Virginia web site houses a complete set of Salem witchcraft documents including all the examination and trial transcripts.[1]

---

[1] http://etext.virginia.edu/ salem/witchcraft/texts/

Let Goody Martin rest in peace, I never
knew her harm a fly,
And witch or not—God knows—not I?
I know who swore her life away;
And as God lives, I'd not condemn
An Indian dog on word of them.

—John Greenleaf Whittier (1807-1892)

Chapter One: Witches Then and Now

Nobody broke the news to me—gently or otherwise—and I didn't find out by delving into family genealogy. As far back as I can remember, I've known I was descended from a witch—or rather, I was descended from a woman who was hanged as one. When I probe my memory, the first family discussion I recall on the subject had to do with the correct form of the past tense of the verb "to hang."

"Pictures are hung," my mother told me. "People are hanged."

My father died when I was young, and the only other male in the immediate family, my brother, went away to college when I was four. The result was my mother, grandmother, and five-years-older sister raised me. Surrounded by three of the feminine persuasion and hearing often about my seven-times-great grandmother who ran a farm by herself and was able to do things women weren't supposed to be able to do—and was hanged as a witch for it—it's no wonder I came to be what you might call an early feminist, believing a woman could do anything a man could do.

In recent years I've wondered if my ancestor really was a witch. Having studied transcriptions of as many original documents from the time of the New England witch hysteria as I could get my hands on, I'm almost certain at least some of the accused were practicing magic, or "witchcraft" as it then was called. I'll hold off until later to give an opinion about my ancestor's guilt or lack of it but will say my mother was convinced she was innocent. It was generally accepted in the Martin household that the words on her memorial in Amesbury, Massachusetts were true. She was, "An honest, hardworking, Christian woman. Accused as a witch, tried and executed at Salem, July 19, 1692. A martyr of superstition."

Perhaps as a result, my parents were what you might call staunchly anti Christian-fundamentalists.

Let me revise that statement. My mother was, which is perhaps a little strange since it was my father's side that had the witch in it. Now that I think about it, I'm not sure what my father felt because I was so young when he passed away. His two brothers were Methodist ministers, and I recall now my mother saying he'd wanted to be one, too, but she'd talked him out of it. She'd said she simply couldn't be a minister's wife. Maybe it had to do with her husband's six-times-great grandmother having been hanged as a witch. Or maybe it was something more than that. As an outward display of contempt for what she considered a narrow-minded and dangerously-superstitious world view, she insisted on naming my older sister "Susannah North Martin" after the family martyr, which makes me wonder now if the connection between my mother, whose name was Evelyn, and the first Susannah Martin wasn't somehow closer than it would appear at first glance.

Whatever the case may be, nowadays you'd think most people wouldn't care one way or the other if you had someone in the family who was tried, convicted, and executed more than 300 years ago for what was then the felony of witchcraft. It's probably true most wouldn't. But one time, when it came out in conversation I was descended from one of the Salem Witches, the mother of a girl I was dating gave me the strangest look. It turned out she was a staunchly Christian lady—what my mother would have called, with a hint of scorn in her voice, a

"Bible thumper." Even in this modern age, this woman believed witches were real, evil, and to be feared and shunned.

I guess she never watched *Bewitched.*

Caution: This Book May Challenge Your Beliefs

What happened in New England long ago was tragic and horrific, which is why I suppose it still fascinates so many of us today. At the very least, it makes us think and wonder. And if someone you are directly descended from was caught up in it and actually killed by it—well, you might say having a witch in the family makes you look at things differently than you otherwise might. For one thing, you don't automatically assume people in authority know what they're talking about. In my own case, I almost always submit to an internal compass what is said by Church leaders, people in positions of authority in government or science, or in practically any discipline for that matter. My tendency is hold off on accepting what they say is true until some evidence or pattern causes it to click into place in my gut. Even when things do resonate with truth, I remain open to the possibility that I, or they, might be wrong, or that whatever I had accepted as being one way might in light of new evidence be subject to revision, however slight. The result of this inherent skepticism is that I've been forced to change my world view many times over the years. This holds even for my mother's assumptions concerning the witch trials in New England, and our ancestor's guilt or lack of it.

Let's talk about belief systems. To me, you might compare one to stack of cans like you might see in a grocery store, containing peas or soup, that forms a pyramid. Each can represents an individual belief. All are in place and fit together to form a world view that makes sense because everything belongs where it is and holds the other cans in place.

What happens if hard evidence turns up that refutes one of the beliefs, especially one of the key supports near the bottom? Suppose if you remove or change that can, the whole stack will come tumbling down?

If you're honest with yourself, that can of peas will have to go, even though you may be left with a helluva mess. If your are a seeker of truth, you will be compelled to remove an erroneous belief even though your pyramid of cans will have to be reconstructed from the ground up.

The Case of the Great Sphinx at Giza

Let me give you an example of the reaction of a scientific community to new information which if accepted would have upset long and dearly-held theories. For many years the body of the Great Sphinx at Giza, Egypt, was covered with sand. The reason was that it is lower than the surrounding area. No one disputes that in its natural state the part of the Sphinx that's now the head was an outcropping of rock sticking out of the ground. The Egyptians, or perhaps some other ancient people, as we will see, thought this rock could be carved into the head of an animal or a king, and they did so. At some point, maybe at the same time, the rest of the rock was uncovered and carved into a body to go with it. Over the years sand storms covered it up again. But today the sand has been cleared away and the body is exposed.

Not long ago, a geologist happened to notice that the body of the Sphinx appears to have been badly worn by water. The rock is clearly eroded, and small gullies can be seen all over it. Other geologists were consulted. The type of rock the Sphinx is made of was compared with the same type of rock that indeed had been worn away by water. Sure enough, without doubt the Sphinx's body has suffered water erosion.

How could this be? As we all know the Sphinx is located in the middle of a desert where it almost never rains. According to textbooks, Egyptologists, and tradition, the head of the Sphinx is a sculpture of King Khafre of Egypt who lived about 4500 years ago. During his rein was when the Sphinx is supposed to have been carved. Yet meteorologists who study ancient weather patterns say the climate of Giza was pretty much the same 4500 years ago as it is today. For there to have been enough rain to cause the type of erosion in evidence, the Sphinx would have to have been in existence for more than twice that long. Way back then—9,000 to 14,000 years ago—the weather of the area would have been similar to the African savanna with a season when rain poured down for several months each year. This would easily have caused the erosion.

When I learned this, my reaction was that the Sphinx must be a heckuva lot older than anyone previously thought. Some sort of civilization must have existed before the Egyptians, or at least a group of people smart and industrious enough to have carved the outcropping into a head, clear away and expose the base, and carve it into the body of the animal. Indeed, such a theory has been put forth. Close examination of the head reveals the current sculpture that resembles King Khafre may have been reworked from an earlier one that depicted an animal's head. It doesn't take a great deal of imagination to picture an ancient civilization of hunter gatherer people on the savanna digging out the outcropping and carving it into the shape of a lion, for example. Humans have had the mental ability to do this sort of thing for at least as long as the cave paintings have existed in France and Spain, and that's 30,000 or 40,000 years. It isn't hard to imagine the Egyptians coming along later and adapting an already ancient monolith for their own purposes.

What do you suppose was the reaction of the scientific community of Egyptologists to all of this?

Why, naturally, it was to reject it out of hand.

No kidding.

They have refused to listen—have totally rejected the whole idea. They have too much invested in the belief that Egyptians created the Sphinx. To admit the possibility of anything else would be to jeopardize Egypt's claim to be the first true civilization on earth. These scientists are simply not going to let something like water erosion on the body of the Sphinx cause them to rethink and let go of positions they hold dear. Accepting the erosion even exists would mean theories they hold about how the Sphinx came to be would have to be revised. For most of them a matter of pride may be as stake since the majority are Egyptians themselves and feel good about their ancestors having produced the first civilization. And for some it may be a matter of religious faith. As followers of Islam they trace their lineage back through Abraham all the way to Adam and Eve. If one calculates how long humans have been around based on the number of generations listed in the Bible, the figure is approximately 4500 to 5000 years. No way the Sphinx could be older than that, right?

My objective in telling you this story is to put you on notice. Be prepared. This book contains information that may cause it to be necessary to reconstruct your world view. If this turns out to be the case, the best way for you to react is to be glad. You will be in closer touch with reality, even though your new world view may be out of sync with that held by many living now, in the early part of the twenty-first century.

Witchcraft in the Seventeenth Century

Let's take a look at New England in the late seventeenth century. It's not an exaggeration to say that in 1692 mass hysteria and rampant paranoia swept the New England countryside. People in the small village of Salem, and indeed across the whole of Essex County Massachusetts, were being accused of casting spells, of consorting with the devil, of being witches. This persecution was a relatively rare phenomenon in America. But there was nothing at all new about it in western civilization. Throughout France, Italy, Germany, and England, witch hunts had been going on and commonplace for 300 years. Some think millions may have been executed, but most historians now dispute this. According to reliable sources, from the fourteenth through the sixteenth centuries, an estimated 40,000 to 50,000 people were executed. Many, like Joan of Arc, were burned at the stake.

Witches Were Condemned by the Bible

In those days, people believed what was written in the Bible was literally the word of God. This isn't hard to believe since plenty of Christians still do today, particularly members of evangelical churches. They call themselves "Bible inerrantists" and say they believe what the Bible contains is literally the word of God put down on papyrus or on clay tablets by Moses, the prophets, the disciples and others who were selected by God for the task. They hold that what is written is inviable, infallible, and that we are to live by it on a daily basis.

Where does it say witches should be put to death?

The Ten Commandments are given in Chapter Twenty of the Book of Exodus, and are followed by a host of smaller commandments and the punishments to be meted out for breaking them. If someone steals an ox, for example, and slaughters it or sells it, and that person gets caught, he must pay back five head of cattle to settle the score. Stealing a sheep, on the other hand, only requires the pay back of four sheep. If a man seduces and sleeps with a virgin who is not betrothed, he must pay the bride-price, presumably to her father, and marry her anyway. And on it goes. Exodus 22:18 says, "Thou shalt not suffer a witch to live." That's the King James translation, which is what our New England forefathers would have been familiar with. A more recent translation, the New International Version puts it this way: "Do not allow a sorceress to live." Either way, it's pretty clear what's to be done with people who conjure up spells and work magic. They are to be put to death, no doubt because they called on spirits other than Yahweh, the Old Testament God of the Jews. As you may recall from Sunday School, the Old Testament God is a jealous God and it was a big no-no to cavort with or worship others. "You shall have no other gods before me" tops the list of the Ten Commandments.

Despite this biblical condemnation, however, the record shows that early Christians were relatively tolerant of paganism and sorcery. The apostle, Paul, who was arguably the most prolific of the early Christian evangelists, spent the majority of his ministry converting as many gentiles as possible. Gentiles were pagans, and what in the seventeenth century would have been labeled "witchcraft" was rampant among them. Paul was a smart guy and realized that putting these heathens to death would not win friends or influence people in a positive way. As a result, he took a "when in Rome do as the Romans" approach and even persuaded other Church leaders of the time, including the top guy, Peter, that gentiles who wished to become Christians should not be required to follow Jewish dietary laws or be circumcised. This became Church canon in spite of Old Testament laws and commandments spelling out what was permissible and what wasn't. So you might say the new followers of "the way," as Christianity then was called, were selective about which commandments—after the big ten—they followed. They even ditched one altogether—remembering the Sabbath and keeping it holy. As God had rested on the seventh day, Saturday, so were the Jews to rest. Christians moved their day of worship to the first day of the week—Sunday. But that was in the days the Church was reaching out for new followers. Some historians say that as the Roman Catholic Church began to consolidate its power—once it became the official state religion of the Roman Empire and, later, of other countries such as Spain and France, heretics were looked upon as enemies. By 1231 Pope Gregory IX instituted the Inquisition in order to expose and punish heresy, and from that point forward the practice of magic and sorcery was dangerous business. After all, what it boiled down to was a religion in competition with Christianity, and a threat to the authority of the Church and its leaders.

In 1484, Pope Innocent VIII declared witchcraft a heresy, the punishment for which was death. Witch hunts often were conducted by superstitious villagers. Some historians think when animosities and tensions arose among people, a witch hunt was a way to get rid of real or imagined enemies. The authorities rarely did anything to stop them. Many people probably did believe their neighbors to be sorcerers and were afraid of them. And I'm willing to bet many actually were practicing magic. After all, some in our modern, twenty-first century world claim to be witches. Why wouldn't witches have existed then?

Witchcraft Today

In Chesterfield County Virginia, which borders on the city where I live, county meetings are opened with a prayer. Apparently the ACLU hasn't learned of this. Anyhow, the honor of giving the invocation is rotated among Christian and Jewish clergy. A resident of Chesterfield, Cyndi Simpson, is a Wiccan priestess, also known as a witch, affiliated with the Unitarian Universalist Association of Congregations—a church that, according to its web site, does not require its members to subscribe to any particular creed. Cyndi asked the Chesterfield County Board of Supervisors to add her name to the list of ministers, rabbis, and priests who give invocations at the meetings. Her hope, she said, was to give a generalized invocation "to the creator of the universe" in order to help rid the community of misconceptions about witches and Wiccans. You see, in Virginia, and probably in many other backward areas, Wicca and other neopagan religions are often associated with Satanism. According to Cyndi this is wrong. She is quoted in the local newspaper as saying, "I wasn't going to talk about the Goddess. I was going to call the elements, maybe offer up an invocation to the highest being— something that would be non secular. But they didn't want any of that. One of the board supervisors called Wicca a mockery."

Cyndi took her case to court and lost.

So, according to Cyndi Simpson and other Wiccans, modern witches are not, for the most part, devil worshipers. "Satanists" are. The web site of the Church of Satan says that the organization has about 10,000 members in the United States today.

But Cyndi says that organization is not to be confused with Wicca and witchcraft, which according a Wicca web site is "a pantheistic religion that incorporates spirituality, divinity and nature." Wicca, it says, is a peaceful, harmonious and balanced way of thinking and life that promotes oneness with the Divine and all that exists. Because most modern witches, it says, believe every living thing springs from and has the Divine at its core, Wiccans do not believe in working evil spells, adding that most believe in the Wiccan Rede, which states, "An [sic] it harm none, do what you will." This web site goes on to explain the threefold rule: that anything a person does, any energy she sends out will come back to her, magnified. Do good and good will return to you. Do evil and evil will come back. Or, as the Apostle Paul wrote, "A man reaps what he sows."[2] On this, Christianity and most religions of the world agree.

Guarding Against Fallacious Witchcraft Accusations

Actually, perhaps Virginia is not so backward. In the

---

[2] Galatians 6:7, NIV translation

middle of the seventeenth century a law was passed in what is now the Old Dominion to prevent people from arbitrarily charging others with witchcraft. Anyone who accused someone and could not produce substantial proof could be fined the amount of fifteen hundred pounds of tobacco.[3] That's the equivalent of a full year's production for a small planter.

But no such law existed in New England, and a number of folks in Salem Village sowed some pretty nasty stuff. It appears at least one individual reaped what he sowed. On July 19, 1692, five women, including my ancestor, Susannah North Martin, were hanged. When one of the women, Sarah Good, stood at the gallows ready to die, she was asked once more by Reverend Nicholas Noyes, assistant minister of the Salem Town church, to confess and in so doing save her soul. Rather than do so, she is said to have screamed, "You are a liar! I am no more a witch than you are a wizard, and if you take away my life, God will give you blood to drink."

The curse came true. Twenty-five years later, as Noyes lay dying, he choked on his own blood.

Stay tuned. In the next chapter, we will begin to take a closer look at the life and the times of Essex County, Massachusetts in 1692.

---

[3] *The Writer's Guide to Everyday Life in Colonial America,* Copyright 1997 by Dale Taylor, Writer's Digest Books

Chapter Two: The World of 1692

In 1626 Charles I of England granted a religious splinter group called the Puritans a charter to settle and govern an English colony in Massachusetts Bay. Their desire was to create a new and perfect society based on the principles of the Bible, a theocracy with no separation of church and state. Their goal was a model community, what they called a "city on a hill," a light to people all over the world. We still have that notion today in the United States, as anyone old enough to recall President Reagan will attest. But among the Puritans, the idea was real and the dream intense.

Of course, not everyone who crossed over from the Old World was a Puritan. Some left because they had no land, no jobs, no wealth. Their lives in England were so difficult that going to the edge of the known world and building a society out of nothing looked better than dealing with the situation they had. That people were there for different reasons is one of the things that produced a natural sort of tension in New England.

The Puritans remained British citizens and like their countrymen were a community that believed in witches. Witchcraft wasn't something on the side. It helps to view it in context of the larger believe system prevalent at the time. They thought about it constantly. The idea witches might be in their midst causing problems was something almost everyone was worried about at least to some degree.

The World View of 1692

This fixation on the supernatural is not surprising when you think about it. In the world of 1692, many events lacked explanations. Children suddenly got sick and died. Animals suffered mysterious ailments. Strange noises were heard or ghostly visions seen. Early New Englanders envisioned themselves as residing in what one writer of the time referred to as a "world of wonders," in which a universe of invisible spirits surrounded them. This was as real as the material world they could see, touch, and feel. The visible and invisible realms coexisted and often intersected. When they encountered harmful events that otherwise seemed inexplicable, New Englanders often were quick to assume a malevolent witch had caused their troubles. And, as shall be discussed, during the early 1690s residents of the Bay Colony had experienced many setbacks that needed explanation.

Imagine you live in seventeenth century New England. A "Big Dig" is when you make a hole in the ground to build the outhouse over. The possibility was real that hostile Indians might give you a haircut to the bone. A savage could be hiding behind any tree in the forest. If you walked through Sleepy Hollow at night you might actually lose your head. To understand fully an early colonist's mind set, start by putting aside practically everything you learned in school about natural science. You see, the Age of Enlightenment was nearly a century away. As a resident of Salem Village, you may or may not be aware, for example, that Copernicus had placed the sun at the center of the solar system. You and most of your neighbors believed the earth, the sun, the stars, plants, animals, man and woman were created by an anthropomorphic God over a seven day period something more than 4000 years ago. Today, in your twenty-first century incarnation, you may wonder about the meaning of life, or if there even is one, but in seventeenth century New England, no uncertainty existed. Life was a test—a test of obedience that the first man and woman failed. Because of Adam and Eve's misstep, you as their descendant, had to undergo a similar test.

How to Pass the Test of Life

What one needed to do to pass the test was clear. God Himself had come to Earth more than 1500 years ago to show the way. He became a man and sacrificed Himself in place of you to make your salvation possible. The formula you needed to follow was simple: Obey the commandments. Accept Him as your savior and believe He is Who He said He is. Confess your sins, ask forgiveness for them, and you would ride into heaven on His coattails.

Sounds easy, and maybe for a Roman Catholic or a member of the Church of England it was. But as a Puritan you believed salvation was questionable even if you followed this formula and all the rules to the letter. It's been said that "puritanism is a religion of endless striving and very uncertain reward." Why? They thought each person's fate was predetermined by God before he or she was born. It was preordained. You might not make it to and through the pearly gates even if you obeyed the rules. This being the case, from time to time you probably felt a palpable level of anxiety and searched for clues as to whether you were a member of the small elect, someone who possessed the spirit of God within him, planted there by God Himself, making you destined for heaven—or one of the unfortunate many who was damned before getting out of the starting blocks. After all, the Apostle Paul had said God had hardened Pharaoh's heart, causing him to play the bad-guy role when Moses led the Jews out of Egypt. But even though Pharaoh's role was essential in God's plan, he did not earn a ticket into heaven. No way.

The idea that some were damned no matter what may have led some to witchcraft. If you came to the conclusion you were not among the chosen, you might as well make a pact with the devil and take up black magic since you were on your way to hell, anyway, so why not live it up?

On the other hand, if you considered yourself saved—one of the chosen—you certainly wouldn't want to derail your train to glory by admitting to a crime you didn't commit—such as witchcraft—even to avoid the gallows. The nineteen who were hanged could probably have saved their lives by publicly confessing guilt and asking God's forgiveness. During the witch hunt of 1692, once a witch confessed and repented, the matter was no longer seen as one for the court—it was between that person and God. More than fifty of approximately 150 who were accused and arrested took this route. The nineteen who were hanged did not. That would have been telling a lie, which was one of the big ten no-nos. It boiled down to a way to save your skin, and lose your soul.

Women Were Viewed as the Weaker Sex

Also at the core of Puritanism was an inherent misogyny. It's possible this is one of the things that set my mother off. Puritan women were expected to be quiet, docile, and submissive helpmates to their husbands. Mom may have been born in 1906, but that didn't mean she bought that women were the weaker sex. But most Puritans did. Women were also thought to be more likely than men to become helpmates to the devil. You see, they were presumed to be more credulous than men, to be more lustful creatures, and to find appealing the idea of sexual relations with Satan. Let's face it, the old goat was thought to be a studly guy, running after maidens on his hooves, horns leading the way. Yeah, he was horny all right. Plus, women were thought to be more malicious and spiteful than men when wronged. And then there was the whole forbidden knowledge thing. Remember Eve? She was proof women could be dangerously curious and seek knowledge humans ought not to have.

The climate of suspicion surrounding women was further exacerbated by social dynamics. Imagine what it was like to live in a community of 500 people. Talk about gossip, plus all the friction that can exist when people are thrown together in a small group. Land disputes erupted continually. There are also indications resentment existed in Salem Village because it was under the political domain of Salem Town, which was on the coast several miles away. Conservative farmers in the village often had disputes with the more liberal and prosperous merchants who dominated Salem Town.

On top of this, life was difficult in seventeenth century New England. It was a dualistic world with God on one side, Satan on the other, and the Puritans in the middle. God demanded their obedience. Satan offered them an easy way, but with huge consequences after death. Of course they might be headed to hell no matter what they did—if they weren't among the chosen. Scratching out a living wasn't easy, and Satan was constantly offering a hand. He delighted in dangling temptation under a nose.

As a faithful churchgoer, you would have heard and read the following many times: " . . . be strong in the Lord and in his mighty power. Put on the full armor of God so that you can take your stand against the devil's schemes. For our struggle is not against flesh and blood, but against the powers of this dark world and against the spiritual forces of evil in the heavenly realms."[4]

But Materialism Has a Foothold

It needs to be made clear that belief in an unseen world was not universal, even in seventeenth century New England. An English philosopher, Thomas Hobbes (1588-1679), had argued that aside from God—the "first cause" who created the material world—nothing existed that is not of the material world. The logic he used was simple. How could it, if God created everything?

Hobbes had a big impact on the Age of Enlightenment, which was to pick up steam a century later, and he probably had his followers in seventeenth century New England, though they were likely to be "closet" followers of Hobbes rather than openly challenge widely-held beliefs of the day. This should not be surprising. At first blush, what Hobbes argued seems to make sense. But before you replace that can of peas, sit back and think. Nobody, Hobbes included, knew about gravity, electromagnetism, gamma rays, radio and TV waves and so on which aren't of the material world, but are nonetheless as real as anything constructed of matter. Nevertheless, Hobbes unleashed a powerful idea. Materialism continues to hold sway with many, even though it requires its adherents to ignore the implications of quantum physics—that matter is

---
[4] Ephesians 6: 10-12, NIV translation

energy and energy is matter[5] —as well as scientifically conducted experiments proving without a doubt some paranormal phenomena are real.

"The universe," Hobbes wrote, "that is, the whole mass of things that are, is corporeal, that is to say, body, and hath the dimensions of magnitude, namely length, breadth, and depth; also every part of body is likewise body, and hath the like dimensions, and consequently every part of the universe is body, and that which is not body is no part of the universe: and because the universe is all, that which is no part of it is nothing, and consequently nowhere."

Hobbes's statement that spirit is "nowhere" is as uncompromising a statement of materialism as one can imagine. You might expect such a man to be skeptical of witchcraft. Someone who did not believe in an invisible world would scarcely give credence to what Cotton Mather called "the wonders of the invisible world," which Mather wrote in large measure to counteract such thinking.[6]

It is true Hobbes was a skeptic, but his skepticism was accompanied by an attitude that would probably not be held by today's skeptics. "As for witches," he wrote in his *Leviathan,* "I think not that their witchcraft is any real power; but yet that they are justly punished, for the false belief they have that they can do such mischief, joined with their purpose to do it if they can; their trade being nearer to a new religion than to a craft or science." If Hobbes had found someone sticking pins in a doll made in the image of a neighbor, or if he'd found them casting spells on a neighbor's cow, he'd probably have made sure they were hanged from the nearest weeping willow. He wouldn't have

---

[5] E = MC2 (Energy equals mass [i.e., matter] times the speed of light squared)

[6] As you will see, the influential preacher Cotton Mather's efforts at countering Hobbes' thesis with his book *Memorable Providences* may unintentionally have been one cause of the Salem witch hysteria.

believed the person really had occult powers, but he'd have executed him anyway for heresy and malice.

The Three Degrees of Magic

It seems safe to say that in seventeenth century New England Hobbes views were not widely known or discussed among ordinary people. As far as most were concerned, practically everything happened as the result of something going on at the ethereal, unseen level of reality. Everyone who used a charm, such as a lucky rabbit's foot or a horseshoe over the door, believed he was making an appeal to occult forces—at possible peril to his soul. But the degree of peril was relative because, like murder, there were three degrees of witchcraft or magic, the first being the practice of white magic. This involved charms or spells used for benevolent purposes. Horseshoes and rabbits' feet fell into this category. Just remember to nail the horseshoe above the door with the open end upward so the shape will suggest the horns of a herd animal—or maybe so the luck won't fallout. I've heard it both ways.

The intention of this sort of thing was innocent enough, and the practice of white magic was usually not sufficient to generate concern among community leaders. It was, however, an appeal to occult forces that were non-Christian, and as such it could, and sometimes did, draw a forceful reprimand from the clergy.

The second degree of witchcraft was black magic. This was magic used maliciously. Black magic was very serious indeed. It was an appeal to Satan, the Prince of Darkness, to accomplish something evil.

The third degree was a pact with Satan. In this case, the witch was no longer merely invoking the devil's aid through charms and spells. He or she actually believed she had made a contract to serve the horny guy.

Up until thirty or forty years ago, the view held by most was that no actual witchcraft was practiced in New England. But examination of transcripts of original documents from the time reveals this to be incorrect. All three degrees of witchcraft were practiced: white magic commonly; black magic not uncommonly, and pact on at least one occasion, as we will see. To these folks, Satan was not some abstract force which might or might not exist. Satan was real. He and his forces were around us, always watching, always looking for an opportunity to have an effect on a Godly community. Satan wanted nothing more than to break down the Puritan way of life.

The State of Science in 1692

If all this seems hard to believe—that people could be so gullible—consider the level of knowledge that existed about how the natural world actually worked. A resident of seventeenth century Salem Village lived at a time when germs, for example, had not yet been discovered. Oh, a few years before, in 1675, a Dutchman named Antoni van Leeuwenhock—an amateur lens grinder and microscope builder—saw for the first time tiny organisms he called "animalcules" living in stagnant water. He also spotted them in scum collected from his teeth. Leeuwenhock didn't know or even speculate that "animalcules" might cause disease. The idea creatures so small they were invisible to the naked eye entered the body to make a person sick and sometimes die would have seemed totally absurd. It would be almost as hard to believe as telepathy, or ESP, or communication with the dead through a medium is to materialists today—at least to those who hold fast to the idea that anything and everything that cannot be replicated in a laboratory simply does not exist.

Back then, however, the unseen world was thought to be very real and very much a factor in people's lives. For example, from the time of the ancient Romans, through the Middle Ages, and until the late nineteenth century, it was generally accepted that some life forms arose spontaneously from nonliving matter. Such "spontaneous generation" appeared to occur primarily in decaying matter. For example, a seventeenth century recipe for the spontaneous production of mice required placing sweaty underwear and husks of wheat in an openmouthed jar, then waiting for twenty-one days, during which time it was alleged that the sweat from the underwear would penetrate the husks of wheat, changing them into mice.

Although such a concept may seem laughable today, it is consistent with the other widely held cultural and religious beliefs of the time.

The first serious attack on the idea of spontaneous generation, by the way, was made in 1668 by Francesco Redi, an Italian physician and poet. At that time, it was widely held that maggots arose spontaneously in rotting meat. Redi, on the other hand, believed maggots developed from eggs laid by flies. To test his hypothesis, he set out meat in a variety of flasks, some open to the air, some sealed completely, and others covered with gauze. As he had expected, maggots appeared only in the open flasks in which the flies could reach the meat and lay their eggs.

This was one of the first examples of an experiment in the modern sense, in which controls were used. In spite of his well executed experiment, however, the belief in spontaneous generation remained strong. Even Redi continued to believe it occurred under some circumstances. The invention of the microscope only served to enhance this belief. Microscopy revealed a whole new world of organisms that appeared to arise spontaneously. It was quickly learned that to create "animalcules," as Antoni van Leeuwenhock had labeled these organisms, you needed only to place hay in water and wait a few days before examining your new creations under a microscope.

The debate over spontaneous generation continued for centuries. In 1745, John Needham, an English clergyman, proposed what he considered the definitive experiment. Everyone knew that boiling killed microorganisms, so he proposed to test whether or not microorganisms appeared spontaneously after boiling. He boiled chicken broth, put it into a flask, sealed it, and waited. Sure enough, micro-organisms grew. Needham claimed victory for spontaneous generation.

An Italian priest, Lazzaro Spallanzani, was not convinced, and he suggested that perhaps the microor-ganisms had entered the broth from the air after the broth was boiled, but before it was sealed. To test his theory, he modified Needham's experiment by placing the chicken broth in a flask. He sealed the flask, drew off the air to create a partial vacuum, then boiled the broth. No microorganisms grew. Proponents of spontaneous generation argued that Spallanzani had only proven that spontaneous generation could not occur without air.

The spontaneous generation theory was finally laid to rest in 1859 by a young French chemist named Louis Pasteur. The French Academy of Sciences sponsored a contest for the best experiment either proving or disproving it. Pasteur's winning experiment was a variation of the methods of Needham and Spallanzani. He boiled meat broth in a flask, heated the neck of the flask in a flame until it became pliable, and bent it into the shape of an S. Air could enter the flask, but airborne microorganisms could not because they would settle by gravity in the neck.

As Pasteur had expected, no microorganisms grew. When Pasteur tilted the flask so that the broth reached the lowest point in the neck, where any airborne particles would have settled, the broth rapidly became cloudy with life. Pasteur had both refuted the theory of spontaneous generation and convincingly demonstrated that microorganisms are everywhere, even in the air.

But Louis Pasteur lived almost two centuries our story takes place. Hardly anyone in seventeenth century New England questioned spontaneous generation or the role played in daily life by spirits and the unseen world.

How Disease Was Transmitted

As a seventeenth century New Englander, for example, what do you suppose caused illness and disease? If you sat in a draft you might "catch cold." If you went out in bad weather and got soaked to the skin, you might "catch a chill." These conditions and results went hand in hand often enough for you to make a connection. And you also realized some diseases were contagious. Germ warfare, for example, isn't exclusively a tactic of the modern age. In his campaign to conquer the Aztecs a century earlier, the Spaniard Cortez was said to have had the bodies of soldiers who'd died of smallpox thrown over the city walls of his enemies.

So some of the conditions that led to illness were known. The important question was why some people got sick and others didn't. The concept of an immune system, much less germs, did not yet exist. No one knew cold air doesn't cause colds—that germs do. If someone got sick it was because the devil made it happen, and God allowed him. The Spanish, for example, were certain God was on their side against the hopelessly heathen Aztecs. It's a safe bet no guilt whatsoever was felt about throwing a small-pox invested body into the pagans' midst. No wonder so many Indians died, they thought. It was God's will.

The Devil Serves God's Purpose

Hold on. What do I mean, the devil did it, and God allowed him?

Have you ever read the story of Job, the guy who is remembered for his patience? In this Old Testament story, a wager is made between God, whom the Hebrews called Yahweh, and Satan. In the story, Satan comes to visit God. God asks what Satan has been up to. Satan says he's been visiting the earth. God asks if Satan happened to see Job, a mortal of whom God is proud in that Job is a particularly loyal subject. Satan is amused by this and in effect says Job worships God because of the good life God has provided for Job. The implication is that no one worships God except for selfish reasons. God disagrees. He thinks Job's loyalty is genuine even though Job is a very pros-perous man. To prove it, God permits Satan to destroy all of Job's material wealth and to kill Job's children. And, as if that wasn't bad enough, Satan then is allowed to give Job a disease which causes him severe and unrelenting pain.

To make a long story short, Job suffers and complains but in effect remains loyal to God throughout the whole ordeal. It wasn't easy, but Job passed the test God allowed him to be subjected to. Job's wealth was then restored, and new children were born to him to take the place of the old.

Suffice it to say, Puritans felt they were constantly being tested in this way. For them, God was all powerful and could smash the devil at any time and in any place. But He didn't because the devil served a useful purpose—testing people, even testing whole communities or nations. Reading though documents from the times, including papers written and sermons given by various Puritan preachers—notably John Hale, Deodat Lawson, Cotton Mather, and Samuel Parris—it seems clear the consensus in the spring and early summer of 1692 was that God had unleashed Satan on New England along two separate fronts. To the north, He had allowed Satan to operate on the physical plane of reality by giving the Indians—who were thought to be devil worshippers—a long leash. Whole communities had been devastated and many Puritans killed or taken away by the Indians to be slaves. Farther south, in Essex County, God had let loose the devil on the invisible plane by allowing him to recruit a whole host of women and a few men as witches to help in his dirty work.

Similar Thinking Exists Today

What we've just covered shouldn't be all that surprising. The idea powers beyond the veil cause difficulties here in physical reality is still alive and well today. My local newspaper recently reported that a Pakistani imam declared the earthquake that struck his region in 2005 was an act of vengeance by a god enraged that some residents had defiled their homes with cable television. Our own Christian evangelist Franklin Graham, son of Billy, said New Orleans had been home to satanic worship and sexual perversion, and "God is going to use [Hurricane

Katrina] to bring revival." A Texas clergyman, Dwight McKissic, suggested Katrina devastated the city because "they openly practice voodoo and devil worship in New Orleans." Jerry Falwell announced that "the ACLU's got to take a lot of blame" for the terrorist attacks for "throwing God out successfully with the help of the federal court system, throwing God out of the public square, out of the schools."

The desire to blame God or Satan for human misery probably arises from a deep seated need to make sense out of the senseless. The notion that many might suffer so much for no reason at all seems too much to bear.

Yet the truth is our planet is a violent place, full of fire and brimstone. Cataclysms strike everywhere, and they have been doing so since long before humanity's forebears crawled out of the prehistoric mire. Scientists continue to study an enormous crater off Virginia's coast created by a huge object that slammed into the planet 35 million years ago. Debris from the impact fell across an area of three million square miles. It's hard to imagine what the creodonts, amblypods, and condylarths that populated the planet back then did back then to make the Almighty so irritated. What was he trying to tell them?

Then again . . .

Several years ago Pat Robertson suggested Orlando, Florida, was "right in the way of some serious hurricanes because of the local [Gay Days] festival. I don't think I'd be waving those [Gay Days] flags in God's face if I were you," he warned. Shortly thereafter Hurricane Bonnie detoured around Florida but slammed into Virginia Beach—home to Robertson's Christian Broadcasting Network.

Hummm. Maybe sometimes the Almighty is trying to send a message.

Chapter Three: Setting the Stage for Hysteria

The first witch trial in Massachusetts was not in Salem. It took place in Charlestown in 1648. A midwife and healer by the name of Margaret Jones was accused. The record indicates some believed she had a malignant touch that could cause deafness and nausea. They also said she was able to tell the future, but what really did her in was that she had a witch's tit.

The Mark of Satan

So what's a witch's tit? *Cold*, right? Yes, correct, but it was a place on the body, too, called a "devil's mark," where Satan or a witch's familiars—such as her black cat or an imp—suckled her blood, thereby drawing upon her life force. If you found a witch's tit on someone you had indisputable proof that person was a live one. But a person had to be careful. It was possible a mark might look like a witch's tit and not be one. So the inspector would test it by piercing it with a needle. If pain was felt or if blood was drawn from the mark, the person was not considered a witch. On the other hand, if after probing with a needle or a pin the inspector found there was no pain or blood, the mark was not normal, and not normal was bad news for the accused. It was unnatural, and that's of course what witches were: unnatural. This, then, was evidence it was a devil's mark.

Margaret Jones had one and she, along with her witch's tit, was hanged.

Other cases followed.

The Malleus Maleficarum

The information used to hang Margaret Jones came from a book written almost two hundred years earlier. You see, once a person was accused, it was still necessary to provide concrete evidence before marching that individual off the gallows or the bond fire.[7] So an important question was how to prove a spell or curse had been cast. Tangible signs of witchcraft were needed.

In 1486, according to one source, and in 1487 according to another, a guidebook was published on witches called the *The Malleus Maleficarum, or The Hammer of Witches.* The Dominican monks Heinrich Kramer and James Sprenger wrote this tome by assembling fairy tales and magic stories, nightmares, hearsay, confessions and accusations. They put it all together as factual information in what became a handbook for witch hunters, examiners, torturers and executioners.

The Hammer of the Witches contained a definition of witchcraft as well as rules concerning how to investigate, try, and judge cases. Two years prior to the book being published, the authors had secured a bull from Pope Innocent VIII, authorizing them to continue—despite opposition from clergy and secular authorities—a witch hunt they had underway in the Alps. They reprinted this bull when *The Malleus Maleficarum* came out to make it appear the book was sanctioned by the Pope. The book stated that one sure sign of a witch was the devil's mark, or witch's tit. Looking for the devil's mark no doubt became great sport in those days before Playboy Magazine or the ability to go ogle images on Google. The search

---

[7] American and English witches were hanged. Burning at the stake was the standard form of execution on the European continent.

involved a careful inspection of the suspected witch's body which could only be accomplished after shaving all of his or her hair, including the genital area.

Another method for determining who was and was not a witch in the middle ages was called "swimming a witch." The idea was that water was pure—after all you got baptized in it—and would reject all evil. So, naturally, a witch would float, while on the other hand an innocent person would sink. The beauty of this, of course, was that the person being tested was a goner either way.

The Malleus Maleficarum also encouraged torture as a way to elicit a confession from a suspected witch. The best way to get a confusion, it was thought, was to apply force. A favorite was to twist someone's arm behind his or her back and push up. If you've ever had this done you know why. It is excruciatingly painful. Torturing suspected witches was justified in the eyes of the law. English magistrates considered witchcraft a crime against the Church and the state. From the days of Henry VIII onward, the king was the head of the Church. So the political leader was also the head of the Church of England. When you turned your back on God or the Church, you were also turning your back on the king. Witchcraft, therefore, was considered an act of treason—a capital offense.

The Work of Reverend Richard Bernard Plays a Role

According to Mary Beth Norton, writing in *In The Devil's Snare's*[8] the magistrates and judges of the Salem witchcraft examinations and trials also consulted another source for guidance. This was *Guide to Grand-Jury Men* by the Reverend Richard Bernard, published in 1627 in England. Reverend Bernard apparently thought many of

[8] Knopf, 2002

those in authority were far too ready to believe witchcraft allocations and urged that caution be exercised. He warned his readers that certain illnesses could mimic diabolical tortures, and for this reason, a skilled physician should be consulted. Signs that would not be present if an affliction stemmed from natural causes included the subject revealing "secret things past or to come," or the ability to speak without moving the lips. This would only occur with "supernatural assistance." Another surefire sign was when an afflicted individual could "speak with strange languages," or was able to demonstrate physical prowess that went "far beyond human strength." Other symptoms included the afflicted's body becoming "inflexible, neither to be bent backward nor forward without he greatest force," or "the belly to be suddenly puffed up, and to fall instantly flat again."

You will soon read about cases that took place after this work was written in which such symptoms were apparent.

Bernard noted that the diagnosis of diabolical activity by itself left many questions unanswered. As previously mentioned, many people of that time thought the devil did not and could not act without God's express permission. Apparently, the concept was out of vogue or hadn't been considered that God had granted sentient beings—humans as well as the devil and other fallen creatures—free will, which made it possible for them to do as they pleased. To me this is what the story of Adam and Eve is about. Humans, having evolved to the point of possessing objective conscious awareness, were able to make their own decisions and, therefore, to disobey God or nature—unlike lower animals who were compelled to follow their natural instincts. Eve made a decision to disobey God, and Adam followed along, and they both suffered the consequences—just as each of us do today when we don't consult or obey the still, small voice within. But Puritans obviously didn't see it this way. As Bernard wrote, "Neither devils nor witches, nor wicked men can do any thing without the Lord's leave." As a result, when it became apparent the devil was at work in a household, all the members of that household needed to spend time in refection and self-examination in order to consider what they might have done to offend God and bring afflictions upon themselves or their loved-ones.

Among the important questions which would have been raised by diabolical activity were, "Was the person possessed?" In other words, had Satan or a demon entered the body and soul of the individual? Or, alternatively, was the person obsessed? In this case, the devil was torturing the victim but had left his or her soul untouched. "Children . . . young folks . . . women" were the most likely to succumb to obsession or possession. The proper treatment was to summon "the finger of God" through prayer and fasting to cast the devil or demon out. Exorcism, as we shall see later, is still practiced today by the Roman Catholic Church and by a small number of psychiatrists who prefer to call it "depossession."

Cotton Mather, who was very much involved in the Salem examinations and trials, wrote about possession in his *Memorable Providences, Relating to Witchrafts and Possessions*, published in 1689. The case had to do with a boy from Tocutt (Branford) Connecticut. The boy never accused anyone of bewitching him. The son of a minister, he carried on long conversations with the devil while in fits. Satan promised him that if he would only enter into a covenant with him, the boy "should live deliciously, and have ease, comfort, and money." When the boy refused, "the devil took a corporal possession of him," tormented him and spoke to those who addressed the boy with barking and hissing, and sometimes voicing "horrible blasphemies against the name of Christ."

According to Reverend Bernard, a third possibility after obsession and possession was that the devil might have one or more witches working for him and be using them as intermediaries to do his malicious work.

If witchcraft was suspected, how did one go about determining if an accused was a witch?

First, one should determine what sort of person the suspected witch was. This might provide a clue because witches were "malicious spirits, impatient people, and full of revenge." Often a person guilty of witchcraft was "to be much given to cursing and imprecations," whether or not there was cause.

A really obvious sign was that after the witch had made threats, "evil [came] to happen, and this not once or twice, to one or two, but often, and to diverse persons." In such a case "a great presumption" of guilt was justified.

Another strong indicator was an "implicit confession," a statement by the accused which could be construed as an admission of guilt. Others included an interest in the afflicted that went beyond the ordinary, such as continually visiting even after being told to stay away, and "The common report of neighbors of all sorts," as well as being "of kin to a convicted witch," such as a sister or brother, child or grandchild.

The testimony of another witch should also be considered, "for who can better discover a Witch, then [sic] a Witch?" And lastly, if those being tormented named people while in their fits, "and also [told] where they have been, and what they have done here or there," or "seeme[d] to see" apparitions of the accused in their fits, "this is a great suspicion."

We shall see a number of these indicators arise at the Salem examination, which no doubt made the magistrates' eyes and ears perk up.

To his credit, Reverend Bernard warned his readers not to jump to conclusions. What he had identified were presumptions only. Someone might look and act like a witch and simply be "rude and ill-mannered" and what he described as "of the poorer sort." He went on to caution that when the afflicted saw apparitions while in their fits, this was in effect, "the devil's testimony, who can lie, and that more often then speak truth." A capital case should not rest on this sort of evidence for even when Satan told the truth he did so with "lying intent," in an effort "to ensnare the blood of the innocent." Reverend Bernard cautioned that Satan "can represent a common ordinary person, man or woman unregenerate [though not a witch] to the fantasy of vain persons, to deceive them and others." By "unregenerate" the reverend meant someone who had not been regenerated or "born again" by the spirit of God or Christ or, in other words, "saved." This distinction became important in Salem when presumably "regenerated" church members were accused of witchcraft.

You will see several of the issues Richard Bernard dealt with surface in Salem.

The Case of Bury St. Edmunds, England

A trial at Bury St. Edmunds, England, from March 10-13, 1662, provides with an interesting case and is likely to have had a profound influence on those presiding over the

Salem examinations and trials. What is known about it comes from a sixty-page booklet entitled, *A Tryal of Witches, at the Assizes held at Bury St. Edmonds for the County of Suffolk;* on the Tenth day of March 1664 (though it actually occurred in 1662). Published in London in 1682, it supposedly was written by an anonymous spectator. According to Cotton Mather, writing in *Wonders of the Invisible World,* this booklet was "much considered by the judges of New England." A contemporary of Mather's, the Reverend John Hale, also wrote about the Salem trials and referred to this case when doing so.

The events leading up to the Bury St. Edmunds trial occurred in Lowestoft, an isolated fishing town northeast of London and about fifty miles east of Bury St. Edmunds. It all started when Samuel Pacy, a wealthy fish merchant and property owner of Lowestoft, rejected several requests from Amy Denny, a widow with a reputation as a witch, to sell her some fish. According to Samuel Pacy, whose deposition is recorded in the 1682 pamphlet, immediately after he turned down Amy Denny a third time, his daughter, Deborah " . . . was taken with most violent fits, feeling most extreme pain in her stomach, like the pricking of pins, and shrieking out in a most dreadful manner like unto a whelp, and not like unto a sensible creature."

Deborah's symptoms continued for three weeks. Finally, Samuel Pacy asked a neighbor, Dr. Feavor, for his opinion. Feavor could not determine a natural cause of the illness. It's interesting Pacy did not seek the help of the clergy. Nor is there any mention in Pacy's deposition at the trial of an attempt to employ religious remedies.

Pacy's deposition states that Deborah Pacy, " . . . in her fits would cry out of Amy Duny [Denny] as the cause of her malady, and that she did affright her with apparitions of her person." After Samuel Pacy made a formal complaint, the authorities put Amy Denny in the stocks. This did not, however, end his daughter's symptoms. Two days later " . . . being the Thirtieth of October, the eldest daughter Elizabeth, fell into extreme fits, insomuch, that they could not open her mouth to give her breath, to preserve her life without the help of a tap which they were enforced to use . . . "

The two sisters suffered other symptoms for two months, including lameness and soreness, loss of their sense of speech, sight, and hearing, sometimes for days. Fits ensued upon hearing the words "Lord," "Jesus" and "Christ." They also claimed that Rose Cullender, another reputed witch, and Amy Denny, "would appear before them, holding their fists at them, threatening, that if they related either what they saw or heard, that they would torment them ten times more than ever they did before." The sisters also coughed up pins, " . . . and one time a two-penny nail with a very broad head, which pins (amounting to forty or more) together with the two-penny nail were produced in court, with the affirmation of the said deponent, that he was present when the said nail was vomited up, and also most of the pins."

On November 30, 1661, seven weeks after the initial illness, the parents of the afflicted sisters relocated them to the home of relatives in hope of a cure. Once there, their aunt, Margaret Arnold, believed they might be faking their symptoms and subjected them to an experiment. She removed all the pins from the children's clothes, yet, " . . . notwithstanding all this care and circumspection of hers, the children afterwards raised at several times at least thirty pins in her presence, and had most fierce and violent fits upon them." Margaret soon became convinced something supernatural was causing the girls' afflictions. She also believed the girls' allegations that bees and flies forced pins and nails into their mouths.

The children continued their fits and hallucinations at their aunt's house until an ominous event occurred. One of the girls " . . . being recovered out of her fits, declared, that Amy Duny [Denny] had been with her and that she tempted her to drown herself; and to cut her throat, or otherwise to destroy her self."

A complaint was filed against Denny. The trial, which began on March 10, 1662, went on for three days. By then, the afflictions had spread to three other neighbor girls: Ann Durrant (probably between the ages of 16-21), Jane Bocking (14 years old), and Susan Chandler (18 years old). Two of the five afflicted were too ill to attend the trial, and family members spoke for the other three, but their presence affected the courtroom atmosphere. The three afflicted arrived "in reasonable good condition: But that morning they came into the hall to give instructions for the drawing of their bills of indictments, the three persons fell into strange and violent fits, screeching out in a most sad manner, so that they could not in any wise give any instructions in the court who were the cause of their distemper. And although they did after some certain space recover out of their fits, yet they were every one of them struck dumb, so that none of them could speak neither at that time, nor during the trial until the conviction of the supposed witches."

Although a good deal of testimony was given, the most dramatic evidence boiled down to the condition and actions of the afflicted children. Elizabeth Pacy created quite a scene, as she "could not speak one word all the time, and for the most part she remained as one wholly senseless as one in a deep sleep, and could move no part of her body, and all the motion of life that appeared in her was, that as she lay upon cushions in the court upon her back, her stomach and belly by the drawing of her breath, would arise to a great height: and after the said Elizabeth had lain a long time on the table in the court, she came a little to herself and sat up, but could neither see nor speak . . . by the direction of the judge, Amy Duny {Denny] was privately brought to Elizabeth Pacy, and she touched her hand; whereupon the child without so much as seeing her, for her eyes were closed all the while, suddenly leaped up, and caught Amy Duny by the hand, and afterwards by the face; and with her nails scratched her till blood came, and would by no means leave her till she was taken from her, and afterwards the child would still be pressing towards her, and making signs of anger conceived against her."

That was pretty dramatic stuff, but there's more. Among other things, the mother of the afflicted Ann Durrant testified that her infant son, William, had suffered similar afflictions about four years prior, and that a Dr. Jacobs, a physician from Yarmouth, had saved him with a prescription for the use of counter-magic. The doctor told Goodwife Durrant to hang William's blanket over the fireplace and to burn anything found in it. When she took it down at night, a large toad fell out, which another boy in the house quickly caught. As he held it over the fire with tongs, the toad exploded in a flash of light.

Goodwife Durrant testified that the next day a relative of Amy Denny had told her Denny had recently suffered serious burns all over her body. When Goodwife Durrant visited Denny, the burned woman cursed her and predicted that Goodwife Durrant would outlive some of her children and be forced to live on crutches.

Denny's predictions proved accurate. Goodwife Durrant's daughter, Elizabeth, soon fell seriously ill, and after seeing Amy Denny's specter, died. After Elizabeth's death, Goodwife Durrant became crippled in both legs and was forced to use crutches for more than three years. But at the end of the court proceedings in which Goodwife Durrant testified, when Amy Denny was pronounced guilty, Goody Durrant was miraculously cured and threw away her crutches.

The Case of Anne Cole

Another interesting case, which likely had an influence on the 1692 witchcraft crisis as well, took place in Hartford, Connecticut, also in 1662. In this one, Anne Cole, "a person esteemed pious," was taken with "strange fits."

According to an eye witness:

"Extremely violent bodily motions she many times had, even to the hazard of her life in the apprehensions of those that saw them; and very often great disturbance was given in the public worship of God by her and two other women who had also strange fits. Once in special, on a day of prayer kept on that account, the motion and noise of the afflicted was so terrible that a Godly person fainted under the appearance of it."[9]

Voices came from her in some of her fits, and these voices were clearly not her own. Anyone who's seen *The Exorcist* or *Ghost Busters* knows what that means, and so did the seventeenth century observers of Anne Cole. Demons had entered and possessed her. The voices seemed to be plotting ways in which Anne Cole might be

[9] "A Case of Witchcraft in Hartford" by Charles J. Hoadly, LL. D., Published in the Connecticut Magazine, November, 1899

further afflicted. Eventually, seeming to realize that they were being overheard, one of the voices announced, "Let us confound her language, [that] she may tell no more tales."

For a while nothing came from her but unintelligible mutterings. Then the conversation resumed, but in a Dutch accent, and this time names were mentioned, names of witches who were responsible for these afflictions.

When she was out of her fits, Anne Cole could recall nothing of what had gone on. She was understandably distressed to find she'd been speaking of things which, to the best of her knowledge, had never been in her mind. It must have been distressing to the local magistrates as well. They now had accusations of witchcraft against several people, but their source was not Anne Cole, the source being a committee of demons who infested her.

The magistrates investigated further, and imprisoned at least some of the accused on suspicion of witchcraft. One of these, a "lewd, ignorant, considerably aged woman" named Rebecca Greensmith sent for the two clergymen who had taken down in writing the demonic conversation which had come through the lips of Anne Cole. The transcript was read to her, and she "forthwith and freely confessed those things to be true," confirming the statement of the voices which had said: "that she (and other persons named in the discourse) had familiarity with the devil." She confessed to a number of other things as well, including that the devil had frequent use of her body with much seeming—but indeed horrible and hellish—delight to her.

During the Salem trials of 1692, people who confessed to witchcraft were eventually set free, provided they apologized and asked God's forgiveness. Perhaps Rebecca Greensmith would not repent, for in 1663 she was hanged, as was her husband, Nathaniel, although we do not know the grounds for his conviction. According to Increase Mather, a prominent New England clergyman and the father of Cotton Mather, Nathaniel Greensmith did not confess, and many of the other persons accused by the demonic voices "made their escape into another part of the country."

Humm. Mayve they went to Virginia to grow tobacco.

The Case of the Goodwin Children

Several additional witchcraft cases followed, but perhaps the one that had the most damning effect on Salem in 1692 took place four years prior in Boston. Much of what I've written below was reported in Cotton Mather's account, which he published in his work called *Memorable Providences*. This piece became what today would be called a bestseller. More than likely almost everyone in New England was familiar with the details of this case when the witch hunt began in Salem Village, either because they'd read Mather's work, or had heard about it.

The story begins when four previously well-behaved children of a "sober and pious" mason, John Goodwin, began having fits. The oldest, Martha, a girl of about thirteen, was the first to show symptoms, but she was soon joined by two younger brothers and a sister.

Parenthetically, before Cotton Mather became a minister he was a medical student, which some historians think gives him a fair amount of credibility in terms of his descriptions and characterizations of their behavior. He spent a lot of time with the children, even taking one into his home, and he gave a thorough account. In his words, the children's strange fits were "beyond those that attend an epilepsy or catalepsy." Sometimes they would be deaf, sometimes dumb, and sometimes blind. On many occasions they were all these at once. Sometimes their tongues would be drawn back and down their throats. At other times the tongues would stretch out of their mouths to what seemed an impossible length to actually touch their chins. Their mouths would open so wide their jaws would seem to go out of joint, then the jaws would clap together like a spring-loaded lock. "The same would happen to their shoulder blades, and their elbows, and hand wrists, and several of their joints." They would at times lie in a daze-like condition and neck and heels would come together as though a rope had been attached between the two and drawn tight. They would cry out pitifully saying they were being cut with knives, and hit repeatedly. Their necks would seem to be twisted so that it appeared their necks were broken. Then all of a sudden their necks would become straight and stiff. Sometimes their heads would be twisted almost completely around.

Sound like *The Exorcist?*

If anyone tried to stop these hideous contortions, the children would cry out in pain. This went on for weeks.

Today, the little Goodwins might be diagnosed as suffering from hysteria neurosis, a psychosomatic condition that is said to afflict those in early adolescence. According to what I've read on the subject, this affliction doesn't occur often nowadays, but it was fairly common in times past—although the symptoms these children displayed would probably be considered well over the top and into the twilight zone. At any rate, hysteria neurosis wasn't a term Mather would have found in his medical books, and besides, he seemed to have had a pretty good idea what was causing the fits. They had started immediately after one of the children had quarreled with an Irish washer woman employed by her family. The washer woman's mother was Goodwife Glover, described by Mather as "a scandalous old woman" whose late husband had complained to anyone who would listen that she was undoubtedly a witch. Those were strong words in that day, and not to be uttered lightly. Anyhow, Mather tells us the old hag "bestowed very bad language upon the girl," which I suppose means she cursed her.

Neighbors advised the family to try white magic to counter the spell, but apparently John Goodwin was a God-fearing man and refused to have anything to do with the occult. Instead, he consulted "skillful physicians," particularly one Dr. Thomas Oakes whose opinion was that "nothing but an hellish witchcraft" could be the cause. Next Goodwin turned to the Boston clergy, who held a day of prayer at the Goodwin house. This seemed to do some good. One of the four children was permanently cured, but the three others suffered a relapse. Finally, Goodwin entered a complaint against Goodwife Glover with the magistrates.

She was examined by the court, and according to Mather "gave such a wretched account of herself" they sent her directly to jail on the charge of witchcraft.

Cotton Mather wrote that when she came to trial and was formerly charged she had a hard time giving a straight answer concerning her innocence or guilt. When she did finally enter a plea it boiled down to a confession. The court ordered the old woman's house to be searched, and you'll never guess what they found. Effigy dolls. Mather described them as "small images, or puppets, or babies, made of rags and stuffed with goat's hair and other such ingredients."[10]

---

[10] The dolls were probably stuffed with goat hair because it is the goat who is deified in Satan's horns and cloven hooves.

The children were present in the court when the dolls were brought forth. Goody Glover was questioned about them and explained she used them to torture people she didn't like.

"How is it done?" she was asked.

Quite simple, really. She averted her eyes from the children and attempted to make herself look small and meek. All she did, she said, was wet her finger with spit and stroke the little buggers.[11]

A doll was handed to her, and she straightened up and took it.

One of the children fell into a fit.

The doll was taken from her. As soon as order in the court was restored, and the child calmed down, the judges asked her to again take the doll and stroke it.

The child fell into another fit.

As you can imagine, this did not help Goody Glover's cause.

The judges asked whether she had anyone who would vouch for her as a character witness.

"Oh, yes," she said. Then, according to Mather, she looked around very pertly in the air.

No doubt her smile quickly turned into a frown.

"No. He's gone," she said. She then confessed she had just one character witness, who was her Prince, and he had skipped out on her.

The next night, Goody Glover, presumably in her cell, was heard "expostulating with a devil." She wanted to know why had he'd run out on her. Doggone it all, she'd confessed everything because of how badly he'd treated her.

Later, a half dozen court-appointed physicians exam-

---

[11] Spit was thought to have occult power, a belief that still survives today in the idea of spitting on one's hands before tackling a particularly difficult task.

ined Goody Glover to determine whether or not she was sane. Even in the seventeenth century, some people must have thought she was a bona fide nut case. They spent a number of hours with her, and decided that everything that came out of her mouth was "pertinent and agreeable."

"What do you think will become of your soul?" They asked her.

"You ask me a very solemn question," she said, "and I cannot well tell what to say to it."

Satan worshipers were not supposed to be able to recite the Lord's Prayer so they asked her to do that. According to Mather, Goody Glover was a Roman Catholic and "could recite her *Pater Noster* ["Our Father"] in Latin very readily," except for a couple of clauses which she couldn't seem to master. When asked why not, she said she could not say them, "if she might have all the world."

In end the doctors agreed she was *Compos Mentis,* or mentally competent, and a death sentence was passed.

Cotton Mather Talks with Goody Glover

Cotton Mather visited Goody Glover twice after her sentencing. He said she never denied being guilty of witchcraft, but wouldn't say much about her relationship and dealings with demons and Satan. She did say she used to go to meetings where her "Prince and four" would be. Mather said she told him who the four were and that her Prince was Satan. But apparently a lot of what she said was in Irish [Gaelic] which Mather didn't understand. She did speak English when Mather said her Prince had cheated her.

"If it be so, I am sorry for that!" she said.

Mather then asked her a number of questions, but she

remained silent. After a while, she told him she'd like to answer, "but they would not give her leave."

"They? Who are *They?*" Mather wanted to know.

She replied that "They were her spirits, or her saints," to which Mather added, "for they say, the same word in Irish signifies both."

Another time she made reference to her two mistresses.

When Mather asked who these mistresses were, she went into a rage and refused to say more about them.

Mather told her she needed to break her covenant with Satan and dedicate herself to Christ before it was too late. Otherwise, she would surely burn in hell.

She said that seemed a reasonable course of action to follow, but she simply couldn't do it.

He asked whether it would be all right for him to pray for her, to which she said, "If prayer would do me any good, I could pray for myself."

He asked her again, and she told him she could not agree to it unless her spirit companions said it was all right.

Mather prayed for her anyway, and when he was done, she thanked him "with many good words."

Finally, Mather left her in her cell. He was no sooner out of sight, than "she took a stone, a long and slender stone, and with her finger and spittle fell to tormenting it; though whom or what she meant, I had the mercy never to understand."

Goody Glover Goes to the Gallows

When unrepentant Goodwife Glover was on her way to the gallows she announced that the children's afflictions would not cease at her death because, in addition to her, others also had a hand in the witchcraft directed at them. Presumably at least one of these was her daughter, who had been the Goodwins' washer woman, and the person with whom one of the four children had argued, setting the episode in motion. But Goodwife Glover didn't identify her accomplices publicly. From what Mather wrote it seems he believed her abettors to include the four whom she'd told him had joined her in meetings with the devil. But Mather kept their identities to himself. Presumably he felt this the proper course to follow on the grounds one should not accept the testimony against others of a confessed witch. The devil was, as Mather often called him, "the Prince of Lies," and this woman had been his faithful worshipper. This is one case in Massachusetts of a pact with the devil we can be fairly certain of, and there is no doubt Cotton Mather and others were thoroughly convinced.

The children's fits did continue as she had predicted, and were even more violent than ever, except that one of the boys could be given sporadic relief by striking at the specters he saw. The theory was that if you could hit the specter you could injure the witch. On one occasion it was reported "that a wound was this way given to an obnoxious woman in the town." But again Mather refused to make the name public, "for we should be tender in such relations, lest we wrong the reputation of the innocent by stories not enough inquired into."

Eventually Mather took the eldest Goodwin girl into his own home, partly in an attempt to cure her through prayer and fasting, and also that "I might have a full opportunity to observe the extraordinary circumstances of the children, and that I might be furnished with evidence and argument as a critical eyewitness to confute the sadducism[12] of this debauched age." From this, it seems logical to assume he recognized this was a classic case. At this point, he had probably decided to publish an account of it in an attempt to convert materialists to the belief in an invisible world.

Once the the girl was in Mather's home she provided a thorough display of symptoms. Most of them have already been described, but new ones appeared as well. Her belly would swell up like a drum, and sometimes croaking noises would come from it. On one occasion Mather was praying for "mercy on a daughter vexed with a devil," and a low booming voice came out of her mouth, saying, "There's three of us!" At other times the girl would go for a ride on a spectral horse, bouncing as though she was riding along. At the conclusion of one such promenade she announced she'd been to a witches' meeting, and had learned the identities of those who were causing her affliction. There were three of them. She named them, and announced that "if they were out of the way, I should be well." But Mather made no move to put them out of the way. After all, this was a girl through whom devils were speaking. Once more he kept the names of the accused to himself. It is a shame the same degree of caution was not exercised four years later in Salem.

One of the girl's more spectacular symptoms was that of flying, which is hardly the stuff of hysteria nervosis. You read that right, *flying*. According to Mather, "she would be carried hither and thither, though not long from the ground, yet so long as to exceed the ordinary power of nature in our opinion of it."

Another was her inability to pray, or to hear prayers

---

[12] The Sadduces were a sect of Jews of Jesus's time who did not believe in an afterlife or spirits. Mather used the term to refer to followers of Thomas Hobbes, who were materialists. (See the discussion of beliefs in Chapter Two.)

said on her behalf, or to read Puritan religious works. "A popish [Roman Catholic] book she could endure very well," and she was able to read "whole pages" of "a Quaker's book," although she could not read the words "God" or "Christ." She simply skipped over them.

Once, Mather urged her to tell him what the word was she'd skipped over.

"I must not speak it," she said. "They say I must not. But you know what it is, it's G and 0 and D."

She couldn't read the Bible, and if someone else read it, even silently, "she would be cast into very terrible agonies."

Puritan catechisms had the same effect. *The Assembly's Catechism*, or Mather's grandfather John Cotton's catechism for children, *Milk for Babes*, "would bring hideous convulsions on the child if she looked into them; though she had once learned them with all the love that could be."

Although the Goodwin girl was unable to utter the name of God or to pray, it appears to have been prayer that finally cured her. Cotton Mather and other members of the community would occasionally join him in prayer for her. According to Thomas Hutchinson, writing in his 1750 publication, *History of the Province of Massachusetts:*

"The children [eventually] returned to their ordinary behavior, lived to adult age, made profession of religion, and the affliction they had been under they publicly declared to be one motive to it. One of them I knew many years after. She had the character of a very sober virtuous woman, and never made any acknowledgment of fraud in this transaction."

Hutchinson was reported to have been an eighteenth-century rationalist who regarded witchcraft as poppycock, so his characterization of the Goodwin girl as sober and virtuous can be viewed as credible.

The Case Is Used to Counter Materialism

The Glover case was as spectacular and mind-boggling then as it is today. While it was still going on Joshua Moodey wrote this to Cotton's father, Increase Mather: "It is an example in all the parts of it, not to be paralleled."

Cotton Mather took the occasion to preach to his congregation a sermon entitled "Discourse on Witchcraft." His main objective was to demonstrate that prayer, faith, and a good life rather than charms were the proper "preservatives" against witchcraft. More important, however, was his use of the case as ammunition in his war against philosophical materialism espoused by Thomas Hobbes. As already noted, persons skeptical of witchcraft did not doubt the practice of it, only whether or not it worked, or worked through spiritual means. For example, the skeptic John Webster conceded there were witches and devils who "have power to perform strange things" in his 1677 publication *Displaying of Supposed Witchcraft*, but he spent the twelfth chapter on the question "whether they do not bring them to pass by mere natural means." What was at issue was the reality of the spiritual world, the "invisible world" as Mather called it. The controversy over witchcraft raised theological issues fundamental to the seventeenth century Christian. "We shall come to have no Christ but a light within, and no Heaven but a frame of mind," said Mather, if the materialists should succeed in destroying the belief in an invisible world.

Chapter Four: Hobbes Won the Battle But the War's Not Over

It seems safe to say Thomas Hobbes's view of reality coupled with Newtonian physics is the bedrock of scientific thinking, today, with the notable exception of quantum physics. The result of this has, for the most part, been positive. The idea that nothing exists that is not of the material world and that everything in nature works strictly according to mathematical and scientific principles has led to enormous advances for humankind in almost every area of our lives. It is likely responsible for the fact that no one has been executed for witchcraft since 1782. Just for a moment envision the growth in the use of mathematics and scientific knowledge since 1692 and all the many benefits that have come about as a result—from medical miracles that save lives, to washing machines that make life easier, and intercontinental passenger jets that allow us to travel in a few hours what took our ancestors weeks or months. You might say this way of thinking has led humanity out of the dark ages and all the way to the moon. For science to adopt the Hobbes-Newtonian world view was in my opinion absolutely necessary for us to have arrived where we are today and to have achieved the quality of life and the high standard of living we enjoy. But for all the good it has done, Hobbes-Newtonian world view is in error. If we are going to understand what really happened in 1692 Salem, we have to update our thinking and our understanding of reality. For this reason, I will now refer to the eighteenth through twentieth century model as the "old world view." Things happen—phenomena have been demonstrated scientifically—that would be impossible if the old world view were true, even though most scientists continue to maintain its validity. It seems to me the old world view has served its purpose and the time has come to embrace a new world view. Our quality of life in general and the quality of life of millions of individuals could be even better than it is today if all human beings understood that there is more to life and to reality than meets the eye, or that can be seen under a microscope, or measured in a laboratory. But that's a discussion for later.

Toward a New Model of Reality

Adherents to the old world view believe awareness and thought are the result of electrons jumping across synapses and that thought remains at all times inside the skull. It's also been said that this doesn't line up with the facts. Quantum physicists know, for example, that the observer of an experiment can affect the outcome. Quite simply, knowledge [thought] possessed by the observer can determine what happens. An example was reported upon in the June 19, 1995 issue of *Newsweek*, in which particles of light seemed to "know" what experimenters had in store during a "double slit" experiment.

Double slit experiments have been around a long time. In 1803, Thomas Young demonstrated that light is waves by means of a simple experiment wherein he placed a screen with two parallel slits between a source of light (sunlight coming through a hole in a screen) and a wall. Each slit could be covered with a piece of material. These slits were razor thin, not as wide as the wavelength of the light. When waves of any kind pass through an opening that is not as wide as they are, the waves diffract. This was the case with one slit open. A fuzzy circle of light appeared on the wall.

When both slits were uncovered what was seen were alternating bands of light and darkness, the center band being the brightest. This pattern of light and dark resulted from what is known in wave mechanics as interference. Waves overlap and reinforce each other in some places and in others they cancel each other out. The bands of light on the wall were where one wave crest overlaps another crest. The dark areas were where a crest and a trough meet and cancel out each other.

In 1905, Albert Einstein published a paper that proved light also behaves like particles, and he did so by using the photoelectric effect. When light hits the surface of a metal, it jars electrons loose from the atoms in the metal and sends them flying off as though they had been struck by tiny billiard balls. Light is both a wave and particles. This, of course, is a paradox, which according to Newtonian physics cannot be.

Now let's take a look at an experiment in which what the person conducting the experiment knows or doesn't know [i.e., what he thinks] changes the outcome. We set up the double slit experiment this time using a photon gun that fires only one photon at a time. In this case[13] both slits were open and a detector was used to determined which slit a photon passed through. A record was made of where each one hit. Only one photon was shot at a time, so there could be no interference. As one would think, the photons did not make the zebra pattern.

Now comes the twilight zone part. When the detector was turned off, and it was not known which slit a photon

[13] This case is summarized from an article entitled, "Faster Than What?" that can be found in the June 19, 1995 issue of *Newsweek*

passed through, the zebra pattern appeared.

Noble-winning physicist Richard Feynman calls this the "central mystery" of quantum mechanics, that something as intangible as knowledge—in this case, which slit a photon went through—changes something as concrete as a pattern on a screen. The old word view simply doesn't allow for this. Thought that remains inside a person's head would be incapable of having an effect on this experiment. Yet thought in the form of knowledge of which slit a proton passed through does have a profound effect.

By the way, quantum physicists tell us it doesn't matter where the researcher is. He or she could be on the other side of the room, the other side of the world, or the other side of the universe and the result would be the same. Thought, it turns out, is everywhere at once. It's part of the seamless whole of reality and is not confined in space or by space. In addition—and get ready for this—thought may not be constrained by time—another finding of the double slit experiment reported upon in the same article in the same issue of *Newsweek*. To prove this, a different version of the double-slit experiment was devised and carried out. In the first, the detectors were in front of the two slits. In the second version, researchers placed a second set between the screen and the two slits. The detectors monitored each photon fired, determining which slit it had just passed through. As in the original experiment, knowing about a photon's behavior at the two slits made the interference pattern vanish. But when the detectors were switched off, the zebra stripes returned. Another variation of this was to determine which slit a proton went threw with the first detector and then to erase that knowledge with the second. The same thing happened. The zebra pattern returned.

Thought Changes Reality

Photons are fired one at a time. If the researcher does not know which slit each photon passes through, a zebra pattern is formed indicating interference as taken place. If the researcher knows which slit each passes through, the zebra pattern disappears. It makes no difference whether the measurement is taken before or after a photon passes the slits, or if it is taken before and then erased. The result is the same. The researcher's knowledge or lack of knowledge causes the difference.

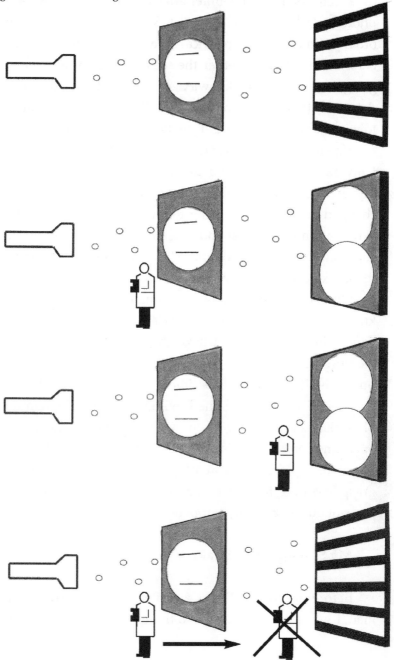

But wait. Whether or not photons create the zebra pattern is determined by their behavior at the double-slit screen. How can what photons do at the slits be affected by a detector they encounter after the slits? How, when a photon reaches the slits, does it "know" how to behave in order to match the presence or absence of the detector behind the slits, or whether the second detector is or is not going to erase the knowledge captured by the first detector? Its past behavior at the slits is made to conform to whether or not it "should" make the zebra pattern.

Versions of this experiment were carried out at the University of Munich and at the University of Maryland. The behavior of the photons, the researchers report, "is changed by how we are going to look at them." A plausible explanation is that past and present are non existent in the subatomic realm of thought. This coincides with another theory concerning thought, which we will take a look later.

Or maybe not. It may be enough that the researcher knows at the start of the experiment that he will know which slit a photon went through, and when or where the measurement is taken is irrelevant. Whatever the case, the point is that this experiment proves thought and knowledge are not confined within the brain. Quantum physicists say it's part of the whole. Anyone who is still operating on old information that indicates otherwise needs to replace this can of peas. This is important to grasp and in order to arrive at potentially accurate conclusions about what really happened at Salem.

My Skepticism Is Shaken

Before my current life as a writer, I was an advertising man. I was also an adherent to the old Hobbes-Newtonian world view. One day, in this capacity, I went to a luncheon given by a television station. A door prize was to be given away—a new Sony TV.

When the time came for the drawing, I pulled my ticket from my pocket, looked at it, and experienced a sensation in my gut that said, *You've won.*

The numbers were read. Each one matched.

Nowadays I wonder if the belief and feeling I'd won was what produced a winning ticket, or if precognition is possible and somehow my intuition looked into the future and saw what was about to happen. If thought is timeless, maybe so. But I'm still not convinced things are destined to happen—likely, maybe, but not preordained. Now, I lean toward the feeling and belief as what caused the winning ticket. At the time, however, coincidence was the only acceptable explanation—although that didn't seem at all adequate and certainly wasn't satisfying.

This little episode actually shook my belief system. Nevertheless, I remained an old world view adherent to anyone who asked because I didn't want to be excommunicated. But on the sly, I started to be on the lookout for more such inexplicable incidents.

The next one came at the end of a vacation in Corsica where my first wife and I, and our then three-year-old daughter, had spent a week at the summer home of one of my wife's childhood friends.

Of Tea Leaves and Tarot Cards

Both my wife of that life and her friend were French. Or, more accurately, the friend was half French and half Corsican. No matter what this mixture might be called, this young woman was most definitely not an adherent to the old world view. Her view of life was even older—more like the seventeenth century one. I suspect this is often the case among those who feel particularly close to a place as Corsicans do to their "Isle of Beauty." I found myself amused by what I considered to be her fantasies of spooks and fairies lurking here and there—in wildflowers called four-o'clocks, in mountain glades and the rugged, fragrant underbrush Corsica is famous for called the *maquis*. She even believed she could tell fortunes by reading tea leaves and tarot cards.

I resisted her attempts to tell my fortune until the last night of our visit. Even then, I limited my participation to only two cards, which I pulled from the deck and handed to her.

She studied them. "You will soon be going on a journey," she said, folding them together and handing them back. "On this journey you will meet a young man. You will know him because he is blond. He will be in need of your help. Whether you come to his assistance is your decision."

She was half right, I thought. I was going on a journey. We were leaving the next morning, as she well knew. That didn't prove a thing.

Before I returned the cards to the deck, I looked at them.

One pictured a young man—blond as a Nordic god. He did look in need of help.

An Encounter with a Blond Young Man

I forgot about this tarot card business until something happened after we landed at the airport in Marseilles. We had to catch a cab. I was afraid I didn't have enough cash, so I took a place in line at an airport bank to change some dollars into francs. (Back then, the Euro hadn't been invented.)

The man directly ahead of me reached the teller window, unfolded an enormous bill, and slipped it through. The teller looked at it, and turned it over.

"Ooh, la, la," he muttered.

He looked up, shook his head, and handed back the bill. The man's face fell. "What's wrong?" he said with a Norwegian accent.

The bank teller spoke in rapid French. He gestured with his hands, his head, his eyes. My glance shifted to the man with the big bill. He was young and blond.

"I've just arrived from Oslo," he said in English. "I have no French money. What will I do?"

The teller waved his hands as if to dismiss the subject.

Then he leaned forward and spoke slowly and loudly in French.

"What? I do not understand." The young man shook his head.

"Please repeat. Oh, no, what am I to do?"

"Excuse me," I said. "Maybe I can help." I leaned forward so I could hear the teller, who explained in French that the bill was too large. He didn't have authority to change that many kroner. The man would have to go to the main branch of the bank in downtown Marseilles and change the bill there.

I turned to the blond young man, and translated. "You don't have something smaller?" I said.

He shook his head. "I'll take a taxi. The driver will have to wait to be paid until I've changed this." He looked me in the eye. "Thank you, thank you very much. You've been most helpful."

I'd assisted him all right, a blond young man, as my

wife's friend had predicted.

This "coincidence" got me thinking again and it wasn't long, only a matter of hours, before I had another incident to chew on.

It happened that same night.

We Stop at Joel's House in Marseilles

Marseilles is not a stop I'd recommend if you have the choice of going elsewhere in the south of France but even this filthy port city has at least one neighborhood with charm—the one where Joel lived, another of my first wife's childhood friends. That day's final destination was her home, which was situated on a steep, curved lane where walls hid quiet gardens—on the southern side of the hill below the statue of Notre Dame.

This icon of the mother of Jesus looks down from atop the highest point in Marseilles. She has a magnificent view of the burning bright, azure harbor and the island fortress of Count of Monte Cristo fame. Joel's house was a hundred feet or so directly below Mary's statue, behind an iron gate, recessed into the side of the hill. The stucco-covered stone house had three levels, the bottom of which was an English basement at grade with a terrace in front. Joel lived there with her widowed mother. Neither of them worked outside the home, and I imagine money was short. Perhaps as a result, they had turned the ground floor of the house into a separate apartment and had rented it out. The first tenant had turned out to be a dashing young man who worked with Jacques Cousteau.[14] This young Frenchman, Philippe Sirot, gallivanted around the world on a converted minesweeper called the Calypso along with Cousteau and

---

[14] Jacques Cousteau was a French marine biologist based in Marseilles who invented the aqua lung. He made many documentaries on marine life which were shown on PBS television in the 1960s and 1970s.

his motley ban of adventurers and marine biologists. The apartment in the quiet Marseilles neighborhood was where he lived when he wasn't gallivanting. As luck and love would have it, he and Joel fell for each other and got engaged. The four of us had chummed around before my wife and I were married, and when we two tied the knot, Philippe had been the French equivalent of my best man and she had been the maid of honor.

That had been in happier times. The mood was somber when we arrived at the house in Marseilles that year. Only a few months prior, the dashing young man had died a tragic death.

I believe Philippe had been possessed of a fascination with death. He sincerely thought it did not represent the end. Rather, he hypothesized that we enter another dimension, that we "cross over" into what may be the mental world of spirit which, according to people who believe in such things, in many ways mirrors the physical side of existence. Looking back with the perspective that time and increased knowledge give, I believe his preoccupation, his burning curiosity, may have led him to harbor an unconscious death wish. I recall vividly how he would barrel down a narrow Marseilles city street on a 750 cc Triumph motorcycle at 120 miles an hour. He did this once with me hanging on in back, praying as no old world view adherent had ever prayed before. He also flew small planes, once taking a Piper Cub to Corsica across open water at night with no instruments. Skydiving was another hobby, and deep sea diving was part of his job. You can still catch sight of him in reruns of Cousteau's documentaries, playing ring around the rosy with a bunch of hungry sharks.

A Young Man Commits Suicide

In the year or two leading up to our visit to Marseilles that August, Philippe had fallen into despair, and his death was thought to have been the result of suicide.

Several things had gone wrong for him. First, by that time the mid 1970s—Cousteau and the Calypso were no longer taking voyages to exotic locations. Replacing a job as a seafaring adventurer isn't easy. But he needed one, and had taken a position as captain of a boat that tended offshore oil rigs in the North Sea. The result was that he was bored to death, perhaps almost literally. Second, his romance with Joel was on the rocks. From what I could determine, they'd broken up after a couple of silly arguments. She was still crazy about him, but was playing a game some people play called "hard to get." She refused to see him, no matter how he tried. Who knows what else had gone wrong. Other factors may have come into play that I cannot recall or of which I was unaware. But the bottom line was, he was found dead one day in his cabin at sea.

On several occasions Philippe had told friends, his ex fiancee included, that he would communicate with them after he died if it was possible. The fiancee, Joel, was all aflutter when we arrived, bursting at the seams to unload a lot of pent up stuff on my wife. For starters, her wristwatch had stopped when his funeral had begun, and had not resumed until the moment the funeral ended. I didn't see that this actually proved anything, but it did make me wonder. Anyway, I didn't have much opportunity to think because Joel was jabbering on and on about black cats and bumps in the night.

Joel, my first wife and my daughter and I had a late dinner that evening. Soon afterwards, I decided it was time for me to turn in. My head was starting to ache from trying to keep up with the conversation, which was in French. It looked as though Joel and my wife were well on the way to staying up all night talking, so I suggested that I put Sophie to bed and then turn in myself.

Sophie was in another room, playing with her dolls. We said goodnight to her mom and Joel, descended a dark, circular staircase, and walked hand in hand through a dimly lit storage room. As in past years, we'd be sleeping in Philippe's apartment. My hand closed around the knob and I pushed the door open.

I Enter the Apartment of a Dead Friend

Nothing had changed. Every piece of furniture, every wall hanging was exactly as he'd left it.

What happened next is difficult to explain. The most bizarre sensation overwhelmed me. I felt Philippe in the room, present among his belongings—the American Indian throw on the bed, the primitive masks and spears on the walls, the little statues and knickknacks from all over the world, including local deities and fertility gods. His presence was palpable, and it grew more so each second, seeming to close in on me, as if he had moved close to examine my face.

I could almost feel his breath, and I felt he wanted to speak to me.

I didn't want to upset my daughter, so I helped her into her pajamas, and went through the usual bedtime routine of a story. At last, I put her down in a child's bed, which had been positioned at the foot of Philippe's and turned out the lights, except for one by the bed I'd use to read by. Then I crawled under the covers.

All was silent. I opened a book, but could not concentrate.

Philippe's presence was strong, particularly when I looked at the primitive wall hanging of a sunburst. The hand woven image reminded me of the rising sun of Japan. My eyes were drawn to the center until the circle filled my vision.

What seemed a disembodied voice said, "Don't think about ghosts. It doesn't do any good to think about ghosts."

It was my daughter, Sophie. I'd thought she was asleep but along with every hair on my body, she was sitting up.

I had no idea she even knew what a ghost was, or rather what a ghost was supposed to be. We'd never talked about them. At that point, I didn't think they even existed. Thomas Hobbes had known what he was talking about, right? Man oh man, I certainly hoped so.

In retrospect I should have asked, "Why do you say that, Sophie?" But I wasn't thinking clearly. Instead, I said, "That's correct, Sophie, honey. It doesn't do any good to think about ghosts."

She laid back down, and I didn't hear from her again that night.

Who Was Doing the Talking?

What do you suppose caused Sophie to sit up and make that rather interesting observation? I believe that three possibilities exist. First, although I don't recall that we'd ever talked about it and neither did my wife when I told her about it later, Sophie may have been aware that

Philippe was dead and that we were spending the night in a dead man's apartment. This unsettling idea may have played on her mind, as it obviously played on mine. She simply may have been reassuring herself—"There's no need to be afraid of the dark. There aren't really any goblins under the bed." Only, my experience as a father of four is that young children believe there are goblins under the bed no matter how emphatically one assures them they're not. Anyway, she didn't say that ghosts aren't real. She said I ought not to think about them.

Second, she may have picked up on my thoughts through mental telepathy. People who believe in such things think those who are closely related such as a mother and son or father and daughter or sister and brother are particularly susceptible to this sort of telepathy—which of course old world view people maintain can't exist. I was indeed thinking about a ghost. Maybe she tuned in on this and decided to give me a piece of worldly, three-year-old daughter advice. I must say, however, that she refrained from dishing it out again until she was approximately nineteen. And as every parent of a nineteen-year-old can verify, at that age the child knows everything and the parent knows nothing—absolutely nothing—encumbered as parents are by the stupidity that comes from having reached one's forties.

The third possibility is that Philippe had crept into Sophie's three-year-old, half-asleep mind and was using her larynx—since he no longer had one—to communicate as he'd promised he would. If so, the message he chose is particularly significant in light of his former preoccupation with death and his reported suicide. "Don't think about ghosts. It doesn't do any good." I've taken that to mean, live life while you can. Death will come soon enough.

Maybe you can think of another explanation. If so, write to me in care of the publisher of this book because I'd be interested in hearing it. Otherwise, take your pick from the possibilities listed above. Be advised, though, that the second two require something to have happened that old world view folks will say cannot—either unspoken thoughts passing between Sophie and me, or unspoken thoughts passing from Philippe's ghost to Sophie and then aloud to me. My intuition—which old world view folks also say cannot exist—tells me it was the latter. Why? Because of the extremely strong sense of Philippe's presence in the room. But that's something I can only tell you about and hope you get some inkling of. You'd have to experience it yourself to understand the full effect that such a presence can have.

So, What Does This Say About What Happened at Salem?

If Philippe was able to somehow enter Sophie and use her body as a vehicle to speak to me, it suggests possession is possible by a disembodied spirit. This raises the question, after the flesh and blood body roams Earth, does a spiritual or "thought" body continue to exist? If what I think I experienced was more than a coincidence and hallucination, that may be the case. This idea would certainly also seem to be supported by the near death experiences (NDEs), which have been reported, written about and researched by a number of medical doctors.

Old world view holders have tried to explain NDEs by telling us people were experiencing some sort of process that takes place in the brain when we die caused by a lack of oxygen. But some think they are grasping at straws.

Consider what one doctor wrote about that:

> The Light is the one element of the near-death experience that brain researchers can't even come close to explaining. The testimony of children is clear on this point: The Light is the key element of the NDE. How can we scientifically explain this light after death? I do not know of any biochemical or psychological explanation for why we would experience a bright light as the final stage of bodily death.[15]

The Unity of Reality Is One Aspect of the Near Death Experience

Quantum physicists speak the unity of all things. It's interesting to note that the sense of unity often is reinforced by an NDE. Raymond Moody tells us in his book, *The Light Beyond,* that NDEers come back to life with a feeling everything in the universe is connected. They don't always find this concept easy to define but most have new respect for nature and the world around them. To illustrate, Dr. Moody quotes a man he described as a hard-driving, no-nonsense businessman who had an NDE during a cardiac arrest at the age of sixty-two:

> The first thing I saw when I awoke in the hospital was a flower, and I cried. Believe it or not, I had never really seen a flower until

---

[15] Melvin Morse, M.D., (with Paul Perry), pat 133, *Closer* to *the Light,* Ballantine Books, New York. 1990.

I came back from death. One big thing I learned when I died was that we are all part of one big, living universe. If we think we can hurt another person or another living thing without hurting ourselves, we are sadly mistaken. I look at a forest or a flower or a bird now, and say, "That is me, part of me." We are connected with all things and if we send love along those connections, then we are happy.

Five steps seem to be common to NDEs:

1. A sense of being dead; sudden awareness of a fatal accident or of not surviving an operation.

2. An out-of-body experience; the sensation of peering down on one's body. NDEers often report back the scene of their near death with uncanny accuracy, quoting doctors and witnesses verbatim.

3. Some kind of tunnel experience, a sense of moving upward or through a narrow passage.

4. Light; light "beings"; God or a Godlike entity. For those having a "hell-like" experience, the opposite may be true darkness or a lack of light.

5. Life review; being shown one's life, sometimes highlighting one's mistakes or omissions. One is said to feel what others felt—good and bad—as a result of actions the person took and words spoken during

the life and to understand what "might have been" had they followed a different course.

An argument can be made that the NDE adheres fairly closely to the Christian idea of heaven and hell. Heaven is generally supposed to be a place or a state of being where one is with God or Christ. This corresponds to the Light and the beings of light described in step four above.

Hell is often thought of as being separated from God, or lost in the darkness so to speak. In her bestseller, *Embraced by the Light*, Betty Eadie writes, "Some who die as atheists, or those who have bonded to the world through greed, bodily appetites, or other earthly commitments find it difficult to move on, and they become earth-bound. They often lack the faith and power to reach for, or in some cases even to recognize, the energy and light that pulls us toward God. These spirits stay on Earth until they learn to accept the greater power around them and to let go of the world. When I was in the black mass [of the tunnel] before moving towards the light, I felt the presence of such lingering spirits."

According the the work of one psychiatrist, Louise Ireland-Frey, M.D., these earthbound spirits roam the earth and can become attached to—or may even come to possess or obsess—living persons. We will delve into Ireland-Frey's work later.

Let's Talk About Ghosts

Certainly the idea of ghosts is far from new. I had an uncle, for example, who told me his best friend dropped in to see him just after having died. My uncle didn't know his friend was a ghost until the next morning, when he found out the friend had passed away an hour before the visit. During that visit the friend explained several aspects of his will and told my uncle where the key was hidden to the safe deposit box in which the will was kept.

Usually, however, we don't see ghosts. We certainly don't see a spirit leave the body when someone dies. After my encounter with what I thought might be Philippe's ghost, I began to wonder how could all this be if things we can't see aren't real?

Ah, but often they are. Let's give some thought to how sight works. It's one of five senses that convey information from the physical world to our brains. Without sight or hearing we'd be like Helen Keller. We'd have a hard time imagining what the world around us is like. But even with 20/20 vision, our knowledge is only an approximation of what exists. For example, at this moment what you see is reflected light that has passed through the lenses of your eyes and struck the retinae. The retinae have translated the light into impulses and these are sent by the optic nerve to your brain. The brain translates these impulses into a picture of the page of a book that looks like the thousands of other pages of books you've seen.

But there's so much you don't see. You don't see the comparatively huge distances between paper molecules and ink molecules. You probably don't see the tiny cotton fibers, and you surely don't see microbes squirming around that were left by the last person who picked up this book.

Okay, you say. But scientists can see microbes with a microscope, and cotton fibers, and even some of the empty space between molecules. We know these exist.

Well, then, look around the room, and think about other things you can't see. For one, the space is filled with television and radio waves. Think of all the cell phone conversations going on you can't see or hear. Maybe one is in your ear right now, and the waves are rotting out your brain.

True, you say. But all it takes is a television, radio, or cell phone tuned to the right frequency to know they're there.

Yes. And with the right kind of lens or photographic paper you'd also be able to detect infrared light, which the eyes cannot. And X-rays. And gamma rays. And who knows what else.

A lot of things you can't see exist, like it or not. Suppose for a moment the instruments to detect them hadn't been invented?

Let's think about a few other invisible things that are unquestionably real. What about a magnetic field? We can't see that or take a picture of it.

We could sprinkle some iron filings on a piece of paper, place a magnet in the middle and shake it gently. Presto, a butterfly shape would form.

How about a gravitational field? That's too big for paper and iron filings, but we know it exists because without it we'd fall off Earth.

Fields Made of Curved Space

What are these fields made of? They aren't material. And how do they work?

These kinds of fields are curved space. The filings are drawn into the pattern of the space around the magnet. This creates what's called magnetic force. The moon follows the curved space created by the gravitational field around Earth. Earth follows the curved space around the sun and so on. These forces are curved space. If life is the fabric of space, perhaps a ghost is curved space, too. Maybe space in the shape of Philippe was the presence I felt that night.

We will consider this possibility later.

Chapter Five: The Milk Turns Sour in the Land of Milk and Honey

During the first third of the seventeenth century, members of the Puritan sect in England believed the country was headed straight to hell. The reason was the Anglican Church continued to employ Roman Catholic ritual, which apparently the Puritans considered devil-inspired. The Church and England needed to be cleansed, they believed, or only God knew what terrible fate would befall the land. They were so sure the Almighty was about to unleash His wrath, many felt the time had come to get out of Merry Old England and find a place where they'd be safe. They may have been mistaken in this regard, but they were quite clever in how they decided to remedy the situation. Like Colonel Potter on the old TV show M*A*S*H, Charles I—the reining monarch—probably didn't realize what he was signing when a Radar-like acquaintance who happened to be a Puritan, shoved a paper called the Cambridge Agreement under his nose and handed him a pen. Charles probably thought he was authorizing another run-of-the-mill commercial venture in the New World. But the Puritans had pulled a fast one. The royal charter, signed on March 4, 1629, authorized the Massachusetts Bay Company, which amounted to a Puritan colony in New England, a theocracy that would have Puritanism as its official religion.

A Great Adventure Is Embarked Upon

In Spring, 1630, the new governor of this enterprise, John Winthrop, led eleven ships and seven hundred passengers—the Winthrop Fleet of 1630—to the Massachusetts Bay Colony in the New World. The was the greatest assembly of vessels up to that time to carry English citizens overseas to a new homeland.

Winthrop, for whom the town of Winthrop, Massachusetts is named, deserves a mention here. As governor—a position to which he was returned many times—he was reported to have been one of the least radical of the Puritans. He did his best to keep the number of executions for heresy to a minimum, and he worked to prevent such innovations as veiling women, which many Puritans supported. Were it not for him, we might have Riyadh on the Charles River, rather than Boston. On the downside, however, he also gave the Puritans a vision which may have helped foster the witch hysteria sixty years later.

Winthrop is well known for his "city on a hill" sermon, in which he declared Puritan colonists emigrating to the New World to be members of a pact made with God to create a holy community. This excerpt gives a taste of the Puritan mind set and reflects widely held beliefs of that time:

> For we must consider that we shall be as a
> city upon a hill. The eyes of all people are
> upon us. So that if we shall deal falsely with
> our God in this work we have undertaken . . .
> we shall be made a story and a by-word
> throughout the world. We shall open the
> mouths of enemies to speak evil of the ways
> of God . . . We shall shame the faces of many
> of God's worthy servants, and cause their
> prayers to be turned into curses upon us til
> we be consumed out of the good land whither
> we are going.

Talk about putting the pressure on. These people had set about the task of building of a society in the New World based on Puritan ideals and a direct relationship with God. The community they would create was to serve as a positive example for the Old World to emulate. It's important to understand this because this belief was likely an important factor that led to the witch hysteria.

My ancestor, Susannah North Martin, was a child of seven or eight when this speech was given, yet it marked such a huge event in her life she probably remembered it to her dying day. The belief the community was especially ordained by God—in partnership or pact with Him—was still very much alive when she was an adult. This had a powerful effect on how people interpreted events and the world around them. After all, for them, breaking a covenant with God was not something to be lightly done. Everyone knew the story of Noah and the Ark. God directed Noah to build one because He was fed up with the people of that day. The people He had created out of clay had become corrupt and "the Lord saw how great man's wickedness on the earth had become,"[16] which caused God to raise more than an eyebrow. He raised his finger, pointed it, and sent a flood that drowned the whole lot—except Noah, his family, and the animals who were all that was left to start over.

Woe be unto him or her who broke a promise to God or got out of line.

A Stable Society Is Formed

To avoid incurring God's wrath, the Puritans tied to maintain perfect order in their society. Even the smallest sins were punished. No one was allowed to live alone for

[16] Genesis 6:5, NIV translation.

fear they'd succumb to sin. Parents were to instruct their children and servants diligently in the Word of God. Skipping church was not an option. And on and on it went.

These conventions and institutions led to an extremely stable and structured society in New England in contrast to the unstable, loosely-bound and perhaps even somewhat bawdy society of the early British colony of Virginia. If you don't believe life down south was different, visit Colonial Williamsburg today and watch and listen as a minstrel strums his mandolin and belts out drinking songs of the Colonial era. Some of the lyrics will make you blush. Heck, in Virginia you might not be able to accuse your neighbor or some old hag of witchcraft without fear of a hefty fine, but you could have a helluva of a time carrying on and swilling ale at the Kings Arms Tavern. And who knew what went on in the upstairs bedrooms.

Suffice it to say the foundation of the witchcraft crisis was laid by the world view passed down to their children and grandchildren from the first settlers of Massachusetts Bay. They were a chosen people, charged with bringing God's message to a heathen land which had long been ruled by Satan.

Did I say Massachusetts was ruled by Satan?

It's true. The Puritans considered the Indians to be devil worshipers. The settlers didn't bother to find out much about or to study the Indians' spiritual beliefs. They could see whatever they were doing must demonic just by glimpsing a witch doctor at work, or by watching the practically naked pagans dance around, chant, and conjure up spirits in the smoke of a campfire. And the Indians had another strike against them in the Puritans' view. Besides these obvious signs of devil worship, north of Massachusetts they were aligned with the French, and the French were followers of that most despicable of all religions, Roman Catholicism.

Talk about heathens. The woods were full of them.

God Speaks to His People Through Events and Circumstances

Puritans believed God spoke to them daily through His Providences—that is, through the small and large events of their lives, and this was certainly true in their adopted homeland. Remarkable signs in the sky (comets, the aurora borealis), natural catastrophes (hurricanes, droughts), smallpox epidemics, the sudden deaths of children or spouses, unexpected good fortune all carried messages from God to his people. There were no accidents. New England's Puritans, even in the third generation, believed themselves surrounded by the invisible world already mentioned in addition to the physical world experienced by way of the senses. Both worlds communicated God's messages, because both operated under His direction and control. Satan, whom they understood to be the leader of a army of fallen angels, played a major role in the invisible world. Like everyone and everything, Satan had been created by God. He was Lucifer, the Light Bearer, who had at one time had been God's right-hand man and faithful helper. But as time passed Satan got too big for his britches and wanted to be like God. He wanted people to worship him instead of the Almighty. So Satan corralled other angels who'd been booted out of heaven and enlisted them as minions to help do his dirty work. And of course, he was always on the lookout for new recruits who might be willing to sell their souls.

Yes, Satan was powerful, all right. But as noted before,

God could squash him if He wanted, anytime he wanted. To believe otherwise would be to deny God's omnipotence. As Pat Robertson said to Disney World's officials, "I wouldn't wave that Gay Days festival in His face if I were you."

God Unleashes Satan in a Devastating War

For a while things went along relatively smoothly for the Puritans and their city on a hill. Then, in the last quarter of the seventeenth century, two successive and devastating wars took place on the northeastern frontier. King Philip's War and King William's War—or the First and Second Indian Wars as they are also called—wreaked havoc on what had been prosperous Puritan settlements to the north of Massachusetts Bay. Since events were interpreted as messages from God, and a reliable measure of His attitude toward His people, it's important to know what was going on in the Puritans' world leading up to and during the witch hysteria.

The First Indian War was extremely costly, but it did end with a victory in southern New England in late summer 1676 and came to a close in the northeast in spring 1678 in what amounted to a standoff. But though they were able to breathe easily for a while, another setback followed.

King James II ascended to the throne of England. Unlike his brother, Charles II, James was a religious man, and to the undoubtedly great horror of the Puritans was a Roman Catholic. Most in England were Protestants, but it is possible they may have submitted to a Catholic king had he not used his official power to change the state religion in England to Catholicism. And King James was not content to confine this to the home country. To the dismay of the Puritans in New England, he revoked the Cambridge Agreement and sent a tyrant, Edmund Andros, to govern.

From 1685, when James ascended to the throne, unrest and turmoil increased both at home and in the mother country, until three years later the opposition was so formidable James fled from England and took refuge in France. When this happened, James' daughter and her husband, the Prince of Orange, became the joint sovereigns of England, known as William and Mary. A distinguished institution of higher learning down the road from me in Williamsburg, Virginia is named for them.

The king of France, Louis XIV, was a Catholic and backed James as the rightful king of England with the result that war broke out between the two nations. King William rejected an offer of neutrality for the colonies, and what is known as "King William's War" was underway. For the colonists this renewed the old problem of French encroachments on the northern border. The French were determined to hold the St. Lawrence country, and to extend their power over the vast Mississippi basin. In addition, both the English colonists and the French were jealous of each other's fisheries and the fur trade, not to mention the intense feelings of animosity generated by religious differences that held sway.

The war began with a series of Indian massacres instigated by Frontenac, the governor of Canada. The first of these was the destruction of Dover, New Hampshire, a town of fifty inhabitants. One night in July, 1689, two squaws came to the home of Major Waldron and begged a night's lodging. He let them in, and in the night they got up and let in a bunch Indians who had been waiting. Waldron was tortured and put to death, the town was burned to the ground, about half the people were massacred, and the remainder were carried away and sold into slavery. In the following month Pemaquid, Maine, met a similar fate. In February, 1690, a group of French and Indians, sent by Frontenac, came to the town of Schenectady on the Mohawk. For nearly a month they had faced the wintry blasts, plowing their way through the deep snow on their mission of destruction. At midnight they fell upon the sleeping village with whoops and yells that some say could have raised the dead. In a few hours it was all over. The town lay in ashes. More than sixty were massacred, many were taken captive, a few escaped into the night and reached Albany. The towns of Casco and Salmon Falls soon after met a similar fate. You can imagine how the Puritans interpreted these Providences. God obviously was unhappy with them.

With the war now well underway, a land force was sent against Montreal by way of Lake Champlain, and a naval expedition set sail against Quebec. The expenses of the former were borne by Connecticut and New York, and of the latter by Massachusetts. Sir William Phips of Maine commanded the naval force. He had thirty or more vessels and two thousand men.

Frontenac's forces successfully repelled the land force, which turned back disheartened. Then Frontenac's men turned their attention to the defense of Quebec, but little effort was required. Phips proved to be a weak commander, and the fleet, after reaching Quebec and finding it well fortified, returned to Boston without striking an effective blow. The people of Massachusetts were greatly disappointed. It appeared God had turned His back, not to mention that outfitting an armada had not been cheap. The debt of the colony had reached an enormous figure, and to meet it, bills of credit, or paper money, were issued to the amount of £40,000, a mighty sum in those days. Phips was sent to England to seek aid of the king and a renewal of the old charter, which had been struck down by King James.

Over on the other side of the pond, however, King William was hard pressed to keep things together in his own backyard and elected to let the colonies fight their own battles. He also refused to restore the old charter, but he did grant a new one, and he made Phips the first royal governor of Massachusetts. New charter in hand, Phips took office in May 1692 in time to set up and oversee the official witch trials that sent nineteen to the gallows. Meanwhile, the war dragged on. In time the towns of York, Maine, Durham, New Hampshire, and Groton, Massachusetts, were the scenes of bloody massacres, and hundreds of people were slain.

People had to be asking, as Jesus had asked on the cross, "My God, my God, why have you forsaken me?"[17]

The Puritans' Faith is Badly Shaken

The success of the Wabanaki Indian heathens and their French Catholic allies called into question whether Puritanism would ultimately triumph over all adversity as its followers had long assumed. Even the most faithful had to be wondering, were they or were they not God's chosen people? Devastating defeat after devastating defeat was attributed not to mistakes by their military and political leaders, but to God's providence or lack thereof. God had, they concluded, allowed Satan to visit these afflictions upon them as chastisements for their many sins of omission and commission.

---

[17] Matthew 27:46, NIV translation.

With the death and destruction of the Second Indian War on their minds, it appeared the Almighty was sending a second plague upon them when He allowed an outbreak of witchcraft in Essex County in 1692. Mary Beth Norton points out in her book, *In the devil's Snare,*[18] that the connection the Puritans drew between the war and the witchcraft epidemic can be spotted in the examinations and trials in the repeated spectral sightings of a "black man," whom the afflicted described as resembling an Indian, and in the threats that the witches and the devil would—as the Indians had—"tear to pieces" or "knock in the head" those who dared to oppose them.

It would be going too far to claim the war caused the witchcraft crisis, but it can be argued it created the conditions that allowed it to get out of hand. What might otherwise have remained a minor episode, snowballed instead—turning into a full-fledged crisis. The incident in Salem Village that started the snowball rolling resembled other New England witchcraft cases we've already covered. The fits experienced by Salem Village girls were not everyday occurrences, but they were no more spectacular than those of the Goodwin children and others. But these new fits occurred in an atmosphere marked by ongoing political conflict and uncertainty, along with war and destruction—in other words, at a time when the Puritans felt under siege—that God had given the devil plenty of rope, then turned His back.

The Magistrates Lose Perspective

In cases before 1692, New England's magistrates had displayed a certain amount of levelheaded skepticism when charges of witchcraft were brought forward. The

---

[18] Alfred A. Knopf, 2002

judges believed in the existence of witches, of course, but they also knew that legally-acceptable proof of guilt was often hard to come by. Someone frequently would allege difficult-to-prove malefic activities by a neighbor viewed as a vengeful witch. But English law required two witnesses to a capital crime such as witchcraft with the result that convictions and executions were fairly rare. But in 1692 circumstances weren't normal. God's people appeared to be under attack by demonic forces with the result that first the Essex justices—and later all the members of the court—may have been more receptive to charges they otherwise might have dismissed.

Besides, these weren't run of the mill accusations made by someone whose cow had stopped giving milk. They weren't brought by a disgruntled neighbor who might have a bone to pick. They came from young girls whose symptoms looked an awful lot like those of the Goodwin children, and no one doubted they'd been victims of a frightful old hag who'd been practicing devil worship and witchcraft. Later, as time passed and tensions grew, the accusations came from teenagers and grown women whose terrible sufferings were obvious to all who witnessed them, and these horrible sufferings were viewed firsthand by everyone packed inside the Salem Village meeting house. Obviously, the men running the show viewed them as ample evidence to convict.

I'm not a psychologist, but I have to wonder whether a subtle, perhaps even subconscious motivation may have been at work on top of other conditions that made officials receptive to belief in an epidemic outbreak of witches. The people who served as judges and magistrates were also the colony's civic and military leaders. Governor Phips himself had led a foray against the French and Indians at Quebec and had failed miserably. The man led a force of thirty vessels and two thousand men and turned back, hardly having firing a shot. Today's pundits on Fox News and CNN, along with leaders of the opposition party, would have placed blame for the setback squarely on his shoulders. Perhaps Phips and his colleagues subconsciously thought that if the devil and his followers were behind the colony's troubles including the disastrous loses in the war—then it was not they who were incompetent. In a twisted sort of way it may have been comforting to believe God and the devil were to blame for the unfortunate state of affairs, and not them. Maybe it's not surprising these men quickly became invested in believing in the reputed witches' guilt.

Chapter Six: The Devil Comes to Zion

Ironically, the events that let to the witch hysteria got rolling in a Puritan minister's kitchen—the reverend Samuel Parris. It's probably not a coincidence Parris had a copy of Cotton Mather's book, *Memorable Providences,* in his library—and a small library at that.[19] Back then, people didn't sit around glued to the TV or playing Game Cube and were actually likely to talk to one another and read books out loud for entertainment. This being the case, it's possible if not probable Parris shared the book with his family, so it's likely they probably knew all about the Goodwin Children, and the fits and the torture they'd endured as a result of the malice and witchcraft of Goodwife Glover. With vivid images of the Goodwin children simmering in their minds, it seems likely the Parris girls were primed and ready for what was coming their way. Later, we will explore what science has to say about the power of suggestion and belief, but at this point in our story, let's just say it can be considerable.

Tituba and Her Magic Tricks

Before sitting down to write this book I did quite a bit of reading about the witch trials and the events leading up to them. According to some accounts, Reverend Parris and his wife spent a fair amount of time away from home in the winter of 1691-92,[20] as any minister and his wife would

---

[19] "Salem Witch Trials" © 1998 by A&E Television Networks.
[20] Dates from this era can be confusing because the Feast of the Annunciation, 25th March, marked the new year. England and its colonies did not adopt the Gregorian calendar until 1752, at which time the start of year date was moved to January 1. As a result, texts often show January-March 25 dates in the year of the hysteria as 1691/2.

have done, visiting the members of their parish. Their daughter, Betty Parris, age nine, and her eleven year old cousin, Abigail Williams, were often left in the care of the family's Carib Indian slave, Tituba. It's likely Tituba warmed the cold New England nights reminiscing about her childhood in sunny Barbados, telling fanciful tales involving magic. There is also evidence she demonstrated voodoo tricks for the girls. Despite their young age, the girls certainly knew this type of behavior was strictly forbidden. The head of the household was, after all, a preacher—and a Puritan preacher at that. But the girls managed to keep it a secret from the adults as their group began to grow. Within a short time it included six other young women and girls, ranging in age from twelve to twenty.

I'm not going to say at this point whether or not I believe there's anything other than imaginations at work in what happens when people take part in occult activities. We will get into that later when we take a look at what experts say about the paranormal. What I will say now is that occult practitioners tell amateurs who dabble in occult activities they do so at their own peril. Apparently, the occultists have a good deal of support in this regard. I just plugged the words "Ouija warning" into Google, and it turned up 123,000 hits.

Beware of Ouija Boards

I only checked out the entries on page one of Google's listings but all were about scary things that happened to people who were messing around with Ouija boards. A typical example is that of a woman and her friend who were in the kitchen speaking to a spirit through the board who told them his name was Dave, and that he was a fireman who died in 1938. They were chatting with Dave when she realized her hands were above her head and no matter how she tried she couldn't bring them down. She also was unable to speak. Imagine her panic. In the meantime, her friend was busy asking Dave questions, and didn't notice. She felt she was beginning to hyperventilate and wanted desperately to get her friend's attention but couldn't move or utter a sound. She said she felt a heaviness pressing down on her like a dead weight and all the while the Ouija board kept her friend busy answering questions. Finally, the friend looked up at her and saw in an instant something was terribly wrong. The friend picked up the board, ran with it to the top of the basement stairs, and tossed it down. The woman was released from her paralysis. Even so, other strange things kept happening until the next morning when they deposited the Ouija board in a dumpster in the alley.

The advice of every entry on Google I read is the same—stay away from Ouija boards and such. No doubt the Parris girls and their friends had heard similar warnings about fooling around with occult activities. But Tituba's lurid tales and voodoo tricks stirred up some measure of excitement in what was without doubt a typically boring New England winter, and their curiosity probably got the best of them. It wasn't long before they began to act in strange and aberrant ways. They fell into fits. They went into trances. They felt pricked with pins, cut with knives. They were tempted to throw themselves into the fire and commit suicide. They had to stop their ears when the minister preached the word of God because they couldn't listen to it. They screamed, cried out, threw things about the room. This was is not the behavior of young Christian girls, certainly not in Puritan New England. And it was a lot like the Goodwin kids.

One Ouija-board-like trick Tituba is thought to have demonstrated was a variation on crystal ball gazing used to divine the future. An egg was cracked open and the white allowed to slide into a glass of water. This was then held up to a candle. The girls were told to look into the egg white, and they would see images that would foretell the occupations of their future husbands.

I once read a book about crystal gazing written by a doctor of psychology. He believed people see in the crystal what's in their own unconscious minds. The gray, shiny image of the glass, or egg white in this case, simply provides a screen or medium on which to project mental images. I suspect the girls must have been feeling pretty guilty about fooling around with magic, and also worried about ending up like the Goodwin children. Often we bring upon ourselves what we worry about, creating a reality we'd rather not have, and this may have been what happened. One thought she saw a coffin in the egg white, which must have really freaked her out.

According to John Hale, a pastor of a church in Boston at the time, the whole Salem witchcraft saga could be traced to experiments made with the occult:[21]

"I fear some young persons, through a vain curiosity to know their future condition, have tampered with the devil's tools so far that hereby one door was opened to Satan to play those pranks, Anno 1692. I knew one of the afflicted persons who (as I was credibly informed) did try with an egg and a glass to find her future husband's calling, till there came up a coffin, that is, a specter in likeness of a coffin. And she was afterwards followed with diabolical molestation to her death, and so died a single person a just

---

[21] *A Modest Inquiry Into The Nature Of Witchcraft*, By John Hale, 1702

warning to others to take heed of handling the devil's weapons lest they get a wound thereby.

"Another, I was called to pray with, being under sore fits and vexations of Satan. And upon examination I found that she had tried the same charm, and after her confession of it and manifestation of repentance for it, and our prayers to God for her, she was speedily released from those bonds of Satan."

The old rhyme "Rich man, poor man, beggar man, thief" is another way for little girls to divine their future husband's occupation. Such an activity would be considered quite innocent in the twenty-first century, but it was anything but innocent for the two seventeenth century girls in Reverend Parris' kitchen and the friends who joined them in such activities. Whether it was brought on by guilt, their imaginations, or something truly paranormal was at work, perhaps it should not be surprising that they began to display hysterical symptoms, and that one of them was "followed with diabolical molestations to her death."

Hale does not name the children, but the one who was cured was probably Betty Parris, the minister's nine-year old daughter. She disappeared from Salem Village late in March, when her father sent her to the household of Stephen Sewall in Salem Town, possibly because fits were known to be contagious and he wanted her removed from contact with those who were still having them. The other girl was probably his eleven-year-old niece, Abigail Williams, although we can't be sure. There is very little information to be found about the later lives of most of the afflicted girls.

White Magic Is Employed to Break the Spell

Parris had been a merchant in Barbados before moving to New England and entering the clergy. He brought with him the slave woman Tituba and her husband John when he moved. Both were Carib Indians, and though the egg and glass is an English rather than an Indian method of divining, she is thought to have been behind it.

In any case, as mentioned, the girls strange behavior grew extremely alarming. Betty Parris and Abigail Williams were obviously very sick as were their friends who had also, presumably, been experimenting with the occult. Chief among these were Ann Putnam, Junior (twelve years old), Mary Warren (twenty), Mercy Lewis (nineteen), Mary Walcott (sixteen), and Elizabeth Hubbard (seventeen). Parris took them to various doctors, but their symptoms grew steadily worse. When Doctor Griggs made his diagnosis of witchcraft, Parris apparently didn't accept it at first. He continued his regimen of prayer and fasting in the hope of curing the girls.

Reverend Parris may not have been anxious to believe the children were bewitched, perhaps because he felt it reflected poorly on him, but his neighbors were. They began to ask the girls who was afflicting them. The girls would not or could not give an answer. It was then that Mary Walcott's aunt, Mary Sibley, decided to employ white magic in an attempt to break the spell, or at least to find out who was behind it. On February 25, she went to the minister's Indian slaves, Tituba and John, and had them prepare a witch cake, the major ingredients of which were meal and the children's urine. Sounds tasty, doesn't it? This was baked in the fire and fed to the Parris's dog, on the theory the animal was a "familiar"—a spirit in animal form assigned to a witch by Satan.

This happened without the minister's knowledge. When he found out about it a month later, he was appalled. Mary Sibley's witch cake was, as Parris put it, "Going to the devil for help against the devil." He lectured her privately about it and before the entire congregation he called her "to deep humiliation for what she has done." In tears, she acknowledged her grievous error, but it was too late. The horse was out of the stable. The witch cake had been baked, and by it Salem's goose was cooked. As Parris said, "the devil hath been raised among us, and his rage is vehement and terrible; and, when he shall be silenced, the Lord only knows."

The Girls Name Their Tormentors

Puritans believed witches could tempt or seduce people into becoming witches themselves, and this was something to guard against. The girls' symptoms, their convulsions and so forth, were seen as a reaction against a witch who was tempting them to join the forces of Satan. In other words, they were struggling not to become witches. Reverend Parris questioned the girls relentlessly, trying to get them to identify the witch who was behind it. Finally, Elizabeth and Abigail named Tituba—an obvious choice, her status being that of a slave. Perhaps the accusation was justified to some degree if it was true she'd been dabbling in magic to amuse the girls.

But the girls didn't stop with Tituba. Next, they accused Sarah Good, the town beggar. Her stooped and wrinkled appearance, her irascible temper and low status in the village no doubt made her an easy mark, and from the girls' point of view, a logical target.

Sarah Good had not always been poor. Her father had been a prosperous innkeeper, but he had drowned himself twenty years earlier, when Sarah was nineteen. She had been cheated of her inheritance by her mother's new husband. Now the wife of a ne'er-do-well and the mother of several young children, Sarah was reduced to begging for food, and she did so in an angry, ill-natured spirit. If refused, she would turn away cursing. A kindly neighbor who put her up for a while at last turned her out, defeated by her bad temper and worried she would set fire to the house with the pipe she smoked.

The girls also accused Sarah Osborne, another logical target. This Sarah had also once been prosperous, having married Robert Prince, the owner of a hundred-and-fifty-acre farm. But when her husband died, she scandalized Salem Village by buying a young Irish immigrant, Alexander Osborne, for fifteen pounds. That is, she bought his "indenture," the right to own him for a period of time as a servant. Fifteen pounds was a substantial sum in those days, but he must have proved worth it because she later married him. The scandal of the transaction lay chiefly in the general belief that the two lived as husband and wife before they actually were. Such an offense, if proved, could be punished by whipping. The eventual wedding did not lessen its wickedness in the eyes of most. Also, Sarah Osborne had made matters worse by contesting her first husband's will to try to keep his lands as her own, though he had left them to her in trust for his sons. This too caused a scandal. In 1692 the dispute, begun fifteen years before, was still unresolved. Sarah and her husband, Alexander, were no longer as prosperous and Sarah was bedridden.

Another strike against both Sarahs was that neither of them attended church. When their names became known, four "yeomen of Salem Village in the County of Essex" by the names of Joseph Hutchinson, Thomas Putnam, Edward Putnam, and Thomas Preston, appeared before a magistrate and swore out warrants for suspicion of witchcraft.

The warrants were issued on February 29, and on March 1 the three accused women were formerly questioned by two Salem magistrates who were to conduct the majority of the pre trial examinations: John Hathorne—whose great-geat-grandson Nathaniel, author of *The House of the Seven Gables,* added a 'w' to the family name—and Jonathan Corwin. On March 1, 1692, the three women were brought before an informal tribunal in the meeting house of Salem Village in order to establish if there was evidence of witchcraft. Back then people often were not defended by a lawyer, and these three women didn't have one. They were obliged to answer the magistrates' questions without the benefit of legal advice, and it was up to each to defend herself.

The purpose of this examination was to determine if sufficient evidence existed to bring the matter to trial. Perhaps due to the sense of being under siege from Satan and his Indian allies, as has been discussed, magistrates and the ministers advising them were willing to accept a type of evidence that had been considered unacceptable in other New England witchcraft proceedings—spectral evidence. Many who took part in the trials later realized it was a grave mistake.

According to the afflicted, a witch sometimes appeared to them in spectral form—in other words, as a ghostly apparition. By allowing this, the accuser didn't have to claim it was the actual person doing the alleged pinching, biting or hitting. All they had to do was testify the person's specter or ghost had done or was doing so.

Sarah Good Is the First to Testify

The preliminary hearing began with the interrogation of Sarah Good. In a deposition taken before the hearing, Ann Putnam Junior had sworn that the specter of Sarah Good had tried to enlist her as a witch by getting her to sign the devil's book.

"I saw the apparition of Sarah Good, which did torture me grievously. She did prick me and pinch me and urge me most vehemently to write in her book."

Several of the other girls confirmed Ann's accusations.

Sarah Good did not help herself when she took the stand by acting as one would expect an accused witch to act. She maintained she had done nothing to the children, but when—after the children fell on the floor in fits—she was asked who did afflict them, she accused her fellow prisoner, Sarah Osborne. This was likely taken by the magistrates as the "implicit confession" one should be on the lookout for, which they'd read about in Reverend Bernard's *Guide to Grand-Jury Men.* As you recall, he'd written that witches were able to see the specters of other witches. If Sarah Good could see the specter of Sarah Osborne, this meant Sarah Good must be a witch. They almost surely came to this conclusion because the summary of evidence later prepared for Good's trial observed, "None here sees the witches but the afflicted and themselves," and Sarah Good, "not being afflicted must consequently be a witch."

Strike three against her may have been that her

husband, William, testified—perhaps in an effort to save his own skin—that "he was afraid that she either was witch or would be one very quickly." When Hathorne asked if he had any evidence she practiced witchcraft, William replied that he did not. He thought she might be a witch because of "her bad carriage to him."

"Indeed," William Good said, "I may say with tears that she is an enemy to all good." The humor in this remark was probably lost on everyone.[22] He added that he'd seen a "strange tit or wart" on his wife's body, and we know what that meant.

Sarah's daughter Dorcas, whose age varies between four and six depending on the source, also testified against her. She said her mother had familiars: "three birds—one black, one yellow and that these birds hurt the children and afflicted persons."

I'll bet mom could have strangled the little darling.

A Pattern Is Set for the Conduct of the Investigation and Trials

John Hathorne asked the majority of the questions and established an attitude toward the accused other judges later assumed in the 1692 proceedings. Rather than the stance of an impartial investigator, as the judge in the Goodwin witchcraft case in Boston in 1688 had taken, Hathorne took on the role of prosecuting attorney. He presumed guilt and attempted to force a confession with bullying questions.

"Sarah Good, what evil spirit have you familiarity with?"

"None."

---

[22] Sarah Good was an enemy to all good, such as all the Good family, herself, her husband, her children—all Good. Get it?

"Have you made no contract with the devil?"

"No."

"Why do you hurt these children?"

"I do not hurt them. I scorn it."

"Who do you employ, then, to do it."

"I employ nobody."

"What creature do you employ, then?"

"No creature, but I am falsely accused."

Another important precedent was set at this examination. Hathorne asked the children to look at Sarah Good and say whether she was who afflicted them. They agreed she was the one, all right, "upon which they were all dreadfully tortured and tormented for a short space of time." When they recovered from their fits the girls charged her with causing them, saying her specter had come to them and tormented them although her body remained "at a considerable distance from them."

The magistrates may have read and been familiar with Reverend Bernard's *Guide to Grand-Jury Men*, but one piece of advice in it was largely ignored, as was already mentioned. You'll remember Bernard had advised that a capital case should not rest on spectral evidence because this was in effect, "the devil's testimony, who can lie, and that more often then speak truth." Yet in Salem, spectral evidence eventually became the central legal issue of the trials with proponents and opponents lined up on either side. On one hand, here were girls afflicted with violent physical symptoms which had no known physical cause, but which a medical doctor had attributed to witchcraft. A malicious and haggardly woman was accused of causing them. When the sufferers had pointed the finger at her they were immediately thrown into convulsions. What could be more plausible than that the convulsions were inflicted as revenge for the accusation. Yet, on the other hand, as one of the recorders noted, "none here sees the [specters of the witches] but the afflicted." If the accused had been allowed to have defense attorneys, a good one would have jumped all over this.

"Your Honor, I move to strike. No one sees these alleged specters but the persons bringing charges. How can this be admissible evidence? Who's to say they aren't making it up, or that the devil himself isn't deluding them?"

Nevertheless, Hathorne was convinced. When the children had recovered and repeated their accusation he turned to the hapless woman.

"Sarah Good, do you not see now what you have done? Why do you not tell us the truth? Why do you thus torment these poor children?"

"I do not torment them."

"Who do you employ, then?"

"1 employ nobody. I scorn it."

Sarah Good Proves to Be Her Own Worst Enemy

Part of what was behind Hathorne's bullying may have been Sarah Good's evasiveness. An example of this can be found in the record. A beggar who often sought charity from people in their houses, she was known to go away muttering when she was turned down. Hathorne asked her what she muttered.

She answered, "If I must tell, I will tell."

"Do tell us, then," Hathorne said.

"If I must tell, I will tell. It is the Commandments. I may say my Commandments, I hope."

"What Commandment is it?"

"If I must tell, I will tell. It is a psalm."

"What psalm?"

She hesitated. Then, "after a long time she muttered over some part of a psalm."

After hearing such an exchange anyone was likely to come to the conclusion Sarah Good was lying, and not very well. It seems probable what she actually muttered as she left her neighbors' houses were curses. Certainly many thought her malicious, since they attributed to her a number of inexplicable events, including the death of a cow which perished in "a sudden, terrible and strange unusual manner."

Sarah Osborne Is Caught in a Lie

So much for Sarah Good. When Sarah Osborne took the stand, she also denied she'd hurt the children. And again, they fell into fits. Hathorne asked her how this happened. Sarah, even without a defense attorney, did all right for herself with her answer though it ended up not doing her any good. Perhaps, she said, the devil took on her likeness and then went around doing harm, but she certainly didn't know anything about it. Thus, she was first at Salem to assert the principle that Satan can impersonate whomever he likes, including an innocent person. This was a matter of debate at that time, but from what I am able to determine, many if not most Protestant authorities agreed with her that, as Shakespeare's Hamlet had put it, "The devil hath power to assume a pleasing shape."

Nevertheless, the issue was quickly sidestepped at this hearing. One reason may have been that Sarah Osborne was caught in a lie, and perjury was considered a serious offense in addition to a mortal sin in the days when the Ten Commandments had not yet become the Ten

Suggestions. A lie under oath was a crime then, and it still is. It happened when Hathorne tried to find out how well she, Sarah Osborne, knew Sarah Good. Goodwife Osborne said she recognized her but did not know her name.

What did she call her when they met, Hathorne asked.

For a while she didn't answer, but at last said she called her, "Sarah."

The afflicted girls volunteered that Goodwife Osborne had said she was more likely to be bewitched than to be a witch. Hathorne asked the accused woman why.

She replied she was frighten one time in her sleep and either saw or dreamed she saw something that looked like an Indian, all black, "which did prick her in her neck and pulled her by the back part of her head to the door of the house."

Hathorne asked if she had ever seen anything else, and she said no. But several of the audience volunteered that she had once said "she would never be tied to that lying spirit any more."

No doubt this raised Hathorne's eyebrows, Satan being Prince of Lies.

"What lying spirit is this?" He asked. "Hath the devil ever deceived you and been false to you?"

"I do not know the devil. I never did see him."

"What lying spirit was it then?"

"It was a voice that I thought I heard."

"What did it propound to you?"

"That I should go no more to meeting. But I said I would, and did go the next Sabbath day."

Hathorne asked if she had been tempted further, and she said no.

Why then, he asked, hadn't she been at church?

She said she'd been sick, and unable to go. But her

husband and others contradicted her. "She had not been at meeting," they said, "this year and two months."

Tituba Spills the Beans

The examinations of Sarah Good and Sarah Osborne certainly raised suspicion and provided grounds for further examination. But the major event of that first day was the examination of Tituba. It began like the first two but quickly changed.

"Tituba, what evil spirit have you familiarity with?"

"None," she said.

"Why do you hurt these children?"

"I do not hurt them."

"Who is it then?"

"The devil, for aught I know."

"Did you never see the devil?"

"The devil came to me," Tituba said, "and bid me serve him."

Can't you almost hear the room break out in a loud murmur? Hathorne probably had to pound his gavel.

Tituba went on, with a minimum of prodding, to provide a detailed confession of witchcraft, the first of about fifty-five that were made during the Salem trials. Over the course of her testimony on March first and second, Tituba said the devil had come to her in the shape of a man—a tall man in black with white hair. At other times he had come in the shape of an animal. He had told her he was God, that she must believe in him and serve him for six years, and in return he would give her many fine things. The devil had shown her a book and she had made a mark in it, a mark that was "red like blood." Tituba said Goody Good had said she had made her mark there, "but

Goody Osborne would not tell. She was cross to me."

Sometimes the man in black had brought other witches with him—Sarah Good and Sarah Osborne and women from Boston whose names she did not know. The group of them had forced her to go with them and afflict the children. She had gone "upon a stick or pole and Good and Osborne behind me. We ride taking hold of one another; don't know how we go, for I saw no trees nor path but was presently there."

In addition, she said both Good and Osborne had familiars.

Sarah Good had a cat and a yellow bird, and the bird sucked her "between the forefinger and long-finger upon the right hand."

Sarah Osborne had a thing with "wings and two legs and a head like a woman." The children had seen it on February 29, after which it turned into a woman.

She also had "a thing all over hairy, all the face [had] hair, and a long nose, and I don't know how to tell how the face looks." The thing had two legs "and is about two or three foot high, and goeth upright like a man, and last night it stood before the fire in Mr. Parris' hall."

Tituba Releases the Contents of Pandora's Box

For almost three days, Tituba spun elaborate tales about talking animals, night flights on broomsticks, and spectral visits intended to harm the children. But perhaps what caused the greatest concern in the community was that the mysterious tall man from Boston bade her to sign the devil's book in blood, and when she was asked how many names were in the book, Tituba replied there were nine—her own, Sarah Good, Sarah Osborne and six others she could not see. This testimony must have sent a cold shiver through the crowd gathered in the meeting house. It meant there were other witches on the loose in Salem. Pandora's box was now wide open.

At the end of Tituba's first examination the children were in fits, and Hathorne asked who afflicted them. Tituba said she saw the shape of Sarah Good tormenting them, and the girls confirmed it.

The convulsions of Elizabeth Hubbard grew even more violent, and Hathorne asked Tituba who afflicted her.

"I am blind now," she said. "I cannot see."

Shortly afterward, Tituba had spells during which she lost her ability to speak or see. Eventually she fell into fits.

Tituba gave people a lot to talk about. But was she really a witch? Was Sarah Good one, too, as Tituba had indicated? Or was Tituba simply a shrewd woman with no fear of or allegiance to the Judeo-Christian command-ment against bearing false witness. She was, after all, a Carib Indian. By confessing and throwing herself on the mercy of the court, she saved her skin. Not being a God-fearing Puritan, it's possible she'd have said whatever she thought Hathorne and Corwin wanted to hear to avoid their bullying and to appear cooperative. If so, she must have had a vivid imagination. Her testimony seems far too detailed and original in its particulars to have merely been the product of the magistrates' leading questions. It could be, of course, she was simply playing back or modifying stories she'd grown up with in Barbados.

Or maybe Tituba was herself possessed by Satan.

Chapter: Seven The Witch Hunt Begins

Tituba might as well have dropped a bottle of strychnine in the Salem Village well. The accusations of witchcraft began to spread in the poisoned atmosphere her testimony created. The first three accused had been of low status in the village. The next was not at the bottom of the pecking order—she was a member of the village church, a privilege not open to everyone—but it does seem likely she had over the years supplied plenty of grist to the village gossip mill. Her name was Martha Corey, and she was the third wife of a much older man, Giles Corey, who was 80. What really had set the tongues to wagging, I'm willing to bet, is that she had borne a bastard mulatto son in 1678 seven years prior to her marriage to Corey. The boy, then fourteen or fifteen, lived in the home of his mother and stepfather, thus providing a constant reminder of an obvious indiscretion many Puritans surely considered scandalous.

Ann Putnam, a twelve-year-old daughter of the parish clerk, Sergeant Thomas Putnam, accused Goodwife Corey of tormenting her. Also known as Ann Putnam Junior because her mother, Ann Carr Putnam (Senior), had the same name and later became one of the afflicted and an accuser herself, she was a one of several girls who'd been hanging out with the Parris children.

Two of those who heard these accusations were Edward Putnam and Ezekiel Cheever, fellow church members of Martha Corey's, who thought it their duty to go to her and see what she had to say about the complaint. I've summarized the account that follows from W. Elliots

Woodward's *Records of Salem Witchcraft* (Roxbury, MA, 1864).

In the morning, the two men agreed to go to visit Martha Corey that afternoon. Before they did, they dropped by Thomas Putnam's house to ask his afflicted daughter, Ann, to tell them what clothes Goody Corey was wearing when Corey came to her as an apparition so they could see if this was what she had on later when they saw her.

The girl said she couldn't describe Goody Corey's clothes because the woman had come to her and blinded her. Goody Corey's apparition had told her she'd be unable to see until nightfall, after which Corey would come again.

Soon after hearing this, Putnam and Cheever went to the Corey home where they found Martha alone in her house.

Goodwife Corey smiled and said, "I know why you're here. You want to talk with me about being a witch. But I'm not a witch. I can't help what people say."

Edward Putnam answered that one of the afflicted girls had said she was being tormented by Corey and that was why they'd come.

"Oh?" Goody Corey said. "Tell me, does she say what clothes I have on?"

No doubt the men gave each other a look.

Goody Corey persisted. "Does she say what clothes I have on?"

"No, she says you came and blinded her and that you told her she would not be able to see again until dark. She said you told her you were doing this so she would not be able to tell what clothes you wore."

Goodwife Corey kept her mouth shut, but it appeared to the men to curve into a smile as though she'd played a clever trick on them.

Now, let's think about this for a minute. How could Martha Corey know the men would try to verify by her clothes that she was tormenting Ann Junior?

Apparently, there had been some discussion going around the village about the afflicted being able to say what clothes the apparitions wore, and Martha was aware of this. Perhaps someone she knew had overheard Putnam and Cheever talking about their plan and had warned her. If so, whoever let her in on what they were up to must not have known the Putnam girl had later said Goody Corey's apparition had come to her later and blinded her. If the person did—if Martha knew this part of the story—it was pretty stupid of her to bring the matter up with Putnam and Cheever.

Here's some pure speculation about what may have happened. Somehow or other Goody Corey knew the mission Putnam and Cheever were on—whether a little bird told her, a friend told her, or Martha Corey had second sight. Maybe a few minutes before the men arrived, she changed into a different outfit than the one she usually wore. Perhaps she put one on she'd *never* worn before, thinking, "I'll fix their little red wagon." Feeling the thrill of anticipation, and patting herself on the back for her cleverly devised plan, she could hardly wait until they told her what clothes Ann Putnam had said she was wearing because whatever outfit it was, she'd made sure it was not what she had on. Then they told her what Ann Putnam had said about having been blinded. Imagine the sinking feeling she must have felt as the air swished out of her balloon. The little smile she displayed was a smile all right, but it was forced.

Her trick had backfired.

Or, then again, maybe she really was a witch, albeit a pretty stupid one.

A few days later, Martha Corey went to visit the Putnams perhaps in an effort to smooth things over with that family and to get Ann Putnam Junior to stop saying her specter was visiting and torturing her. But her effort at offering an olive branch backfired. As soon as she entered the house, Ann "fell in to grievous fits of choking, her feet and hands twisted in a most grievous manner. She told Martha Corey to face that she did it, and immediately her tongue was drawn out of her mouth, and her teeth fastened upon it in a most grievous manner. "[23] When Ann finally regained control of herself, and got her tongue back in her mouth, she told Martha that "there is a yellow bird a sucking between your forefinger and middle finger. I see it." Ann moved closer to see the bird, and Edward Putnam saw Martha put her finger on the place Ann had just spoken of "and she seemed to give it a hard rub." Immediately, Ann was blinded.

Of course, everyone knew about Tituba's testimony stating that Sarah Good had a spectral yellow bird for a familiar. The implication was clear. Good and Corey shared the same familiar. Ann also described how Martha Corey's specter had put its hands upon Bathshua Pope's face during Sunday services the day before. Ann demonstrated what she she meant by placing her hands on her own face and immediately her hands became stuck to her eyes and could not be pulled off by anyone present.

All this was bad enough for Martha Corey but more was to come. Ann said she saw Goody Corey at the fire turning a spit with a man on it. Mercy Lewis, who was also present at the Putnams, took a stick and struck at the spectral torture scene. Ann reported that the scene

[23] Salem Witchcraft Papers.

vanished, but then it quickly reappeared. Mercy said she would strike again, but Ann said, "do not if you love yourself." Mercy ignored this warning and stuck. Mercy "cried out with a grievous pain in her arm." Ann said she'd seen Martha Corey's specter hit Mercy Lewis with an iron rod. The two "grew so bad with pain" Edward Putnam wrote, "we desired Goody Corey to be gone."

It appears Edward Putnam was a master of understatement.

Reverend Deodat Lawson Witnesses the Afflicted

On Saturday, March 19, two days before Martha Corey was scheduled to take the witness stand to be examined, the Reverend Deodat Lawson arrived in Salem Village. He'd been Salem's minister from 1684 to 1688 and would be its visiting preacher on his visit. But he came this time for personal reasons as well. The afflicted girls had said Lawson's wife and daughter, whom he had buried there, had been killed by witchcraft.

His writings indicate that by the time he arrived there were ten individuals who claimed to be afflicted—three girls from nine to twelve years old, Elizabeth Parris, Abigail Williams, and Ann Putnam, and three adolescent girls—Mary Walcott, Mercy Lewis, and Elizabeth Hubbard. Also, there were four married women, Goodwives Putnam, Pope, Bibber, and Goodall.

Reverend Lawson conducted both the morning and the afternoon services on Sunday, March 20, during which several of the afflicted persons were present. Lawson wrote that they had fits during the first service which interrupted him during his first prayer. After psalm was sung, Abigail Williams said to Lawson, "Now stand up and name your text." This was hardly something you'd expect from an eleven year old girl, especially in a seventeenth century Puritan church.

After the text was read Abigail piped up again. "It is a long text," she said.

At the outset of his sermon, Goodwife Pope, one of the now afflicted adults, said, "Now there is enough of that!"

And in the afternoon service, Abigail Williams told him when he referred to his doctrine—she knew of no doctrine he had.

"If you did name one I have forgot it," she said.

Goodwife Corey was present in the meeting house, and during the sermon. Abigail Williams called out, "Look where Goodwife Corey sits on the beam, suckling her yellow bird between her fingers."

Then Ann Putnam Junior said a yellow bird was sitting on the preacher's hat where it hung on a pin in the pulpit.

A Bite by a Phantom Leaves Teeth Marks

The night before, Lawson had stayed at Ingersoll's Ordinary.

Mary Walcott, one of the afflicted adolescents, had been standing by the door when she appeared to be bitten by something or someone no one could see. When Mary cried out in pain, Lawson and others rushed to her and looked where she pointed on her wrist. They saw what appeared to be teeth marks on either side, an upper and lower set.

Reverend Lawson had also visited the parsonage where Abigail Williams "had a grievous fit." He would see more such fits on Monday, at Martha Corey's examination.

Hathorne Pours on the Heat

During Martha Corey's examination, on March 21, Hathorne was even more brutal than he had been with the first three accused.

"You are now in the hands of authority. Tell me now why you hurt these persons."

"I do not."

"Who doth?"

"Pray give me leave to go to prayer."

She asked this several times. Hathorne told her they had not sent for her to hear her pray.

"But tell me why you hurt these."

"I am an innocent person. I never had to do with witchcraft since I was born. I am a gospel woman."

"Do you not see these complain of you?"

"The Lord open the eyes of the magistrates and ministers. The Lord show his power to discover the guilty."

"Tell us who hurts these children."

"I do not know."

"If you be guilty of this fact, do you think you can hide it?"

"The Lord knows."

"Well, tell us what you know of this matter."

"Why, I am a gospel woman, and do you think I can have to do with witchcraft, too?"

"How could you tell, then, that the child was bid to observe what clothes you wore, when some came to speak with you?"

She said she had learned it from Cheever, but he denied this was true. Hathorne persisted, and she said her husband had told her.

"Goodman Corey, did you tell her?"

The old man denied he had.

"Did you not say your husband told you so?"

No answer.

"Who hurts these children? Now look upon them."

"I cannot help it."

"Did you not say you would tell the truth [about] why you asked that question? How came you to the knowledge?"

"I had no knowledge. I did but ask."

"You dare thus to lie in all this assembly! You are now before authority! I expect the truth. You promised it. Speak now, and tell us who told you [about the] clothes."

"Nobody."

There was more, but nothing more of relevance. Hathorne was never more brutal nor more intolerant than in his examination of Martha Corey. He obviously thought she had tried to fool everyone with her trick about what clothes she wore while torturing Ann Putnam from a distance. It didn't occur to him that maybe it was Ann Putnam—or whatever demonic spirit may have possessed Ann Putnam—who was pulling a fast one by saying she'd been blinded.

It seems possible Goodwife Corey's husband had warned her, and then lied about it to save his own skin. Or it could be someone else had told her what the men coming to see her were up to, and she protected that person by keeping her mouth shut. Or, maybe she just guessed.

Martha Corey commits the Sin of Doubting there Are Witches

Something else about Martha Corey probably got John

Hathorne's back up. It was known she'd been skeptical about the whole witch business. She had even tried to prevent her husband from attending the examinations of Tituba, Good, and Osborne, going so far as to remove the saddle from his horse.

During her own examination, she protested, "We must not believe all that these distracted children say."

Distracted persons, said Hathorne, varied from minute to minute, but these were constant in their accusations.

Later he asked whether she believed "there are witches in the country," to which she answered that she did not know of any.

"Do not you know that Tituba confessed it?"

"I did not hear her speak."

That Martha Corey's skepticism was held against her indicates that by this time the magistrates' attitudes had hardened into those ot witch hunters. Who besides a witch hunter believes that anyone skeptical of witchcraft must undoubtedly be a witch?

The Accused Are Thought to Use Their Own Bodies for Image Magic

A particular kind of behavior first appeared at Martha Corey's examination that remained standard throughout the proceedings. Martha bit her lip, and several of the afflicted children complained they were bitten. She was called down for biting her lip, and quite naturally she asked what harm there was in it.

The Reverend Nicholas Noyes of Salem Town explained, "I believe it is apparent she practiseth witchcraft in the congregation. There is no need of images."

What the good reverend was driving at was that

instead of tormenting images or effigy dolls, she was using her own body as an image, biting the children by biting her own lip, and pinching them by clenching her fingers together. From Martha Corey's examination onward, any motion on the part of the accused was likely to produce a corresponding effect on the afflicted. It must have been a most convincing spectacle, as though black magic were being worked before the eyes of the beholders. The effects produced on the children were obviously painful which made them quite convincing. In some cases marks of bites or pinches were visible on the children's flesh. On other occasions pins were found literally stuck in their flesh.

This indicates to me the children may have worked themselves into a hysterical or hypnotic-like state, perhaps unconsciously, and that they really believed the woman on the witness stand was using image magic to harm them. Skin lesions are among the commonest of psychosomatic symptoms, and plenty of credible accounts exist of this sort of thing happening under hypnotism. For example, a real blister has been known to appear on a hypnotized person's arm when the person is told he or she is being touched by a red hot needle, which in reality may be nothing more than a wooden pencil at room temperature. How the pins could have materialized is another matter. At that time pins were often used instead of buttons or snaps to hold clothes in place, and this may be where they came from. The girls probably did plenty of sewing and may have had some in their pockets. Perhaps they stuck themselves, but did so unconsciously. Or maybe they were possessed by evil spirits. Later, we will touch on cases of pins and other hardware showing up during exorcisms conducted not so long ago. Whatever was going on, when Goody Corey leaned against the a seat where she was standing, "being the bar at which she stood," the afflictions grew worse. Bathshua Pope, complained of "grievous torment in her bowels as if they were torn out," and she hit Martha Corey on the head with a shoe. If the woman shuffled her feet, the afflicted "stamped fearfully." Reverend Deodat Lawson noted in his *Brief and Turn Narratives* that the afflicted "asked her why she did not go to the company of witches which were before the meeting house mustering? Did she not hear the drumbeat?" Indeed, the afflicted declared that "23 or 24" witches were "in arms" outside the building. It seems strange that no one considered that the afflicted might themselves be witches or possessed by demons since they were the ones who heard the drumbeat and everyone knew, "None here sees the witches but the afflicted and themselves."

This, of course, raises the question as to whether spirit possession or bewitchment is actually possible. Eighteenth, nineteen and twentieth century historians have assumed it is definitely not, in an almost knee-jerk reaction against what they likely perceived as the sort of childish superstition and ignorance that led so many to their deaths. On the other hand, I have made a conscious effort not to dismiss any possibility out of hand and later will take a look at what investigations into spirit possession in recent years have revealed.

No matter what the case really was, all this was just too much for Martha Corey to combat, and Hathorne and Corwin committed her to jail for further examination and eventual trial.

By sending Martha to jail, the leadership of Salem had very nearly committed itself to a witch hunt. Yet there would be moments when the course of events would seem to hesitate and waver—moments when a small change of circumstances might have been enough for the final catastrophe to be averted. As it turned out, perhaps the biggest opportunity for the direction to change, and for disaster to be averted, came about with the next individual accused, a woman named Rebecca Nurse.

Chapter Eight: Rebecca Nurse Is Accused

Ann Putnam Junior at first could not identify the specter tormenting her this time, except it was that of a woman she'd seen in church. When she told her family this woman sometimes came and sat in her grandmother's seat at church, however, the others knew who she was talking about. It was Rebecca Nurse. Rebecca's natal family had long been at odds with the Putnam clan over property rights. Some historians have questioned whether this wasn't the real motive, albeit perhaps a subconscious one, for her being accused. Maybe. Whatever the case may have been, however, Ann Putnam Junior knew her by sight because Goody Nurse, a member of the Salem Town Church, often attended services at the Salem Village Church because it was more conveniently located for her.

Ann Putnam Senior Is Visited by the Specter of Rebecca Nurse

Early on the morning of March 22, the apparition of Rebecca Nurse, dressed in a shift, appeared to Ann Putnam Junior's mother, Ann Carr Putnam, wearing a shift. Rebecca, apparently not yet dressed for the day, had brought with her "a little red book" for Ann Senior to sign. And, according to Ann Senior, Rebecca threatened to "to tear my soul out of my body" if she didn't put her John Hancock in it. For almost two hours Goody Putnam argued with Rebecca's specter about several passages of Scripture. Finally, Rebecca's apparition departed, but Ann remained tortured for most of that day.

Rebecca Nurse hardly fit the image of a witch. First, she was a church member in good standing with no apparent skeletons in her closet. Second, she was a rather matronly 70 or 71 years old, apparently almost deaf, and was also described as infirm. I picture her as one of those little old ladies you see shuffling along who's one step away from needing a walker, with a slightly hunched back and wearing a hat with fake flowers and fake baby's breath over silver hair tied back in a bun. Her face may have been wrinkled, but she did not have a long nose with a wart on the end of it as it seems to me Sarah Good might have had. In other words, she was not an obvious person to have been singled out. It's likely a shutter went through the community when her name came up.

A Church Delegation Visits Rebecca Nurse

Elizabeth Porter, the sister of magistrate John Hathorne, went to visit Rebecca Nurse along with several other prominent citizens when they learned she'd been accused. The small group reached her house and found her looking ill and weak. She told them she'd been sick almost a week.

They asked how she'd been otherwise and she quoted Scripture and said that with God's help she thought she'd make it through. Then, of her own accord, she began to speak of the witchcraft scourge among them, and in particular of Reverend Parris his family, and that she felt sorry for them. She said she had not been to see them, but she used to have fits herself and knew how terrible it was. She pitied them with all her heart, and prayed to God for them. She also said she'd heard that people who were likely innocent had been accused.

Then they told her she had been accused.

No doubt she gasped and brought her hand to her mouth. "Well, if this is true," she said, "may the will of the Lord be done." She sat very still for a few minutes, digesting this dreadful news. Then she said, "As to this thing, I am as innocent as the child unborn." Then, revealing her Puritan theological beliefs, she added, "What sin hath God found me unrepentant of, that He should lay such an affliction upon me in my old age?"

The small group went away in agreement she had not known the true purpose of their visit when they'd arrived.

Dorcas Good, a Five Year Old, Is Accused

Back on March 3, Ann Putnam Junior had complained that the specter of Sarah Good's young daughter, Dorcas, "did immediately almost choke me an tortured me most grievously." Nothing came of it, however, until three weeks later when Mary Walcott said that Dorcas had "come to me and bit me and pinched me." As a teenager, Mary may have been viewed as more credible than Ann Junior, and, too, witch fever had risen in the meantime. The result was, when Deacon Edward Putnam and his cousin Jonathan Putnam filed a formal complaint against Rebecca Nurse for having afflicted Ann Carr Putnam, her daughter, Ann, and Abigail Williams, they also filed one against Dorcas Good. In short order, the Good child and Rebecca Nurse both were arrested and held at Ingersoll's Ordinary until their examinations.

Reverend Lawson Helps Dispel a Tormentor

On Wednesday, March 23, visiting reverend Lawson

went to visit Ann Senior where he witnessed her having a terrible fit.

After a while, she seemed to come out of it somewhat and began to argue with Rebecca Nurse's apparition. According to Lawson, "She thought that telling it a passage from the Bible would make it vanish. Said she, 'I am sure you cannot stand before that text!' Then she was sorely afflicted, her mouth drawn on one side and her body strained for about a minute, and then she said, 'I will tell, I will tell. It is, it is, it is!' three or four times, and then was afflicted in a way that kept her from speaking. At last she broke forth and said 'It is the third chapter of the Revelations.'"

Reluctantly—apparently because he wasn't sure if this constituted using magic against magic—the Reverend began to read the passage. Before he had finished the first verse, Ann Putnam Senior opened her eyes and was well.

Reverend Deodat Lawson Raises Doubts about Spectral Evidence

Thursday, March 24, the day Rebecca Nurse was to be put on the stand, was Lecture Day at Salem Village. Visiting preacher, Reverend Deodat Lawson, preached a sermon, which he soon published, entitled, *Christ's Fidelity, the Only Shield Against Satan's Malignity.* Several historians have characterized it as an attempt to stir up the emotions of the community. Intended or not, it probably did so. But in my analysis it also contains some pretty good advice. It's true Lawson reaffirmed that the girls' afflictions were the "effects of diabolical malice and operations, and that it cannot rationally be imagined to proceed from any other cause whatsoever." He urged the magistrates to care for the afflicted girls and do their utmost to find the cause of their afflictions, and he also urged them to "to approve yourselves a terror of and punishment to evildoers, and a praise to them that do well."

He warned the community that there was ultimately no legitimate secular defense against witchcraft. There was, for example, no sure way known of testing to see whether an accused person was a witch—

"We find no means instituted of God to make trial of witches."

Nor could one effectively defend oneself against witchcraft with white magic, such as boiling one's urine or nailing a horseshoe over the door, because such charms were in themselves "a kind of witchcraft," and might well give a more secure foothold to the devil.

Lawson warned that careless accusations of suspected persons might backfire. "Rash censuring of others, without sufficient grounds, or false accusing any willingly . . . is indeed to be like the devil, who . . . is a calumniator, or false accuser." Most important, he warned his listeners that the devil might appear in the shape of an innocent person. Indeed, he suspected this was precisely what had happened when church members saw the apparitions of other church members afflicting them.

The devil had taken "some of the visible subjects of our Lord Jesus and [used] at least their shapes and appearances to afflict and torture other visible subjects of that same Kingdom. Surely his design is that Christ's Kingdom may be divided against itself."

On the "stirring up of emotions" side of the coin, Reverend Lawson said Satan had especially targeted God's own "covenant people." The Lord was "lengthening the chain of the roaring lion . . . so the devil is come down in great wrath," but God did so "to serve His own most holy designs, in the world." Lawson then explained what he saw as God's intended designs. The Lord was speaking to the Salem villagers "with an unusual and amazing loudness," calling on them to ask themselves, "What meaneth the heat of this great anger?" The Lord was insisting on "true and unfeigned reformation" of the "provoking evils" into which God's people had fallen. Then came the *coup de grace.* He addressed anyone in his audience who might have entered into a covenant to serve Satan. "All mankind is now . . . set against you," and so are God and Christ. "You are utterly undone forever . . . doomed to those endless, easeless, and remediless torments." In other words, they were sure to burn in hell for all eternity. This fate awaited witches even if they managed to evade the judgment of men and by some twist of fate escape the detection of the court and the magistrates.

Giles Corey Comes Forward with New Evidence Against Martha

Also on March 24, Giles Corey gave testimony that the previous Saturday, after the formal complaint had been filed against his wife, Martha, he'd oddly been prevented from praying in his usual manner.

"My wife hath been want to sit up after I went to bed, and I have perceived her to kneel down to the hearth, as if she were at prayer, but [I] heard nothing."

The implication was she had not prayed to God but to Satan, and that his own attempt to communicate with the divinity had been blocked by this prayer to Satan. With such a husband, Martha Corey had no need of enemies.

Rebecca Nurse Is Examined

When John Hathorne conducted Rebecca Nurse's examination on that same day, he was for the first time plainly unsure of himself. perhaps this had to do with hearing the cautions given in Reverend Lawson's sermon. Or maybe his own sister had expressed doubts to him that Rebecca was a witch. The woman was, after all, a church member in good standing whose reputation, unlike Martha Corey's, seemed unassailable.

He first asked her what she had to say with respect to the accusations.

She answered, "I can say before my eternal Father I am innocent, and God will clear my innocency."

To this he replied, "Everyone in this assembly desires it." But if you be guilty, pray God discover you."

He was to repeat this sentiment later in the examination. "I pray God clear you if you be innocent, and if you be guilty discover you."

But how was one to decide whether or not she was innocent or guilty? The afflicted girls were present, of course, crying out in pain and agony. Clearly they were enduring the most frightful tortures, and they accused Rebecca Nurse of being the cause. The most casual movement of her body was echoed in grotesque twistings and turnings of their bodies. Yet Rebecca Nurse seemed as unlikely a candidate for witchhood as anyone in Essex County as she meekly called on her God for help in the middle of this demonic uproar. Hathorne plainly did not know what to make of it. The afflicted girls testified that the apparition of Rebecca Nurse was tormenting them. They said they had seen it leave her body and return to it.

But Rebecca Nurse's Christian character and demeanor, and perhaps Lawson's sermon, had cast temporarily doubt on his previously clear faith in the validity of apparitions as evidence.

"What uncertainty there may be in apparitions I do not know," he said. "Yet you are at this very present charged [by your accusers] with familiar spirits. This is your bodily person they are speaking of. They say they see these familiar spirits come to your bodily person. Now what do you say to that?"

Rebecca Nurse denied she was doing harm to them, or that she had any familiar spirits.

It was at this point that Hathorne for the second time prayed that she be cleared if innocent and discovered if guilty. He must have been in a mental quandary. He did not doubt the girls' afflictions were genuine, and he also had to wonder whether Rebecca Nurse wasn't telling the truth—at least so far as she knew it.

He may have thought the devil had made her into a witch without her knowledge. He said to her, "Possibly you may believe you are no witch, but have you not been led astray by temptations?"

"I have not," she answered.

Hathorne could reply only by reflecting on "what a sad thing" it was to see church members accused of such a crime.

What, he asked, did she make of the girls' behavior? "They accuse you of hurting them, and if you think it is not unwillingly, but by design, you must look upon them as murderers."

"I cannot tell what to think of it."

The fits certainly must have looked genuine if Rebecca Nurse—as was the case with the majority of the accused—

could not tell what to think of them.

Later, when Hathorne asked whether she thought the afflicted persons were bewitched.

She answered yes, "I do think they are."

So he appealed to her again. "When this witchcraft came upon the stage there was no suspicion of Tituba. She professed much love to that child, Betty Parris, but it was her apparition that did the mischief. And why should not you also be guilty, for your apparition doth hurt also."

"Would you have me belie myself?" Rebecca said.

To repeated testimony that her apparition was tormenting people she replied "I cannot help it. The devil may appear in my shape."

It seems quite possible it was at that moment Ann Putnam Senior became overwhelmed by "a grievous fit . . . to the very impairing of her strength, and wasting of her spirits, inasmuch as she could hardly move hand, or foot."

Her husband rose and asked the magistrates' permission to carry her out of the meeting house. Later, Ann Senior recalled that as soon as she came out of the building "it pleased Almighty God for his free grace and mercy sake to deliver me out of the paws of those roaring lions, and the jaws of those tearing bears."

She suffered no more fits for the next two months.

Back in the meeting house, the magistrates committed Rebecca Nurse for further examination.

Dorcas Good Confesses

The questioning of Rebecca Nurse marks a critical point in the developments at Salem in the spring of 1692. If she had held the stage alone on March 24, a slight chance exists her evident sincerity might have raised enough doubt in the minds of leaders of the community for them to begin to wonder if they weren't making a mistake. It might have occurred to them to consider whether the afflicted might be obsessed or possessed by demons or the devil, and that this obsession or possession might be independent of the help or assistance of witches. But unfortunately someone else was examined on the same day—Dorcas Good, the approximately five-year-old daughter of Sarah Good—and Dorcas provided Hathorne and Salem with a second confession.

Oh yes, she told the examining magistrates, she had a familiar. It was a little snake that liked to suck her at the lowest joint of her forefinger.

To their credit, the examiners were not willing at first to take her confession at face value. They wanted to know, where did the snake suck?

"Was it here?" she was asked, as they pointed to other places on her body.

No, said the child, not there. Here. And she indicated her forefinger, where the examiners "observed a deep red spot, about the bigness of a flea bite."

Maybe it was a flea bite, and the child had only imagined she had a familiar who sucked her blood there. Perhaps a leech or a tick had made it. Leeches suck blood and look something like a snake. No one can say at this distant point in time. But it's not hard to imagine the feelings of the examiners when they saw it. All of them had heard that a demon in the shape of an animal came to a witch and sucked her blood, and here was what seemed to be physical evidence of just such an "accursed suckage" on the finger of a five-year-old child—pointed out by the child herself as corroboration of her confession. They must have been horrified. If five-year-old children were suckling demons, then the devil had a far surer foothold in Massa-chusetts than anyone had previously imagined. Strenuous investigation would be necessary to uncover its extent.

Yet their horror must have been mixed with triumph. The child accused her mother as well as herself and did it without prodding. Dorcas Good's confession confirmed the rightness of their having imprisoned Sarah Good.

Who had given her the little snake, they asked her. Was it the Black Man?

Oh no, Dorcas replied, it wasn't the Black Man. It was her mother, whom she continued to accuse, testifying later at her trial that she had three familiars, birds, "one black, one yellow and that these birds hurt the children and afflicted persons."

Not only did Dorcas Good confess, her very presence in the meeting house was as powerful as any grown woman suspected of being in Satan's service. Deodat Lawson reported later that the magistrates and clergymen present "unanimously" told him "that when this child did but cast her eye upon the afflicted, they were tormented," and even the non afflicted became afflicted when she looked at them. This, along with her confession and the accompanying physical evidence of her devil's mark, must have dampened the doubts which had arisen among many when Rebecca Nurse had been arrested. From this time on expressions of sympathy for Rebecca Nurse were likely to be met with suspicion.

Reverend Parris Drives a Few More Nails in Goody Nurse's Coffin

On Sunday, April 3, the Reverend Parris preached on John 6:70 in which Jesus is quoted as having said, "Have not I chosen you twelve [disciples], and one of you is a devil?"

The implication was clear. Puritans believed church members had been chosen—selected by God. Thus Parris' text suggested that a church member had betrayed her election just as Judas had betrayed his selection by Christ. Thus, Parris was comparing Martha Corey and Rebecca Nurse to Judas, and implying they were guilty before they had been tried.

Parris directly addressed the arguments offered by Goody Corey and Goody Nurse that the devil might be taking on their likenesses. Speaking to Martha Corey's contention she couldn't be a witch because she was "gospel woman," the minister argued that since devils could be found in churches, "let none then build their hopes of salvation merely upon this, that they are church members." In response to Rebecca Nurse's observation that "the devil may appear in my shape," he admitted that Satan would undoubtedly misrepresent "the best saints" in that way "if he could . . . [but] it is not easy to imagine that his power is of such extent [as] to [be of] the hazard of the Church." In this line of reasoning, Parris was using the Puritan belief in God's power over Satan to maintain it was unlikely God would give the devil enough rope to allow him to deceptively take on apparitions of Godly persons, or saints, when appearing to the afflicted. One can argue he was thus adhering to Reverend Richard Bernard's statement, covered earlier, that the unregenerate,[24] but not by inference, the regenerate,[25] could be falsely represented in spectral form. Again, this is like saying a serial killer like Ted Bundy would not be able to impersonate the Pope

---

[24] Those not born again through Christ, i.e., not regenerated through Christ's indwelling spirit.

[25] Those who are informed by the indwelling spirit of Christ, ie., reborn or regenerated through Christ.

because God would not allow him to do so, thus setting aside the doctrine of free will.

At least one person in the church that day was enraged by the preacher's remarks. As soon as Parris had finished, Sarah Cloyse, a sister of Rebecca Nurse, rose from her seat, stormed out of the meeting house, and slammed the door, "to the amazement of the congregation." They were amazed, of course, not at her resentment of Parris, but at her public expression of it in the midst of a church service—this was an unthinkable action in Puritan Massachusetts.

It should not be a surprise that eight days later Sarah Cloyse was accused of witchcraft.

Chapter Nine: Accusations Escalate

The arrest of Rebecca Nurse and perhaps Reverend Lawson's warnings resulted in a pronounced split in Salem. Most of those who supported her lived on the east side, held more liberal views, and were more prosperous than their neighbors. In general, the accusers were poor farmers and of lower status, who lived in the western part of the village. A total of 39 people signed a petition attesting to Rebecca's Nurse's moral character. This is not something these folks would have done lightly. When you signed a petition meant to aid someone who'd been accused of witchcraft, you were putting your own neck on the line. Who could be sure accusations would not be made against them?

Nevertheless, the number of accusations escalated. Eventually, both of Rebecca Nurse's sisters—Mary Easty and Sarah Cloyse—joined her in jail. As previously touched upon, some authors of accounts of the Essex County witch hysteria argue that the sisters—women of the Towne family from neighboring Topsfield—were singled out by the Putnams because of a feud resulting from land disputes between the Putnam and Towne families that went back a generation. It's certainly true the witch hysteria gave people an opportunity to even the score with old rivals. Almost no one was safe. Just about anyone who spoke out against the proceedings was immediately suspect. Even Reverend George Burroughs, the former minister of Salem Village, who now lived in Maine, was held for trial and was eventually convicted and executed.

The authorities had reason to believe that forty or more witches were living among them based on the sworn testimony of Abigail Williams, who said she had seen a witches' sacrament take place near her uncle's house. That's right. About forty witches attended, she said, and the "deacons" were Sarah Cloyce and Sarah Good. She'd actually spoken to Goody Cloyce, and had asked her, "Is this a time to receive the Sacrament? You ran away on the Lord's day, and scorned to receive it in the meeting house. Is this a time to receive it?"

Abigail added that since that first meeting she'd seen another gathering of witches in spectral form, which had taken place near Ingersoll's Ordinary. Nathaniel Ingersoll was a deacon of the church, so the witches seemed to be thumbing their noses at the religious leadership of the village. Abigail said that Goodwives Cloyce, Nurse, Corey and Good each had participated. Perhaps it's no wonder as the weeks ticked by, the accusations spread. More people sighted witches' gatherings in the night, and others joined those already afflicted in naming Goodwives Nurse, Corey, and Good, while adding others to the list including John Proctor and his wife Elizabeth. Proctor had made the grave error of publicly stating he did not believe the afflicted were actually afflicted—his maidservant, Mary Warren, in particular. On the morning of March 25 he announced to Samuel Sibley that he'd come to the village "to fetch home his jade he left her there last night," meaning Mary Warren, and that he would "thresh the devil out of her," because he believed the afflicted persons "should rather be had to the whipping post" because "if they were let alone so we should all be devils and witches quickly." I'll bet he didn't know how right he was.

A Third Confession Takes Place

About the middle of April the magistrates obtained their third confession. This one was from a teenager who did not live in Salem Village or in Salem Town. Abigail Hobbs, daughter of William Hobbs of Topsfield, had not been shy about talking about the devil, which probably got many tongues wagging, and no doubt brought her to the attention of the afflicted. When scolded for her "wicked carriages and disobedience to her father and mother" or for her "rude" and "unseemly" behavior, she had said quite frankly she was not "afraid of anything" because of a pact he'd made with Satan. Abigail told several people she had "sold herself body and soul to the old boy" and had "seen the devil and . . . made a covenant or bargain with him." One of her contemporaries said she'd asked Abigail why she wasn't ashamed of her disgraceful ways, and Abigail had told her to "hold my tongue and to look because there was old nick [i.e., Satan] sitting over the bedstead." Abigail may not have realized what a hole she was digging for herself. Shortly before she was accused of being a witch, when visiting a neighbor, she had remarked that "my mother is not baptized, but [Abigail] said she'd baptize her. Whereupon she took water and sprinkled it on her mother's face and said she did baptize her in the name of the Father and the Son and the Holy Ghost."

This sort of sacrilege was to a seventeenth century Puritan almost as bad as a cartoon poking fun at Mohammed is to a twenty-first century radical Muslim.

Ann Putnam Junior was the first to complain of torment at the hands of the specter of Abigail Hobbs. Next, the young woman's apparition attacked Mary

Walcott and then Mercy Lewis. In less than a week, on April 19 to be exact, Abigail was questioned at the Salem Village meeting house.

Hathorne began his examination as he had the others before this one.

"Are you guilty or not?"

"I have seen sights and been scared," Abigail said. "I have been very wicked. I hope I shall be better, if God will keep me."

"What sights did you see?"

"I have seen dogs and many creatures."

"What dogs—ordinary dogs?"

"I mean the devil."

"How often—many times?"

"But once."

"Tell the truth."

"I tell no lie."

"What appearance was he in then?"

"Like a man."

All eyes were fixed on Abigail, and the room was hushed. Even the afflicted did not fidget, nor did they make a sound, their eyes glued on the teenage girl.

"Where was this?"

"It was at the Eastward at Casco Bay."

"Where, in the house—or in the woods?"

"In the woods."

"In the night or in the day?"

"In the day."

"How long ago?"

"Three or four years."

"What did he say to you?"

"He said he would give me fine things, if I did what he wanted."

"What would he have you do?"

"Why, he would have me be a witch."

"Would he have you make a covenant with him?"

"Yes."

"And did you make a covenant with him?"

"Yes, I did, but I hope God will forgive me."

"May the good Lord give you repentance," Hathorne said. "You said you saw dogs, and many sorts of creatures?"

"I saw them at that time."

"But have you not seen them at other times too?"

"Yes.

"Where?"

"At our house."

"What were they like?"

"Like a cat."

"What would the cat have you do?"

"She had a book and would have me put my hand to it."

"And did you?"

"No, I did not."

"Tell the truth, did you at any other time?"

"Yes, I did, that time at the Eastward."

"What other creatures did you see?"

"I saw things like men."

"What did they say to you?"

"Why, they said I had better put my hand to the book."

"You did put your hand to the book, you say?"

"Yes, one time."

"What, would they have you put your hand to their book, too?"

"Yes."

"And what would they have you do, then? Would they

have you worship them?"

"They would have me make a bargain—for so long. And do what they would have me do."

"For how long?"

"Not for more than two or three years."

"And what did you agree to? How long?"

"But for two years."

"And what would they then do for you?"

"They would give me fine clothes."

"And did they?"

"No."

"When you set your hand to the book the last time, how long was that for?"

"It was for four years."

"How long is that ago?"

"It is almost four years, now. The book was brought to me to get my hand to it for four years, but I never put my hand but that once at Eastward."

"Are you not bid to hurt folks?"

"Yes."

"Who are you bid to hurt?"

"Mercy Lewis and Ann Putman."

"What did you do to them when you hurt them?"

"I pinched them."

"How did you pinch them? Do you go in your own person to them?"

"No."

"Doth the devil go for you?"

"Yes."

"And what doth he take—your spirit with him?"

"No. I am as well as at other times. But the devil has my consent, and goes and hurts them."

"Who hurt your mother last Lord's day, was it you?"

"No."

"Who was it?"

"I heard her say it was Goody Wilds at Topsfield."

"Have you been in company with Goody Wilds at any time?"

"No, I never saw her."

"Well, who are your companions?"

"Why I have seen Sarah Good once."

"How many did you see?"

"I saw but two."

"Did you know Sarah Good was a witch, when you saw her?"

"Yes."

"How did you know it?"

"The devil told me."

"Who was the other you saw?"

"I do not remember her name."

"Did you go and do hurt with Sarah Good?"

"No, she would have me set my hand to her book also."

"What mark did you make in the devil's book when you set your hand to it?"

"Just a mark."

"Have you not been at other great meetings?"

"No."

"Did you not hear of great hurt done here in the village?"

"Yes."

"And were you never with them?"

"No, I was never with them."

"But you know your shape appeared and hurt the people here."

"Yes."

"How did you know?"

"The devil told me, if I gave consent, he would do it in my shape."

"How long ago?"

"About a fortnight ago."

"What shape did the devil appear in then?"

"Like a black man with an hat."

"Do not some creatures suck your body?"

"No."

"Where do they come, to what parts, when they come to your body?"

"They do not come to my body, they come only in sight."

"Do they speak to you?"

"Yes."

"How do they speak to you?"

"As other folks."

"What do they speak to you, as other folks?"

"Yes, almost."

Abigail suddenly and conveniently could no longer hear.

Having remained silent to this point, the afflicted now spoke up, saying they saw Sarah Good and Sarah Osborne run their fingers into Abigail's ears.

Before long, Abigail was blind, though her eyes were wide open.

At last she said, "Sarah Good saith I shall not speak." Hathorne and Corwin ordered her taken away to prison.

By the way, if you noticed inconsistencies in Abigail's testimony, it's because there were some. But the magistrates expected this from witches.

After Abigail Hobbs was gone, three of the afflicted— Mercy Lewis, Abigail Williams, and Ann Putman—stated that they were sorry for Abigail Hobbs.

Bridget Bishop Is Examined

On the same day, April 19, 1692, another non Salem Village or Salem Town resident was examined by Hathorne and Corwin—Bridget Bishop of Beverly, Massachusetts. The rumor was she had bewitched her first husband, Goodman Wasslebee, to death. People had been whispering behind her back about her being a witch and even saying so to her face for a long time. In 1679 or 1680, during her second marriage [to Thomas Oliver] she had been brought before the Court of Assistants for witchcraft. The records of that trial no longer exist, but it's likely a big factor in her release was the good opinion of her clergyman, John Hale of Beverly, who later wrote that he was "hoping better of Goody Bishop" than others were in the community. Hale had changed his mind by 1692. Her husband at that time also accused her of witchcraft. Two women testified that Goodman Bishop had said, "the devil did come bodily unto her, and that she was familiar with the devil, and that she sat up all the night long with the devil."

Bridget Bishop was aware of her reputation. Once she'd asked William Stacey "whether his father would grind her grist. He wanted to know why she asked. She answered, because folks counted her a witch."

During her examination by Hathorne, when he used his usual bullying techniques, she startled him with these words: "If I were any such person [i.e., a witch], *you* should know it." In other words, she would make him know it. But even more damning evidence than her reputation and a sharp tongue was produced against Bridget Bishop. Two men who had been employed by her testified that they had taken down the cellar wall of a house where she'd lived. In holes in the old wall they'd found "several puppets made up of rags and hog's bristles with headless pins in them."

As you and I know, a doll with pins in it is a classic black magic talisman employed by witches. According to my research, placing such dolls inside the walls of a house is still done today. Whether this testimony would hold up in a twenty-first century court is doubtful, of course, since no one actually saw Goody Bishop sticking the pins in the dolls or placing them inside the walls. But according Cotton Mather, she could give no account of them to the court "that was reasonable or tolerable."

Another bit of evidence is an indication she may actually have been practicing black magic. Samuel Shattuck, a Quaker and the local dyer, testified she had brought him "sundry pieces of lace, some of which were so short that I could not judge them fit for any use." In other words, they were too small to be worn by a human being. It seems likely they were meant for dressing effigy dolls. A witch would have made an effort to dress one in the same materials and colors as the clothing worn by the intended victim.

It should be noted Shattuck had an ax to grind with Goody Bishop. Some years before, one of his children had been ill and having fits. "His mouth and eyes [were] drawn aside . . . as if he was upon the point of death."

Someone suggested the child was bewitched and offered to take the boy to Goodwife Bishop's and scratch her face. You see, drawing blood from a witch's face was a way to break a spell. Shattuck agreed and added some white magic of his own.

"I gave him money and asked him to to ask her for a pot of cider."

Obtaining property and then subjecting it to occult abuse was a common technique of both black and white magic.

But Goodwife Bishop would not be tricked. She refused to sell the cider, and she chased the stranger off, threatening him with a spade. Not only did she keep her own face from being scratched, she actually scratched Shattuck's son's face.

"Ever since," Shattuck testified, "this child hath been followed with grievous fits as if he would never recover more, his head and eyes drawn aside so as if they would never come to rights more; lying as if he were in a manner dead; falling anywhere, either into fire or water if he be not constantly looked to; and generally in such an uneasy and restless frame, almost always running to and fro, acting so strange that I cannot judge otherwise but that he is bewitched, and by these circumstances do believe that the aforesaid Bridget Oliver, now called Bishop, is the cause of it. And it has been the judgment of doctors . . . that he is under the evil hand of witchcraft."

Others testified against Goody Bishop as well. It should not surprise anyone to learn that in less than two months, on June 10. 1692, she would be the first one hanged.

In the meantime, as the weeks ticked by, accusations spread throughout the entire region to Gloucester, Lynn, Malden, Amesbury, Billerica, Marblehead, Boston, Charlestown, and Andover. Many more were examined and some confessed. Before it was over, about a hundred and fifty men and women were arrested.

The pain and suffering this hysteria caused innocent people is immeasurable. Consider, for example, the treatment little five-year-old Dorcas Good received in prison. A special set of chains was made just for her. Her hands and feet would simply side out of a standard set intended to hold an adult.

Dorcas remained chained in a dungeon of a prison in Boston seven or eight months until the autumn of 1692. During the first half of her time there, her infant sibling—"a suckling child" died. In July her mother was executed. One would expect such treatment and events to be highly detrimental to the psyche of a child, and this was the case with Dorcas Good. In a letter written in 1710 by her father to the court seeking damages for his family's imprisonment and treatment, William Good stated that Dorcas "hath ever since [her incarceration] been very chargeable, having little or no reason [with which] to govern herself."

Gosh. I wonder why.

Chapter Ten: Susannah Martin Is Accused

As far back as I remember I heard that the witch in the family was a spunky little woman—hardworking, extremely bright, full of energy—who successfully ran a farm by herself. She is also described in the historical record as having been "of remarkable personal neatness." When I close my eyes the woman I picture is my mother. My mom didn't run a farm by herself, but she did raise two children on her own. Her husband died in 1952, leaving her with life insurance worth about $2000. That would be more than it is now, but it still wasn't all that much. Yet she managed to raise my sister and me and send us to good colleges at a time when woman's liberation hadn't yet been dreamed of. We knew we were poor but it was never looked upon as an impediment. My mother always made sure to drill into my head that I "could do whatever [I} set [my] mind to." She had strong faith in the power of positive thinking.

Looking back, it seems clear my mother identified with Susannah. Susannah's husband, George Martin, was a blacksmith and farmer. He'd been dead at least five years[26] in 1692 when she was accused by the Salem girls. At that time, her children were all grown and had children and homes of their own. Susannah must have been a tough old bird because she herself had had eight of them—five boys and three girls—seven of whom survived to adulthood. Her youngest, William, would have been 30 at the time of the witch hysteria. The oldest, Richard, was 45.

In Puritan New England, running a farm—even a small one was something no woman was supposed to be able to

---

[26] George Martin's will was dated January 19, 1682/3 and probated November 23,1686, so he probably died in the fall of 1686.

do, especially not in the seventeenth century, and especially not all by herself. Naturally, her neighbors thought she must employ witchcraft to get things done. Between the ages of 67 and 72[27] at the time of the Salem fiasco, she was certainly what then would have been considered elderly in years, but she must not have seemed so. Rebecca Nurse was about the same age, and she was referred to as elderly and infirm, but not Susannah. No reference at all is made concerning her age.

She was short of stature and was described as outspoken, contemptuous of authority, and slightly plump—all characteristics that also defined my mother. Maybe one thing was a little different, though. My mother could hold her tongue when it made sense to do so, and she often would display a certain amount of humility. She never made anyone feel uncomfortable around her. Susannah, on the other hand, apparently could cut a person to ribbons when her dander was up and leave that person sitting in tatters in the middle of the floor. I know there were times when my mother would have liked to have done that, but to my knowledge she never did.

How could a small, old woman like Susannah or my mom be able to plant and till and harvest? Not to mention fell trees, chop, and split wood to keep the home fire burning throughout the cold New England winters? My guess is she did it because she was full of spit and vinegar. Apparently most people thought she employed witchcraft. Maybe she did. If so, it's a shame she didn't write down some of her spells and pass them on to others in the family—like me, for instance. I wouldn't mind saying something like "bibbity bobbity boo" and having a tree fall

---

[27] The Martin family tree lists Susannah's date of birth as "about 1620" but other documents indicate she may have been as much as five years younger.

down, chop itself into firewood, and stack itself by the chimney.

In digging into everything I could find about Susannah—and a lot has survived—I learned that at least one adjective used above to describe her may be slightly off. She wasn't just "spunky." The truth is, she could be downright "feisty." She had a hot temper and, as you will see, she apparently didn't suffer fools well. It appears some people were downright afraid of her. Quite a number were convinced she was a witch and had done such as cause their livestock to run off and drown themselves, or a cow to drop dead out of the blue.

Susannah's notoriety in greater Essex County must have widespread. She didn't live in Salem and yet was known to the afflicted Salem girls. Her home was twenty miles away in Amesbury,[28] and in those days, that was a long way. There weren't any cars or expressways, much less telephones, televisions, or iPods. Walking a normal three miles per hour, it would have taken almost seven hours to cover. Riding a horse would have taken four or five—unless the horse was galloped all the way.

Probably one reason Susannah was singled out was that she'd been hauled into court before on a charge of witchcraft. In 1669 her husband posted a 100 pounds bond for her, which was a tidy some in those days. The records of that trial have not survived, but she must have been found not guilty since she was still around 23 years later to be tried again.

Around the time of Susannah's first trial, her husband, George Martin, sued a man named William Sargent, Junior for slander. Apparently, Sargent had been spreading a rumor about Susannah, saying that almost 25 years

---

[28] She would be become known after her death as "the witch of Amesbury."

prior—before she'd married Martin—she'd had a child out of wedlock. The story was that someone had walked in on her while she was wringing the infant's neck. This was supposed to have taken place at what must have been a public stable owned by a Captain Wiggins. Sargent said she'd collared the man who'd seen her in the middle of this act and told him she'd kill him if he squealed. The record indicates Martin sued William Sargent for "saying his wife was a witch and he would call her a witch."

These slander and witchcraft court actions must have been related because Martin also sued another man, Thomas Sargent, " . . . for saying that his son George Martin [Junior] was a bastard and that Richard Martin [another son] was Goodwife [Susannah] Martin's imp" [a witch's familiar]. Obviously, discord among neighbors had reached the level of a screaming match and spilled over into court.

Eventually George Martin dropped the charges against Thomas Sargent, but William Sargent, Junior was found guilty of slandering Susannah in saying she was guilty of "fornication and infanticide." In what appears to have been a public insult, Susannah's husband was awarded "a white wampum peague [colonial currency] or the eighth part of a penny damage" by the magistrates. They must have thought she was fully capable of fornication and infanticide even though no one could prove it.

The year 1669 appears to have been a tumultuous one for the Martins, full of suits and counter suits. George Martin was sued by Christopher Bartlett because Susannah had called him a liar and a thief. The verdict was against the Martins so Susannah's reputation for having a sharp tongue was upheld. But that was not the only problem they had to deal with. At the same court session, their son Richard was "presented by the grand jury at the Salisbury Court, 1669, for abusing his father and throwing him down, taking away his clothes and holding up an ax against him." The court found him guilty and sentenced Richard to be "whipped ten stripes."

All this happened when Susannah was 45 or 50. You'd think that after twenty-plus years had passed, Susannah would have mellowed, but apparently she hadn't. It's impossible to know what thought occurred to her when she saw the Amesbury constable—her longtime acquaintance, Orlando Bagley—coming up the road around the first day of May, 1692. But after he read the subpoena demanding she appear in Salem on the charge of witchcraft, she must have thought, "Here we go again."

A pretty thorough record still exists of the testimony given at Susannah's examination. In what follows, I've tried to bring it to life.

Orlando Bagley and Susannah probably left Amesbury at dawn on May 2, 1692, in order to cover the twenty miles to Salem Village where she was required to appear. Nevertheless, the record shows they arrived late. That's not surprising, given the distance.

Bagley would have escorted Susannah into the great room of the clapboard meeting house and presented her to magistrates John Hathorne and Jonathan Corwin. No doubt her arrival had been eagerly awaited. There was not an empty seat.

As soon as she came through the door, her accusers—the afflicted girls—fell into fits. Their bodies twisted in grotesque contortions, a cacophony flowed from their mouths to fill the room like a swarm of demons humming, shouting, and screaming as their lips curled back bearing their teeth, eyes bulging, tongues protruding so far out of their mouths some actually touched their owner's chins.

John Hathorne, always the outspoken of the two magistrates, conducted most of the questioning throughout the witch examinations. He is likely to have spoken first, directing a question to the afflicted.

"Do you know this woman?"

Eleven-year-old Abigail Williams spoke up, gasping, "It is Goody Martin. She hath hurt me often."

Others tried to speak but could not, their faces contorted in fits.

Elizabeth Hubbard, age seventeen, was one of the few not groaning in agony. She said she had not been hurt by Goody Martin.

John Indian, husband of the confessed witch, Tituba, and now one of the afflicted,[29] also seemed unfazed. He said he had not seen her before, while Mercy Lewis, age nineteen, pointed to the defendant and fell into a fit, unable to force words out of her own mouth.

Ann Putman, twelve, had also been struck dumb. In the spastic gesture of one enduring terrible pain, she threw a glove at Susannah.

Unprepared for the spectacle playing out before her, Susannah apparently did not believe the group was playing with a full deck. They must have seemed to her to be a bunch of crazies or maybe clowns putting on a show, and she laughed at them.

But Hathorne believed every spasmodic gesture and was not amused. "What do you laugh at?" He asked.

Susannah took a breath and made herself as tall as possible. "Well, I may at such folly."

---

[29] One has to wonder if John Indian didn't notice that others related to accused witches were themselves being accused, and decide to become one of the afflicted in order to save his own skin. Smart move.

"Is this folly? The hurt of these persons."

"I never hurt man, woman, or child."

Mercy Lewis cried out, "She hath hurt me a great many times, and pulls me down at this very moment."

Susannah laughed again. Never had she seen or heard such balderdash.

Mary Walcott, sixteen, said, "She tells not the truth, your honor. This woman hath hurt me many times."

Susannah Sheldon, about nineteen, accused her also.

"What do you say to this?" Hathorne wanted to know.

By now Susannah realized the magistrates believed these people were serious.

Susannah said simply, calmly, "I have no hand in witchcraft."

"How does this happen, then? Did you bid someone else do it on your behalf?"

"No, no—never in my life."

The howling and fits continued.

"Well, then, what ails this people?"

"I do not know."

"Certainly you must have an opinion. What do you think ails them?"

Susannah felt a flash of anger and her face flushed. It was clear, now, she was being framed. She must stay in control of herself.

"I do not desire to spend my judgment on it," she said.

"Do you not think they are bewitched?"

"No. I do not think they are."

"Tell me your thoughts about them."

"I will not," she said. "When they are in, my thoughts are my own, but when they are out they are another's. Their master—"

"Their Master?" Hathorne interrupted. "Who do you

think is their Master?"

"Hath it occurred to you that perhaps it is they who are dealing in the black art? Surely, you are able to see this possibility, as well as I."

From the way he rolled his eyes, Susannah understood Hathorne was unwilling to consider this. Gesturing to the afflicted, he said, "Tell us, what have you done towards this?"

"Nothing. Absolutely nothing."

The afflicted piped up louder than before. They cringed, wailed, and cried out that Susannah's apparition had descended upon them—flailing them.

Hathorne said, "It is you, or your appearance, is it not—who torments them?"

"If it is my appearance, I cannot help it."[30]

"Perhaps your apparition is your Master."

Susannah felt like shouting, but said in a controlled voice, "I have nothing to do with Satan. I desire to lead my self according to the word of God."

Again, Hathorne gestured to the afflicted. "Is this according to God's word?"

"I am a Godly person. I tell the truth."

The afflicted wailed—cringing away from something invisible to all but them.

"Well, how comes your appearance just now to hurt these?"

"How should I know? I have naught to do with it."

Hathorne furrowed his brow and stared at her. "Are you not willing to tell the truth?"

"Consider this," Susannah said. "Satan came to Saul in the shape of Samuel—Samuel, a glorified saint. If Satan can do thus, he can appear in any person's shape—mine,

---

[30] No doubt the humor in this statement was lost on Hathorne.

yours—anyone's."[31]

Susannah had just offered evidence taken from Holy Scripture that refuted Reverend Richard Bernard's and Reverend Samuel Parris's claim Satan could not take on the appearance of the "regenerate," or spiritually reborn, but Hathorne was unmoved. He simply shrugged.

"Do you not believe they are speaking the truth?" He said.

Susannah fumed. "They may lie for all I know."

"And you. May not you lie?"

"I dare not tell a lie if it would save my life."[32]

"Then you will speak the truth."

"I have spoken nothing else. I would help these poor people if I could."

"I do not think you have such affections for them, whom you just insinuated had the devil for their master."

Elizabeth Hubbard screamed in pain. She told a nearby marshal of the court Susannah had pinched her hand. Then several of the afflicted cried out and pointed to the rafters.

"There she is," they shouted. "She's sitting on the beam." Hathorne shook his head. "Pray God discover you, if you be guilty."

"Amen," Susannah said. "Amen. A false tongue will never make a person guilty."

Nineteen-year-old Mercy Lewis shouted, "You have been a long time coming to the court today! Yet you come fast enough in the night!"

---

[31] In 1 Samuel, Chapter 28 of the Bible, King Saul, wishing to consult Samuel who had died, went to the Witch of Endor, who conjured up what Saul believed to be Samuel's spirit. While modern Biblical scholars debate this point, Puritans were confident that Satan took on Samuel's appearance in order to trick Saul. This reference to Scripture, which backed up Susannah's claim that Satan could take on her likeness without her knowledge, should have been a powerful argument in a Puritan New England court. Yet the magistrates ignored it without comment. Apparently, they had already decided Susannah was guilty.

[32] For a God-fearing Puritan, to lie was to break one of the Ten Commandments at the peril of one's soul.

"No, sweetheart," Susannah said, sarcasm spilling out of her. "It wasn't I."

Mercy Lewis and the others groaned and writhed in agony. Susannah bit her lip as she watched this spectacle.

Now, John Indian fell into a seizure. "It was that woman, she bites, she bites!"

Hathorne shouted, "Have you no compassion for these afflicted?"

Susannah shook her head, "No, I have none."

Some of the afflicted cried out, "There he is! The black man! He is with her."

Magistrates Hathorne and Corwin whispered to one another.

Then Hathorne spoke.

"We will try an experiment," he said. "Mary Walcott, approach the accused."

Mary Walcott drew her hand to her mouth as her jaw dropped. "Me, your honor?"

"Stand, please, and walk towards her."

Tentatively, Mary Walcott stood. She took a step. Then another, and another, until she fell down as though she'd tripped on an invisible barrier.

"I can go no further. I am blocked."

Next, the magistrates had Abigail Williams and Goody Bibber attempt to approach Susannah. They, too, reached an invisible barrier and fell.

John Indian stood, shouted "I will kill her!" and ran at Susannah. But when he reached the spot where the others had been impeded, he bounced backward and fell onto the floor as though he'd run into an invisible wall.

The packed room erupted. Hathorne called for order.

When relative calm returned, he said, "What is the reason these cannot come near you?"

Susannah shook her head. "I cannot tell. It may be the devil bears me more malice than another. Has it not occurred to you that if I were in league with him, this would not be the way that he would help?"

This was another argument Hathorne and Corwin refused to hear. Hawthorne said, "Do not you see how God evidently discovers you?"

Susannah said, "No, not a bit."

"All the congregation think so," Hathorne said.

"Let them think what they will."

"What is the reason these cannot come near you?"

"I do not know, but it is not I who stop them. If you wish, I will come to them."

"That will not be necessary. What is the black man whispering to you?"

"No one whispers to me."

The accusations persisted, and the magistrates continued to ignore Susannah Martin's arguments and protests concerning her innocence. At the end of the day, she was committed to prison where she would await her trial for the capital offense of witchcraft.

Chapter Eleven: The Power of Belief

One thing is certain. Virtually everyone involved in the witchcraft hysteria thought witchcraft, or black magic, was real and that it worked. From their points of view, this was "knowledge" they held, just like the researchers conducting the double-slit experiment had knowledge concerning which slit a photon had passed through. This knowledge was held by the afflicted, the magistrates, the ministers, the accused, onlookers, and by innocent bystanders.

In the double-slit experiment, knowledge held by a researcher actually seemed to bring about the result that person believed would occur, or should occur. If a single proton was shot through a particular slit, the researcher believed it could not and would not form part of a zebra pattern since interference was required for that to happen. But if the researcher didn't know which slit each of many protons went through, the zebra pattern reappeared, even though the photons each were shot and passed through the slits one at a time. The possession of concrete knowledge seems to have been the difference.

Since knowledge [thought] is not contained within a person's cranium but is *everywhere* at once as was indicated by the double-slit experiment, belief or knowledge held jointly by a group of people would logically seem to be more powerful than that held only by a single individual. The mind of each person would reinforce the others. There's a great deal of anecdotal evidence to support this contention in the form of crowd behavior and the formation of what has been called "group minds" as in Nazi Germany. Often, crowds or groups behave in ways those who make up the assembly would never behave as individuals. A good example might be a lynching. Another is that a team that believes it is going to win is usually very hard to beat. The point is, the afflicted in 1692 believed they were bewitched and would suffer certain symptoms. Everyone around them believed it as well. It's possible this was sufficient to produce symptoms that were real, whether or not their cause was witchcraft.

My Own Experience with the Power of Belief

In the spring of 2000, a startling realization came to me after I'd done a local radio interview on one of my novels. It was about seven o'clock in the evening. I was really tired, you might say beat, having just spent an intense hour doing my best to be entertaining and witty. On the way home from the station, I stopped at my local Seven Eleven for a bottle of beer. A sign caught my eye as I approached the register.

"We I.D. under 27 years of age."

I took my place in line behind a couple of teenagers with Slurpies. An acquaintance from college took the spot behind me, and we exchanged pleasantries. My turn at the register came, I put the bottle on the counter, and reached for my wallet.

The clerk eyed me. "Sorry, I'll have to see your I.D.," she said.

"Excuse me?" I said.

"I'm going to have to see your I.D.," she repeated.

"You're kidding," I said.

She let out an exasperated sigh. "No, I'm not. I need to see your I.D. before I can sell you that beer."

I placed my driver's license it in her hand, turned to my

friend, whose mouth hung agape, and gave her a little shrug.

"It's true," my old acquaintance said, shaking her head. "You really do look young."

On the way home, I sipped, kept an eye out for the cops, and pondered the fact that I'd been asked to prove I was old enough to buy alcohol. You see, I was 55 years old at the time—more than twice what the clerk was required to I.D. It's definitely true that I felt much younger. Now, at 62, I am beginning to notice some indications of aging. But at 55, I felt no different than I did 27.

I started wondering why, and after a while, a possibility surfaced in my mind. Thirty years before, when I was 25, I'd read an article about a study conducted among people who'd been consuming large doses of vitamin E for a period of ten years. The article said that no measurable signs of aging had occurred among them. So I'd gone out and bought a bottle, and I'd been taking it since.

For years, I believed I wouldn't age. And for years, it seemed I didn't age.

Much later, I read that researchers had concluded that vitamin E in pill form cannot be proven to retard aging. As has often been the case, newer studies refute older ones. But I kept taking it anyway.

According to recent articles, we've come almost full circle. No researcher is ready to say vitamin E stops aging altogether, but new research indicates that taking the vitamin results in lower incidence of heart disease and cancer, while helping mitigate all sorts of health problems. Even so, I've come to believe it may have worked for me in large measure due to the placebo effect. But it worked. Thirty years before I'd read an article that said I wouldn't age if I took it. I expected it to work, so it did. If the following week I'd read another article that said the anti-aging qualities of vitamin E were hogwash, I probably would not have experienced the same result.

The Placebo Effect

Belief is extremely potent. The effectiveness of placebos has been demonstrated time and again in double-blind scientific tests. The placebo effect—the phenomenon of patients feeling better after taking inert pills—is seen throughout the field of medicine. One recent report says that after thousands of studies, hundreds of millions of prescriptions and tens of billions of dollars in sales, sugar pills are as effective at treating depression as antidepressants such as Prozac, Paxil and Zoloft.[33] What's more, placebos bring about profound changes in the same areas of the brain these medicines are said to affect—according to this research. For anyone who may have thought otherwise, this proves beyond doubt that thoughts and beliefs can and do produce physical changes in our bodies.

In addition, the same research reports that placebos often outperform the medicines they're up against. For example, in a trial conducted in April, 2002, comparing the herbal remedy St. John's wort to Zoloft, St. John's wort fully cured 24 percent of the depressed people who received it. Zoloft cured 25 percent. But the placebo fully cured 32 percent.[34]

Taking what one believes to be real medicine sets up the expectation of results, and what a person believes will happen usually does happen. It's been confirmed, for example, that in cultures where belief exists in voodoo or magic, people will actually die after being cursed by a

[33] "Against Depression, a Sugar Pill Is Hard to Beat," by Shankar Vedantam, *The Washington Post*, May 7, 2002.
[34] Ibid.

shaman. Such a curse has no power on an outsider who doesn't believe. The expectation causes the result. If you've read my novel, *In My Father's House*, you know I used this phenomenon as a major factor in the plot.

A Real-Life Example of the Power of Belief

Let me relate a real-life example of spontaneous healing that concerned a woman I've known for more than a dozen years, which I think took place because of belief.

Nancy is a minister's wife. She's a devout Christian— as firm a believer in her religion as a bushman who'd drop dead from a witch doctor's curse is in his, or a Puritan in seventeen century New England was in the efficacy of witchcraft. Five years ago, a lump more than half an inch in diameter was discovered in one of her breasts. Her doctor scheduled a biopsy.

A prayer group gathered at Nancy's home the night before this procedure was to take place. They prayed not that the lump would be benign, but rather, that it would disappear entirely.

Nancy is a member of a denomination that takes the Bible literally. In Matthew 18:19-20, Jesus is reported to have said, "Again, I tell you that if two of you on earth agree about anything you ask for, it will be done for you by my Father in heaven. For where two or three come together in my name, there am I with them."

As you can imagine, it was more than two or three. It was a living room full. As in my case and vitamin E, quite naturally, Nancy expected the prayers to work.

Jesus also said, "Therefore I tell you, whatever you ask for in prayer, believe that you have received it, and it will be yours."[35] Notice the tense change in this verse. Jesus is

---

[35] Mark 11:24

saying to believe that you already have what you ask for and it will be given to you in the future. It seems as if he knew thoughts are timeless as indicated by the double slit experiment. Maybe what we hold in mind as a belief already does exist in some way as a thought form. According to one well-known metaphysician, Edgar Cayce (1877-1945), thoughts are things ready to materialize on the physical plane.

The Power of Belief Is Demonstrated on Television

I once saw an experiment concerning belief conducted before the television cameras of the Discovery Cable TV Network. In this case, two subjects participated in the same ESP experiment in the same laboratory using the same equipment. Great pains were taken to keep everything identical except for one thing. One subject believed ESP worked, and the other did not. Like many other scientists, he believed thought remains inside the skull, which would make ESP impossible. Both tests were supervised by impartial observers, including the Discovery Channel crew.

The experiment that employed the researcher who believed in ESP had a statistically significant number of correct hits, meaning the experiment was successful. In other words, ESP was demonstrated under scientifically controlled conditions because the outcome could not have occurred by chance. But the number of correct hits in the experiment that had involved the skeptical researcher fell within parameters that could be accounted for by chance. So this time the experiment failed to demonstrate the validity of ESP. Apparently, the one and only variable—belief—made the difference. The first researcher believed and the second did not. Each got the result he expected.

A great deal of anecdotal evidence supports this finding. Researchers into the paranormal report that even the presence of someone who flatly does not believe can derail such an experiment. Belief, it seems, may be a requisite for at least some paranormal phenomena to happen. Perhaps this is the reason non believers rarely experience anything that would lead them to doubt their position as skeptics.

Nancy Is Miraculously Cured

Let's get back to Nancy, the believer in the efficacy of prayer. The next morning, upon self examination, the lump in her breast seemed to have vanished. Even so, Nancy kept her appointment at the hospital where she was to have had the biopsy. But first, her doctor conducted a thorough examination.

The physician confirmed the lump was gone. No trace could be found, and the bewildered doctor sent her home.

How could a solid lump of tissue disappear? The same question might be asked of the afflicted of 1692. How did they cough up pins, vomit blood, produce lesions on their bodies? Perhaps it is true that belief creates our individual and collective realities.

How Thought and Belief May Create Reality

An explanation of how belief works to create our personal and collective reality may be contained in lectures I came across a few years ago, given by a man named Thomas Troward. He first delivered these lectures in 1904 at Queens Gate at Edinburgh University in Scotland.

Called *The Edinburgh Lectures on Mental Science,* they outline a theory that I believe is worthy of consideration. It's noteworthy that this theory fits with the assertion by quantum physicists that time and distance are not factors on the subatomic level of thought.

According to Troward, thought and life are manifestations of the same thing.

If I were to day, "What's life?" assuming you're old enough, you'd probably say, "a magazine."[36] And no wonder. If you're like me, you don't remember learning what life is when you studied science—not even biology—in school. My college biology textbook devotes not one sentence to the subject. I can only conclude that to have included this in the curriculum would have presented a problem for the biologists who wrote the book. Answering simple questions such as where does it come from and where does it go are not within the capability of biology as it is constituted today. Yet just about everyone knows what life is when they see it. Life is the force that animates what would otherwise be a dead body. A deer strapped to the fender of a car contains no life. A deer running from a hunter is full of it—although perhaps only temporarily.

According to Thomas Troward, life and thought are the same thing and are in fact the fabric of the universe—the ground of being that underlies everything, roughly comparable I suppose to the invisible "strings" quantum physicists now theorize form the basis of all that is. Thought or life may not be apparent in a rock or a stone, but it is there, and it becomes more apparent in manifestations that appear to be more "alive" than others.

To grasp what Troward is driving at, it helps to begin by considering the difference that appears to exist between

---

[36] Life Magazine was published as a weekly from 1936 to 1972 and as a monthly until 1984.

what we think of as "dead" matter and something we recognize as alive. A plant, such as a sunflower, has a quality that sets it apart from a piece of steel. The sunflower will turn toward the sun under its own power. When first picked, it possesses a kind of glow. This quality might be called the life force, or energizing spirit. On the other hand, the piece of steel appears totally inert. Yet, at the quantum level, steel is alive with motion. In fact, quantum physicists tell us that motion or energy is what comprises all matter. They theorize that infinitesimally small string-like bits of space—which contain ten, eleven, or twenty-six dimensions depending on whose version of the theory you buy—rise up in vibration to form the subatomic components of atoms, and as we all know, atoms combine to make molecules and molecules combine to make stuff. But strings, subatomic components, atoms, and molecules are not solid things. They are energy. Vibrations. Some would say the whole universe is alive, as though it were a single giant thought—the thought of an infinitely vast mind of organizing intelligence.

But let's get back to what we can see. By outward appearances the sunflower is alive, and the steel is not. Few would argue this. But one might argue that a plant's state of "aliveness" is different from that of an animal. Consider the difference in aliveness between a sunflower, an earthworm, and a goldfish. Each appears to be progressively more alive.

Now, let's add a dog, a three year old child, and a stand up comedian on the Tonight Show. Each has a progressively higher level of intelligence. So, to some extent, what we call the degree of "aliveness" can be measured by the amount of awareness or intelligence displayed—in other words, by the power of thought.

As was written above, intelligence, or thought—according to Thomas Troward—underlies and creates the entire universe. But it becomes more evident to us—we can see it more clearly—as this intelligence becomes more self-aware. So the distinctive quality of spirit, or life, is thought, and the distinctive quality of matter, as in the piece of steel, is form.

Form Versus Thought

Now let's talk about form versus thought. Form implies the occupation of space and also limitation within certain boundaries. Thought [life] implies neither. When we think of thought or life as existing in any particular form we associate it with the idea of occupying space, so that an elephant may be said to consist of a vastly larger amount of living substance than a mouse. But if we think of life as the fact of "aliveness," or animating spirit, we do not associate it with occupying space. The mouse is as much alive as the elephant, notwithstanding the difference in size. Here is an important point. If we can conceive of anything as not occupying space, or as having no form, it must be present in its totality anywhere and everywhere—that is to say, at every point of space simultaneously—like the thought of researchers in the double-slit experiment.

Life/thought does not occupy space and it transcends time. The scientific definition of time is the period it takes a body to pass from one point in space to another. So when there is no space there can be no time. That life/thought is devoid of space must also mean it is devoid of time. The bottom line is that all life, or thought, must exist everywhere at once in a universal here and an everlasting now.

How does this help us understand how we create our own reality as well as how the afflicted in Salem suffered real symptoms—whether or not they were psychosomatic?

Objective and Subjective Thought

First, it is implicit in the discussion above that there are two kinds of thought. We might call them lower and higher, or subjective and objective because what differentiates the higher from the lower is the recognition of self. The plant, the worm, and perhaps the goldfish possess the lower kind only. They are unaware of self. Perhaps the dog, and certainly the boy and the comedian possess both. The higher variety of self-aware thought is possessed in progressively larger amounts as if ascending a scale.

According to Troward's theory, the lower mode of thought, the subjective, is the subconscious intelligence or "mind" present everywhere that, among other things, supports and controls the mechanics of life in every species and in every individual. It causes the plant to grow toward the sun and to push its roots into the soil. It causes hearts to beat and lungs to take in air. It controls all of the so-called involuntary functions of the body. And, as we will see, it controls a lot more.

That this lower kind of thought is everywhere at once coincides with the theory of Carl Jung who maintained that we humans share a universal subconscious mind. Moreover, we each have our own portion, our individual subconscious mind that blends into the collective mind. We also have a conscious mind, the producer of higher thought that makes us self-aware. The two types of mind are inextricably linked in that our conscious mind arises out of the subconscious. It evolved over the course of millions of years until the point was reached recounted in the myth of Adam and Eve. That's when we were capable of objective thought and therefore of ignoring our instincts—the still small voice within—and of doing as we pleased. We now had free will. The gradual emergence of self-aware thought out of the subconscious is implicit in our consideration of the plant, earthworm, goldfish, dog, boy, comedian and so forth up the scale.

Objective Thought Directs Subjective Thought

Now let us consider an important point made by Troward in his Lectures. The conscious mind has a power over our subconscious mind that creates our reality. I discovered this firsthand in college when I taught myself to hypnotize others. I would put a willing classmate into a trance and tell him he was a chicken or a dog. Much to the amusement of my audience, he would then act accordingly.[37]

Hypnotism works because the hypnotist bypasses his subject's conscious mind and speaks directly to his subject's subconscious. Troward maintained, and it makes sense to me, the subconscious mind has no choice but to bring into reality that which is communicated directly to it as fact by a conscious mind.

Deductive Versus Inductive Reasoning

Being totally subjective, the subconscious mind cannot step outside of itself and take an objective look. As such, it is capable only of deductive reasoning, which is the kind that progresses from a cause—the conscious mind's

---

[37] Do not try this at home. It may be dangerous. As a college student, I didn't know any better.

directive—forward to its ultimate end. It does not stop to question or to analyze. It is the reasoning that a criminal might use in committing a crime. He may walk into a room, see a man counting his money, and think, "I need money, so I will take his. Since the man is protecting the money, I will get rid of him. I'll shoot him. He'll drop to the floor. I will then take the money and run. I'll leave by the window."

On the other hand, the conscious mind, being objective and self-aware, can step outside. It can reason both deductively and inductively. To reason inductively is to move backward from result to cause. A police detective, for example, would arrive at the crime scene and begin reasoning backward in an attempt to tell how the crime was committed and who might have done it.

The result is that the subconscious [subjective] mind is entirely under the control of the conscious [objective] mind. With utmost fidelity, the subconscious will work diligently to support or to bring into reality whatever the conscious mind believes to be true. Since the individual subconscious blends with the collective subconscious and is present everywhere, it is able to influence circumstances and events so that whatever the conscious mind believes to be true is likely to become true. So, for example, if I believe I am a sickly person, I will be a sickly person. If I believe that by sitting in a draft I will catch cold, I will catch cold when I sit in a draft because my immune system will accommodate me by letting in cold germs. If I believe that I am bewitched I will be bewitched and exhibit the symptoms I understand bewitched persons to exhibit, in the same way my friends in college behaved like chickens and dogs when I hypnotized them because they thought they really were chickens and dogs. If I think my cow has a curse on it and will go belly up in two days, my cow may actually go belly up in two days. One way this may happen is that I may subconsciously help the cow along by allowing it to eat wolfsbane, corn cockle, or some other ordinary plant that's poisonous to cattle."

As you will see, Susannah Martin's neighbors believed bad things would happen to them as a result of her "discontents." No wonder bad things happened.

Beliefs Create Reality

Most people go through life hypnotized into thinking they have little or no control over their circumstances. I have become convinced that to a great extent they create their circumstances with their thoughts and beliefs. The message of the *Edinburgh Lectures* is simple. Change your beliefs and your circumstances will change. In 1692 Salem, people created a reality they believed to be true. In a society that believes in witchcraft, witchcraft is real. It works. Not only that, it seems quite possible the afflicted may have developed the symptoms associated with being bewitched because they believed they would.

But what about possession? Weren't some of the afflicted possessed or obsessed?

Could be. But for someone to be possessed means there would have to be a disembodied spirit to possess them. This would have to mean Satan and perhaps his minions are real, or at the very least that a person's spirit continues to exist after death, and that such a spirit can obsess or possess a living person.

Could Cotton Mather have been right about an invisible "World of Wonders?"

Before long, we'll see.

Chapter Twelve: The Witch Hysteria Moves into the Trial Phase

The Massachusetts Bay Colony had been without a governor for quite some time on May 14, 1692, when Increase Mather, Cotton's father, returned from England with a new charter for the colony and a new governor, Sir William Phips. The ranks of accused witches had been growing for more than two months, and it was clear something needed to be done. With a new governor in place it was possible to move the proceedings from a series of inquires, statements, and depositions to the status of an official trial of suspected witches. Accordingly, on June 2, 1692, Massachusetts Governor William Phips convened the Court of Oyer and Terminer[38] at Salem. The court, made up of seven judges and twelve jurors was presided over by the deputy governor of Massachusetts, William Stoughton.

Ordinarily, capital cases were tried in Boston before the highest court. In this instance, the Court of Oyer and Terminer was convened in the affected county of Essex, so the justices had to spend the first day of June traveling from Boston to Salem for the initial court session which was to take place the next day. Several prisoners also had to be carted from the Boston jail to the Salem jail for trial. The accused in this caravan included John and Elizabeth Proctor, my seven-times-great grandmother, Susannah Martin, Alice Parker, Rebecca Nurse, Bridget Bishop, John Willard, Tituba the slave, and Sarah Good.

---

[38] This translates as "To hear and determine."

Ann Carr Putnam Is Visited by Three Spirits

As the leaders of the colony prepared to cleanse the physical world of witches, activity continued unabated in the spirit world. Early on the morning of June 2, the ghosts of Samuel Fuller and Lydia Wilkins came to haunt Ann Carr Putnam, hovering near her as she lay in bed. They—as had the specters of people she'd accused of being witches—threatened to tear her to pieces if she didn't let John Hathorne know that one John Willard had murdered them. The ghosts of Fuller and Wilkins told her that if Hathorne didn't believe her, they might just materialize in court and thereby disrupt the proceedings. Next, in a move that doesn't strike me as particularly intelligent, the specter of John Willard himself came to Ann to boast of additional victims he and a buddy named William Hobbs had done away with—mostly Ann's own children who had died— during her life she gave birth to twelve—as well as other children in the neighborhood.

Let me pause for a moment to interject. If you had been John Hathorne when Ann Senior told you this, don't you think your first question would have been, "Why would someone who didn't want to be hanged send his specter to tell you he was a murderer?"

Whether it makes sense or not, Goodwife Putnam must have spent a busy morning in bed. The ghost of a deceased man named Joseph Fuller was her third visitation. He came and implored her to accuse Martha Corey of causing his death.

Bridget Bishop Is the First to Be Tried

Later that day, Bridget Bishop was the first to be called for trial, probably because the court felt it had the strongest case against her. Not only had she had been accused of witchcraft in the past, not only did bad things seem to happen routinely to just about anyone she had a disagreement with, but there was the matter of what looked an awful lot like effigy dolls found stuffed in her basement walls. A record of what she had to say to the court about these poppets no longer exists, but whatever it was did not convince the court they were something other than what they appeared to be.

The justices were not in unanimous agreement about her guilt, but they did agree to convict, ignoring the fact no single act of witchcraft had been proven to have been performed by Goody Bishop. She was hanged eight days later at gallows hill in Salem, the second victim of the witch hysteria, and the first to be hanged. The first victim had been Sarah Osborne who died in prison on May 10 in Boston.

Thorough Body Examinations Are Conducted

Also on June 2, the "woman's jury" led by a Salem Town surgeon and apothecary, Dr. John Barton, issued two reports. Having inspecting the bodies of Bridget Bishop, Rebecca Nurse, and Elizabeth Proctor "by diligent search"—and believe me from their account they left no square millimeter of flesh unscrutinized—the jurists explained they'd found "apreternathurall Excresensce of flesh between the pudendum and Anus much like to Tetts

& not usuall in women . . . & that they were in all the three women neer the same place."[39] On the other hand, they did not see anything unusual on the bodies of Alice Parker, Susannah Martin, or Sarah Good, whom they also strip-searched. Several hours later, however, a reexamination revealed that the teat-like "piece[s] of flesh" on the first three women had disappeared, being replaced by "dry skin," and that Susannah Martin's breast, which in the morning had "appeared to us very full," was now "all lancke & pendant." These findings implied that between the morning and the afternoon the four women had each been suckled by their animal familiars.

A Baptist Minister Gets in Trouble for Cautioning the Court

Apparently, the Court of Oyer and Terminer took a break from convicting accused witches until the end of the month while other business was attended to. During that time, Governor Phips and his council received two petitions composed by Boston's Baptist minister, William Milborne. One was signed by him, "and several others"— identities now unknown—signed the other. Both petitions objected to the use of spectral evidence in the trials for fear it served to condemn the innocent. "A woeful chain of consequences will undoubtedly follow. . . . [We] therefore request that the validity of specter testimony may be weighted in the balance of your grace and solid judgments, it being the womb that hath brought forth inextricable damage and misery to this province, and to order by your votes that no more credence be given thereto than the word of God alloweth."

---

[39] I have not updated the language spelling or capitalization of this text because it seems to me to have more impact in its original form.

The council was greatly offended by this unsolicited opinion that bordered on accusation and at its "very high reflections upon the administration of public justice." This indicates to me the people running the show had begun to doubt the validity of spectral evidence, anger being the second stage of the five stages people pass through before they accept a truth that conflicts with firmly held beliefs.[40]

Governor Phips signed a warrant for Reverend Milborne to answer for the "scandalous and seditious paper." The sheriff brought him before the council posthaste and Milborne admitted he'd written both papers and had signed one. The council ordered him to appear before the Superior Court—once it was formed—at its first sitting. In the meantime the good reverend had to post a post a 200 pound bond, a huge sum, plus two sureties in order to guarantee he'd appear in court. His only option would have been to wait in jail.

Sarah Good Is Tried

Sarah Good's trial began at nine o'clock on June 28 in the Salem Town meeting house. This was a woman who had experienced great misfortune during her 39 or so years of life. Her father had committed suicide, her stepfather had wrestled away what she believed was her rightful inheritance, her first husband had died and left her deep in debt, her present husband seemed incapable of earning a living, and to add grief upon hardship, a few days before her trial Sarah Good's infant daughter had died in prison where both were being held along with Sarah's five year old daughter. It's not surprising that by all accounts Sarah seethed with anger. Anyone who took time to think about

---

[40] The five stages are denial, anger, bargaining, depression, and acceptance.

it should not have wondered why. The problem was that her anger alarmed people especially if their cattle died after she had let some of it out.

The people of Salem Village testified about Sarah Good. Samuel and Mary Abbey recounted how they'd taken in the homeless woman and her husband Will, but had come to regret this action. Not only was Sarah a pipe smoker, but the Goods' rows were simply too much with the result that after about six months the Abbeys turned them out "for quietness sake." Despite their previous generosity, Sarah "spitefully and maliciously" expressed her anger and resentment to them and to their children. Like clockwork, the Abbey's cattle began to get sick. Seventeen animals died over a two year period, not to mention some sheep and hogs that also went belly up. Will Good, Sarah's husband, told Samuel Abbey at the time— about a year before the trial—that when he mentioned the Abbeys' losses to Sarah, she'd told him she didn't care if they lost all their cattle.

These weren't the only animals people thought Sarah had bewitched. It also came out that one of Thomas Gadge's cows had died around the time the Abbeys had evicted the Goods. Why, do you suppose? Gadge's wife had refused to let Sarah so much as set foot in their house because smallpox was going around, and she was afraid Sarah might be carrying it. But that wasn't all. When Sarah's kinsman Zachariah Herrick refused to put her up, and hustled her and her pipe off this property, she snapped that such might just cost him two of his best cows. As sure as day follows night, two of his best were mysteriously replaced by beasts of lesser quality.

Imagine yourself in Sarah Good's position. Here she was on trial. Her four or five year old daughter Dorcas was back in Boston alone in jail on suspicion of witchcraft, her infant daughter had just died, and her husband was testifying against her. Could things be any worse?

The spectral evidence from her earlier examination was brought against her, plus numerous reports of her specter's activities since that time. Perhaps Reverend Milborne's petitions and the objections of others concerning spectral evidence had begun to undermine the court's faith in it, but nonetheless, the judges and jury had been witness to the obvious suffering of the afflicted during the past five months. And, at that very moment during Sarah's trial— they were having more seizures.

The Judges Accept Obviously Bogus Evidence

According to a later critic of the trials, one of the afflicted roused from a fit claiming that Sarah had stabbed her in the breast with a knife, and had broken its blade in the process. A sliver of metal was found in her clothes.

An unnamed young man came forward and volunteered that he had discarded a fragment from a broken knife blade in the presence of the witness the day before. He produced the damaged knife, which the court then compared with the sliver. It fit exactly, but do you suppose they threw out the evidence and marched the witness to the slammer? No, these particular judges must still have been in the denial stage. They said this was not the first time specters reportedly had used physical objects to hurt their victims, and dismissed the young man with a warning to be truthful. Then they allowed the afflicted witness to continue her testimony.

Followers of Hindu and Buddhist teachings would have to conclude that Sarah Good had one heckuva lot of bad karma to work off during her seventeenth-century lifetime, and that her surly way of dealing with it did not help her cause one bit. Not surprisingly, the jury found her guilty of witchcraft and sentenced her to be hanged by the neck until dead.

Susannah North Martin is Tried

My seven-times-great grandmother, Susannah North Martin, was tried the next day, on June 29. She pleaded "not guilty" to the charge of witchcraft. While making her plea, the afflicted choked, convulsed, screamed, jerked, and writhed as usual. The Reverend Deodat Lawson of Boston was in attendance and commented later that the judges demonstrated considerable patience in ferreting out testimony between spectral attacks. He also related how grotesquely twisted the afflicted were, as if every joint had been dislocated, and how one of the afflicted actually vomited blood. Some were not sure what the red stuff was, and a finger was dabbed in the gore to check it out. It was blood, all right.

The first order of business was to review the testimony given at Susannah's examination, including how she'd laughed at the afflicted as though she enjoyed seeing them in misery, and how when the afflicted had tried to approach her—they had been thrown to the floor. Next, some of her neighbors testified.

Not Very Neighborly Neighbors

Lieutenant John Allen of Salisbury testified he'd once met Goody Martin on the road and refused her request to let his oxen carry a load for her. He'd just finished a big timber-hauling job and wanted to get the animals to pasture and a rest. She'd expressed displeasure at this, and the two of them had quarreled.

She supposedly had said his oxen would be of little more use to him.

To this, Allen had replied, "Are you threatening me, you old witch? I'll throw you into the brook."

He rushed at her but she escaped his grasp and "flew over" a nearby the bridge.

As Allen was going home, one of his oxen became so tired he had to unyoked the beast. Allen took it and others he owned, apparently a total of fourteen oxen, to Salisbury Beach "where cattle did use to get flesh" or graze.

A few days later Allen returned, and all of them were gone.

But he spotted their tracks. They'd run into the Merrimack River.

The next day the beasts were found on Plum Island. But they refused to be yoked, and ran away with "a violence that seemed wholly diabolical." They ran furiously until they reached the mouth of the Merrimack and kept on running into the sea, "swimming as far as could be seen." Only one turned around and came back, "with a swiftness amazing to the beholders," who were ready to help what they expected to be an exhausted animal. "But the beast ran furiously up into the island," and from there galloped through the marshes into Newbury and on into the woods. They finally found this oxen near Amesbury.

Out of fourteen, only this one was saved. The rest were later found dead in one place or another, their carcasses washed up on shore.

According to testimony that followed, for twenty-five years or so people had been experiencing the death of cattle after one of "Martin's discontents"—if they refused her beef or tied to pay with an animal she didn't want. One of her sons traded a cow once to a neighbor against Susannah's wishes and the beast, which had been gentle before, acted crazed all the way to the ferry, breaking the ropes that bound it, and plunging into the river.

Susannah Martin's Specter Stalks a Farmhand

Twice, according to sworn testimony, Martin's specter had stalked a middle-age farmhand named Bernard Peach. He said she had come into his bedroom in the middle of the night, took hold of his feet, "drew his body into a heap and lay upon him near two hours." Finally he was able to move a little and was able to bite her fingers, "as he judged, unto the bone." She fled from his bedroom, ran down the stairs and out the door.

No one besides Peach saw her apparition, naturally, but he said he found a drop of blood on the snow-covered doorstep, the footprints of a woman leading away from the house, and unmarked whiteness beyond. No doubt by then she had become airborne.

Once Peach had refused to help Goody Martin—in the flesh this time—with husking corn. Her specter and that of someone else had crept up on him in the barn. He swung his quarter staff, hitting mostly the beams, but he did manage to land a blow, he said, on Susannah's specter. Soon she was rumored to be unwell, but Peach admitted he did not check to see if her illness was due to the blow from his quarter staff.

Susannah Sics Spectral Dogs and Cats on People

When Susannah had been acquitted of witchcraft back in '69, a fellow named Robert Downer had made the mistake of telling her he thought she was guilty. Her retort had been something to do with a she-devil fetching him away. That night, Downer was attacked by a catlike creature.

Another witness, John Kimball, who already had doubts about the death of some cattle, argued with her about the sale of a puppy.

She was said to mutter, "If I live, I'll give him puppies enough."

One evening Kimball was on his way home, walking along with an ax on his shoulder, when he was caught in a squall and overtaken by what apparently seemed to him a supernatural "force." He ran to elude it, but was tripped up by a puppy-like creature. This apparently spectral being disappeared when he chopped at it with his ax, and was instantly replaced by a larger, more vicious dog. This canine lunged for his throat, missed and veered over his shoulder. It circled about him until the now frantic Kimball called on God and Christ for help, whereupon the creature disappeared.

Both men had long kept these embarrassing encounters to themselves, they said, but according to Cotton Mather writing in *Wonders of the Invisible World,* Goodwife Martin seemed to know all about them, anyway.

A man named John Pressy testified that twenty-four years back, he became lost in familiar territory near the Martins' land at dusk on a Sabbath evening. A moving light as big as a bushel basket accosted him and ruffled like a turkey cock when he prodded the light with his stick. He panicked, whacked it with his stick, but this seemed to have no effect. Then he veered off, and scrambling away fell into a hole he could never find after that day. When he emerged, the light had disappeared, but he saw Susannah Martin watching him, and later he heard that she was ill. He was too frightened to ask if her illness was the result of his blows or not.

Goody Martin Is Blamed for the Insanity of Another

William Brown of Salisbury described how his wife Elizabeth had been a sober, sensible woman until twenty-odd years before when she saw Susannah Martin vanish. Afterward, she felt prickling on her legs every time Goody Martin came by supposedly "pretending" to be neighborly. The pain rose to her stomach like a knot of nails, then arrived in her throat where it felt like a pullet's egg.

"Witch," Goody Brown had cried, "you shan't choke me!" Members of Elizabeth Brown's church had prayed and fasted on her behalf, and she did recover enough to testify against Susannah at her earlier trial on witchcraft charges. Once acquitted, Goody Martin was unneighborly enough to let her displeasure be known, which reduced poor Elizabeth to a flood of tears. Two months or so later, William Brown returned home from a journey to find his wife beside herself, raving that they were divorced. She remained in this condition, healthy in body but distempered and frenzied in mind. No doctor was able to help, but they all concluded she most certainly was bewitched.

Susannah's Specter Is Spotted at Witches' Gatherings

Yet another man named Joseph Ring of Salisbury said that for two years he had been abducted intermittently and taken to witchcraft meetings. There he saw Susannah Martin. Each time he was taken to one of these gatherings he felt a blow on his back that would leave him paralyzed and able only to watch the witches feast and dance. Others verified that he had definitely been absent from his house on those occasions. He had even been seen on the road, only to vanish from view. From the prior August to April, when Goody Martin had been arrested, he had been completely mute, but his ability to speak had returned when she had been carted off to jail.

Even when Goody Martin was not perceived as menacing, she often seemed uncanny, spooking livestock. Once Nathaniel Clark and Joseph Knight, while looking for stray horses in the woods, saw her carrying a dog under one arm. But when she came near and passed by them, the thing under her arm was seen to be a keg. They commented about this to her, which proved to be a mistake. Due to her wrath they spent the better part of the day chasing the horses around and around a knoll. In the meantime, Susannah paused at Clark's house, where she was bitten by his dog.

"A churl," she had muttered. "Like his master."

Goody Martin Takes Flight Two Centuries Before the Wright Brothers

Sarah Atkins testified that one time Susannah Martin

had walked all the way from Amesbury to visit her in Newbury—more than eight miles—during a very rainy season. The road was very muddy, and it hardly seem possible to Sarah anyone could make the trip on foot.

When Susannah entered the house, Goody Atkins shooed her children away from the hearth to make room for Goody Martin, but she flourished her petticoats, and said thank you very much, but she was quite dry.

Goodwife Atkins gave her a close look, and not even the soles of her shoes seemed wet. "Why this is nothing short of amazing," Goody Atkins had said, or words to that effect. "If I had taken the same trip on foot, I'd have been wet up to my knees."

To this Susannah replied that she "scorned to have a draggled tail."

Okay, let's think about this for a moment. It seems logical to me, Susannah probably held her skirts up as she walked, and perhaps even went barefoot, washed and wiped her feet, and put her shoes on just when she arrived. But that's only because I'm trying to think how this feat could have been pulled off—since helicopters hadn't been invented. Apparently, this sort of reasoning was foreign to the judges and the jury. Goody Atkins and others quickly arrived at the conclusion she'd used witchcraft.

The record does not indicate whether, upon hearing that Susannah didn't like getting mud on her skirt and up her back, and indeed had none, Goody Atkins said, "Well, then, did you park your broom outside? You know, you're welcome to bring it in. Or doesn't it like associating with ordinary brooms?"

Apparently, Susannah Martin did not take kindly to being snatched away from her farm for what must have seemed to her no reason whatsoever, being thrown in prison, being accused by a bunch of idiotic girls who had worked themselves into fits, and then being defamed by neighbors who imagined she'd done all sorts of things she herself had probably never dreamed of. I've reached this conclusion because of a note Cotton Mather made at the end of his account of her trial. He wrote, "This Woman was one of the most Impudent, Scurrilous, wicked creatures in the world; and she did now throughout her whole Trial discover herself to be such an [sic] one. Yet when she was asked what she had to say for herself? her Cheef Plea was, That she had Led a most virtuous and Holy Life!"

Chapter Thirteen: Susannah and Four Others Are Executed

Five women were tried and convicted during the last few days of June. On July 19, all of them—Susannah Martin, Rebecca Nurse, Sarah Good, Elizabeth Howe, and Sarah Wildes—were taken from the Salem Town jail and loaded into horse drawn carts for what would be their final journey on earth.

Until Bridget Bishop had been hanged on June 10, Salem Town did not have a place designated for executions. All prior capital cases had been tried in Boston, and the condemned had been executed there. But for Goodwife Bishop's demise and for those who would follow her into the afterlife, Salem officials selected what they surely felt was a good spot away from the center of town, yet visible to anyone who wished to come and gawk. No doubt there were plenty of gawkers on hand that summer day. The condemned women in chains, their hands bound, were flanked by guards and mounted officers who formed a procession down Prison Lane to the town's main street. Soon they left the village and proceeded southwest where the road angled toward Salem Village and Boston and the North River bent sharply to run between bedrock hills. A stream flowed from the high ground on the south into a salt marsh pool that met the river bend. The procession and the crowd accompanying it headed north and crossed the stream on a causeway and bridge that ran between the pool and the river. The procession then turned left off the main road onto a trail that climbed the ledge above the salt marsh pool to what would become known as Gallows Hill.

Five Women Prepare to Meet Their Maker

It was customary for those in a Puritan society who were to die to do their best to face death in a spirit of forgiveness. They were, they believed, about to come face to face with God. This would certainly have been foremost on the minds of seventeenth century Christians who were about to be executed, and from what I'm able to determine it was likely the case with four of the five women, including my seven-times-great grandmother, Susannah Martin. Sarah Good, on the other hand, would have none of it, and played the role of victim to the last. As previously written, at the gallows Reverend Nicholas Noyes urged her to repent by confessing to God what he believed the courts had proven—that she was a witch. From where he stood, this was a way—the only way—for her to save her soul. She would not, after all, be the first to accept Christ and His offer of salvation a few moments before death.

But Sarah denied she was guilty.

Noyes told her she knew perfectly well she was a witch.

"You are a liar," she snapped. "I am no more a witch than you are a wizard, and if you take away my life, God will give you blood to drink."[41]

As you know, at his death Noyes did choke on his own blood. Such is the power of suggestion and belief, as we have discussed. But Noyes' death and any satisfaction Sarah Good might have gotten from him choking on blood from a cerebral hemorrhage was many years off, and that day, rumors were circulating the devil might attempt a

---

[41] The phrase about having blood to drink is loosely based on a verse in the Book of Revelation.

last-minute rescue of his followers. But that did not happen. All five hanged as scheduled on the ledge above the tidal pool.

It isn't clear if a temporary structure or the few trees that grew from the clefts in the rock served as the gallows. But a noose would have been put around each woman's neck, her hands would have been fastened behind, and legs and petticoats tied so they wouldn't end up in an undignified way. Then each would have been blindfolded, or a hood placed over her head, and positioned halfway up a ladder. Either she would have been pushed off, or the ladder kicked away, so that her body would drop and stop with a sudden jerk of the rope. If her neck did not break at once, as it seldom did, death took some time. In these cases, the face beneath the hood would have turned dark red from dammed up blood. Blood would have oozed from eyes, nose, and mouth. Starved lungs would have struggled for air they could not breathe. The whole body would have thrashed against its bonds as it convulsed uncontrollably, clenching and unclenching—expelling waste.

Finally, after a last jerk, the body would have become still, absolutely still, empty now of life as it twisted in the breeze.

The Executions Continue

On August ninth, five more people including Reverend George Burroughs were put to death on Gallows Hill The Reverend went to his maker as a good Christian would wish to. He stood straight and faced his accusers and recited the Lord's Prayer, word for word from beginning to end, making no errors.

As you and I know, witches were not supposed to be able to say this or any Christian prayer properly. As you will see, Burroughs final act—and similar acts by others— apparently caused some New Englanders to think long and hard about what was going on. Nevertheless, on September 22 another eight people were hanged. They were the last to die. But the terror was not yet over.

During the course of the Salem witch hysteria, about 150 people were accused and arrested, and twenty-four lost their lives. Contrary to what some may think, no one was burned at the stake. English law had forbidden the practice of burning witches almost 150 years earlier. Of those who died, 19 were hanged, four died in prison, and one man, Giles Corey—husband of Martha—was pressed to death. He refused to enter a plea of either innocent or guilty, knowing that the court could not proceed without it. So the decision was made to squeeze a plea out of him. First, a thick board was laid on him, then large stones were placed on it. Rock was piled upon rock, but Corey said nothing. Finally, when the pile was high, he said what may have become the most famous two last words ever spoken:

"More weight."

His request was granted, and his chest collapsed.

Death was not the final judgment rendered upon the accused witches. Convicted witches were expelled from the Church. They could not be buried in a holy cemetery or consecrated land. They were considered as pariahs. The bodies were cut down and laid in shallow graves. It was as though they had been wiped from the face of the earth. Their deaths are not recorded in the vital records of the period.

A New Season Heralds a Change in Attitudes

As the leaves began to change in the fall of 1692, so finally did attitudes toward the girls who started it all. Their denunciations became too outrageous for the authorities to support. They began to accuse people who were not thought of as witches, including men, children, ministers, and the upper classes of the community. Resistance grew to the idea that spectral sightings were valid evidence. Rumors began to circulate that the wives of Increase Mather and Governor Phips were about to be accused of witchcraft. Martin family lore has it that the specter of Susannah Martin appeared to Phips and told him that if he allowed this madness to continue, his wife would be next. It seems more likely, however, that the opinions held and shared by two prominent men were what led the governor to change the ground rules of the trials. On October 3, Increase Mather gave a sermon in which he questioned the validity of spectral evidence. The sermon was then published as *Cases of Conscience concerning Evil Spirits personating Men.* Increase wrote, "It were better that ten suspected witches should escape than one innocent person be condemned." In doing so, Increase had broken ranks with his son, Cotton, who apparently continued to maintain that spectral evidence should be acceptable.

At about the same time, on October 8, a letter was sent by Thomas Brattle to Governor Phips, which probably had an important impact on the governor's thinking. Brattle put his thoughts into a pamphlet as well, "giving a full and candid account of the delusion called witchcraft." A Harvard graduate, he was an accomplished amateur mathematician and astronomer, a very successful and wealthy businessman, and an official of Harvard College. He was reported to have preferred the Church of England to alternatives, which may not have endeared him to Cotton Mather and other Puritans. Nevertheless, he was apparently well acquainted with Governor Phips, who must have respected his opinion and and the influence he had on other leaders of the Colony.

Thomas Brattle Argues Against the Trials

Essentially, Brattle laid out four cogent arguments against the trials as they were being conducted:

The first was that the afflicted children and those who had confessed to being witches were likely possessed by evil spirits or the devil himself and as such their testimony against others and themselves could not and should not be viewed by the court as reliable. It was as though, said Brattle, the court was accepting the devil's own testimony. The following is taken from his letter to Phips: " . . . these afflicted children . . . do hold correspondence with the devil . . . for when the black man, i.e., devil, does appear to them, they ask him many questions, and accordingly give information to the inquirer; and if this is not holding correspondence with the devil, and something worse, I know not what is." Moreover, "the confessors . . . are deluded, imposed upon, and under the influence of some evil spirit; and therefore unfit to [give] evidence either against themselves, or anyone else." And finally, "as to about thirty of the fifty-five confessors, they are possessed (I reckon) with the devil, and afflicted as the children are, and therefore not fit to be regarded" as reliable witnesses concerning "themselves or others."

The second argument was that spectral evidence should not be allowed. "The afflicted persons . . . do take their oaths, that the prisoner at the bar did afflict them . . . when the afflicted do mean and intend only [that] the appearance of and shape of such a one . . . did afflict them. This . . . may lead [the jury] into a very fundamental error, and occasion innocent blood. "

Third, many of those who'd been executed had conducted themselves as faithful Christians to their last breath, forgiving their accusers and executioners, and generally behaving in a way one would expect of a faithful Christian, but would certainly not expect of a witch. "They protested their innocence as in the presence of the great God, whom forthwith they were to appear before: they wished, and declared their wish, that their blood might be the last innocent blood shed upon that account. . . . they forgave their accusers . . . they prayed earnestly for pardon for all their other sins . . . "

And finally, number four, some accused by the afflicted who happened to be related to people in authority had not been arrested or brought to trial. Such unbalanced treatment was unseemly, to wit, " . . . some particular persons, and particularly Mrs.[42] Thatcher of Boston, [have been] much complained of by the afflicted persons, and yet . . . the justices [have] never issue[d] out . . . warrants to apprehend them . . . Mrs. Thatcher [being] the mother in law to Mr. Corwin, who is one of the justices and judges. . . . "

The Court of Oyer and Terminer is Terminated

On October 12, a few days after receiving this letter, Governor Phips forbid the jailing of any more suspected

---

[42] The title "Mrs." was reserved for upper class women.

witches. On October 29, he dissolved the Court of Oyer and Terminer. In late November, he had the cases moved to a superior court. Spectral evidence, which had damned all of the witch hunt's victims in the past, was not allowed. Even so, three were found guilty, but Phips gave each of them a reprieve. He also gave reprieves to five others who had been sentenced previously.

As a result of the trials under new rules and the reprieves, all but three of the remaining 52 prisoners were released from prison. The three remaining, including Tituba the slave, stayed there until May when Governor Phips ordered all remaining accused witches released once their fees for prison board were paid. In those days, jail time in Massachusetts didn't come with a free lunch. Someone had to pay if the person who'd been imprisoned could not. The families of two picked up this tab, but Tituba's owner, Reverend Parris, refused to do so. When public sentiment toward the accusers and the trials had begun to change, Tituba had recanted her confession, claiming her master had beat her and forced her into making a confession. This was said to have enraged Parris, who in retaliation refused to pay the jailer's fee. As a result, she was sold to someone else in order to recoup the cost of thirteen months in jail.

Reality and Remorse Settle in

Two of the Essex County ministers most concerned with the trials other than Samuel Parris—John Hale of Beverly and Nicholas Noyes of Salem—quickly realized the mistakes which had been made in allowing spectral evidence. Each of these men frankly and openly acknowledged the error and, as a result, were soon reconciled to those in their parishes who had been injured.

They each lived useful and productive lives thereafter. Parris, on the other hand, would not admit he had followed mistaken principles until 1694. Then, in an attempt to reconcile the dissenting members of his church to his ministry, he read from the pulpit his "Meditations for Peace" in which he stated that he now realized God did sometimes allow the devil to assume the shape of innocent and even pious persons. It's doubtful that by then anyone considered this a revelation. The attorneys of the village had already concluded the afflicted had been suffering from demonic procession, and not from witchcraft. Parris never actually made an apology, and managed to remain in his position only for another three years. He was finally ousted in 1697. Although he did land a couple of short stints as a preacher, he was never able to obtain a permanent position and spent much of the balance of his life working in menial jobs. He died in 1720.

Also in 1697, The Massachusetts General Assembly declared January 14 a Day of Fasting to honor and commemorate the victims of the trials. Twelve trial jurors signed a statement admitting they convicted and condemned people to death on the basis of insufficient evidence. One of the trial judges, Samuel Sewall, who together with the other Oyer and Terminer judges condemned nineteen to death, joined with these jurors in the apology. Sewall's private diary and the books he published during his lifetime convey the agony he felt over what he had been a part of. He also apparently was fearful of God's judgment on himself and his family, and this led him to proclaim his humiliation to God and the Colony in a confession of guilt which he read before the congregation of South Church in Boston. He also made a public apology on January 14. Here is what was read to those who gathered on the Day of Fasting:

> SAMUEL SEWALL, sensible of the reiterated strokes of God upon himself and family; and being sensible, that as to the Guilt contracted upon the opening of the late Commission of Oyer and Terminer at Salem (to which the order for this Day relates) he is, upon many accounts, more concerned than any that he knows of, Desires to take the Blame and shame of it, Asking pardon of men, And especially desiring prayers that God, who has an Unlimited Authority, would pardon that sin and all other his sins; personal and Relative: And according to his infinite Benignity, and Sovereignty, Not Visit the sin of him, or of any other, upon himself or any of his, nor upon the Land: But that He would powerfully defend him against all Temptations to Sin, for the future; and vouchsafe him the efficacious, saving Conduct of his Word and Spirit, January 14th, 1697.

In 1702, *A Modest Inquiry into the Nature of Witchcraft* was published by Reverend John Hale. The book includes one of the most famous and poignant apologies for the trials:

"Such was the darkness of that day, the tortures and lamentations of the afflicted and the power of former presidents, that we walked in the clouds and could not see our way."

Another public apology was given on August 25, 1706 by Ann Putnam Junior. By the time the witch hunt was over, she had accused 62 people. In the years that followed, her life had been difficult. Both her parents died, leaving her to raise nine brothers and sisters on her own. But she did something none of the other circle of girls would do—she publicly denounced her role in the trials, and proclaimed her regret. While she stood before the congregation of the Salem Village Church, the pastor read a statement she had prepared, making her the only accuser to apologize for her actions.

This is what he read:

I desire to be humbled before God for that sad and humbling providence that befell my father's family in the year about '92; that I, then being in my childhood, should, by such a providence of God, be made an instrument for the accusing of several persons of a grievous crime, whereby their lives were taken away from them, whom now I have just grounds and good reason to believe they were innocent persons; and that it was a great delusion of Satan that deceived me in that sad time, whereby I justly fear I have been instrumental, with others, though ignorantly and unwittingly, to bring upon myself and this land the guilt of innocent blood; though what was said or done by me against any person I can truly and uprightly say, before God and man, I did it not out of any anger, malice, or ill-will to any person, for I had no such thing against one of them; but what I did was ignorantly, being deluded by Satan. And particularly, as I was a chief instrument of accusing of Goodwife Nurse and her two sisters, I desire to lie in the dust, and to be humbled for it, in that I was a cause, with others, of so sad a calamity to them and their families; for which cause I desire to lie in the dust, and earnestly beg forgiveness of God, and from all those unto whom I have given just cause of sorrow and offense, whose relations were taken away or accused.

[Signed] Ann Putnam

Ann never married. She died in 1716 at age 37.

In 1711, the Commonwealth of Massachusetts reversed the verdicts of 22 of the 31 people convicted of witchcraft, exonerating them and restoring their civil rights. Susannah Martin was not one of them. The State paid 600 British pounds restitution to the survivors of the trials and their families. It would not be until 1957 that the guilty sentence of the remaining nine people, including Susannah Martin, was reversed.

Chapter Fourteen: Is Possession Really Possible?

Were the witches' accusers possessed? Is such a thing possible? Historians and academicians of the eighteenth, nineteenth, and twentieth centuries have almost universally assumed—without much if any critical analysis—that the afflicted were faking their symptoms and that their accusations were made for sport, spite, or personal gain. This would have to mean the young girls, and those who later joined them, pretended to be afflicted, and in truth were little more than sociopathic monsters who delighted in being the center of attention and in watching others suffer at their whims. Some have said they were blinded by the power they suddenly found themselves in possession of—female children and women normally being low in the pecking order—and that they must have delighted in wielding this power.

Now that you know what actually happened, what do you think?

After careful study and analysis, I find I have a difficult time accepting what has become the conventional explanation. I cannot help but consider how much pain and suffering the so called afflicted would have had to endure in order to pull it off. Even if the eyewitness descriptions of symptoms and suffering are only 80 percent accurate, it is very hard to believe all of the so-called afflicted were faking it. Maybe John Indian was, and the girl who produced the broken knife blade. There could have been others who simply went along with the group and got caught up in a role. But from what was described, some of the symptoms appear simply too dramatic to have been an act. I know of no one, for example, who can vomit blood on demand, force their jaw out of joint, or produce teeth marks or lesions in their skin.

Why, then, would highly-educated people arrive at such a conclusion? The answer is simple. As already noted, Thomas Hobbes won. Perhaps largely in reaction to senseless tragedies such as the Salem witch hysteria and the "ignorant superstitions" that produced them, eighteenth and nineteenth century thinkers and leaders of the Age of Enlightenment rejected the notion of an invisible world in exchange for an unshakable belief in a universe comprised solely of material substance. People like Thomas Jefferson and a number of founding fathers, for example, became what is know as Deists. For them, God was the great clock maker. He had created the universe, wound it up and let it go, and was now no longer involved in its operation. Spirits and ghosts and heaven and hell all were regarded as superstitions—fantasies of the mind—and potentially dangerous fantasies at that. Many still feel this way, which may be one reason the adherence to a world view that postulates a purely material universe has persisted in academic circles to the present day in spite of what quantum physics indicates as well as laboratory studies that refute Hobbes' contention that nothing exists that's not of the material world.

Minds Like Steel Traps—Rusted Shut

People who hold this view aren't likely to change it because a few statistically significant studies say other-wise. Consider this. For years, Drew Westen, a psycho-logist at Emory University, has been studying how people think, particularly in the area of politics. For my money, those who hold steadfastly to materialism in the face of data indicating a universe comprised of something more are much like members of a political party who refuse to see where their own party or candidate has veered off track. In experiments using MRI scans, Westen has demonstrated that persons with partisan preferences believe what they want to believe regardless of the facts. Not only that, they unconsciously congratulate themselves—the reward centers of their brains light up—when they reject new information that does not square with their predetermined views.

In one test, subjects were presented with contradictory statements made by George Bush and John Kerry. Republicans judged Kerry's flip-flop harshly, while letting Bush off the hook for his. Democrats did the reverse. Interestingly, the brain scans showed that the parts of the brain governing emotion were far more active during the experiment than the reasoning parts. Anyone who follows politics will not be surprised by this. The truth is, Westen's research does not relate anything new. Solzhenitsyn characterized this phenomenon as "the desire not to know," and in 1915 George Santayana acknowledged in a letter to his sister that "when I read [newspapers] I form perhaps a new opinion of the newspaper but seldom a new opinion on the subject discussed." Yet Westen's research offers value because it backs up impressions with empirical facts—brain scans.

In another experiment Westen conducted before the 2004 presidential election, participants were told a soldier at Abu Ghraib was charged with torturing prisoners and wanted to subpoena Bush administration officials. Different participants were given different amounts of evidence supporting the soldier's claim that he had been told the administration had suspended Geneva Convention rules regarding treatment of prisoners. But it didn't matter how much information they had. Westen said, "Eight-four percent of the time, we could predict whether people believed the evidence was sufficient to subpoena Donald Rumsfeld based on just three things: the extent to which they liked Republicans, the extent to which they liked human rights groups like Amnesty International, and the extent to which they liked the U.S. military."

Results such as this might help explain why some debates never seem to end. People are invested in the positions they take. So, as Westen puts it, they have a tendency to weigh not just the facts, but also, "what they would feel if they came to one conclusion or another, and they often come to the conclusion that would make them feel better, no matter what the facts are."

How would you feel if you were presented with compelling evidence that we continue to exist after we die, that the devil is real, and that disembodied spirits can possess or obsess individuals? If your immediate reaction is to dismiss all this as impossible, I urge you to suspend judgment until you've finished reading this book. Then wait a day or two mulling it over before you decide if it's really poppycock or not.

There's a reason I ask this. If you are invested in the belief nothing exists but the material world, you are likely to instantly reject any evidence to the contrary no matter how compelling it is, and many very intelligent people— perhaps you included—are highly invested in this belief, particularly scientists who have their careers at stake because they have written books, presented papers, and taught students for years based on strict adherence to a materialistic world view. For them to give an inch would be to risk having their world turned upside down. Think about it. If matter is all that is, then awareness, mind and intelligence are created by the brain and are therefore the result of evolution, which works exclusively through survival of the fittest. Awareness is a natural phenomenon created by the brain and confined within the brain—a byproduct of electrons jumping across synapses—in the same way a rainbow is caused by light passing through water droplets and is visible only to those in position to see it. When the electrons stop jumping, it ceases to be. But if it can be demonstrated—which in fact it has been many times—that mind and awareness do not always remain inside the brain, then the implications for these scientists are enormous—you might even say earth-shattering. For example, instead of life being a gigantic accident, the equivalent of millions of monkeys pounding on typewriters and one of them turning out by chance a letter-perfect copy of *War and Peace*, it may just be that intelligence came first and life and evolution are guided by mind and intelligence, rather than the products of evolution as these scientist now maintain. In other words, what has evolved may not be intelligence itself, but the means to express this intelligence through a brain and a body of flesh and blood. If this is true, primal intelligence became imprisoned in the mineral, stirred a little in the plant, unfolded in the animal, and became released in man—where it has reached its highest expression in the physical realm so far.

Scientific Minds Closed to New Information

Before we look dispassionately at the possibility of possession, let me give you another example of a knee-jerk, minds-like-steel-traps rusted-shut reaction to knew information by a group of scientists. Kristle Merzlock was in a coma after having been pulled from the bottom of a swimming pool in the spring of 1982. Her heart had not been beating for 19 minutes when she arrived at the hospital in Pocatello, Idaho. Bill Longhurst, the physician who received Kristle in the emergency room quickly summoned Melvin Morse, then 27, the only doctor at the hospital who'd performed a significant number of resuscitations. Miraculously, he was able to get her heart going and put her on an artificial lung machine.

Morse had topflight academic credentials—a medical degree with honors from The George Washington University and a research fellowship funded by the National Cancer Institute. Even so, he was not prepared for what was about to happen. Kristle's pupils were fixed and dilated and she had no gag reflex. A CAT scan revealed massive swelling of her brain, a machine was doing her breathing, and her blood pH was extremely acidotic, a clear indication of imminent death. Morse said, "There was little we could do at that point."

But somehow, against all odds, Kristle survived. Three days later she came out of her coma with full brain function. Needless to say, Morse was amazed. But something else amazed him even more and eventually forced him to completely rearrange his pyramid of cans.

Kristle recognized him.

"That's the one with the beard," she told her mother. "First there was this tall doctor who didn't have a beard, and then he came in." This was true. Morse had a beard, and the admitting doctor, Longhurst, was clean-shaven and tall.

Kristle then described the emergency room with astonishing accuracy.

Morse said, "She had the right equipment, the right

number of people—everything was just as it had been that day." She correctly related the procedures that had been performed on her. "Even though her eyes had been closed and she had been profoundly comatose during the entire experience, she still 'saw' what was going on."

Kristle was able to do this, she said, because she was outside her body—that is her mind and awareness were outside floating above it, observing was was going on. As you might expect, Morse had a hard time believing what she told him about her out-of-body experience, and his skepticism showed through. Kristle patted him shyly on the hand and said, "Don't worry, Dr. Morse, heaven is fun!"

Morse wrote up her case for the American Medical Association's pediatric Journal as a "fascinoma," meaning a strange yet interesting case. Then he returned to cancer research. One night he saw Elizabeth Kübler-Ross on television describing to a grieving mother what her child went through when she died. Kübler-Ross said that the girl floated out of her body, suffered no pain, and entered into heaven. Morse thought this was unprofessional of a psychiatrist, and vowed to prove her wrong.

He teamed up with Kimberly Clark Sharp, a clinical social worker in Seattle to begin researching near-death experiences (NDEs) in children. Their work later became known as The Seattle Study. At Seattle Children's Hospital they designed and implemented the first prospective study of NDEs, with age and sex matched controls. He studied 26 children who nearly died and compared them to 131 children who were also quite ill, in the intensive care unit, mechanically ventilated, treated with drugs such as morphine, valium and anesthetic agents, and often had a lack of oxygen to the brain, but never reached the near-death state of actually being clinically dead and then being resuscitated.

Before 1975, not much had been published on NDEs, but in that year a medical student named Raymond Moody published what became a best-selling book called *Life After Life*. Moody interviewed patients who had been resuscitated after being clinically dead and described what he found to be common occurrences in such instances: a sensation of serenity, separation from the body, entrance into a dark tunnel, a vision of light, and the appearance of deceased family members who offer help.

Morse said working with kids had its advantages. "The adult near-death experience is cluttered by cultural references and contaminated by the need for validation." he explained. "But with kids, it's pure. Kids don't repress the memory or fear the ridicule that might come from talking about it."

He found that twenty-three of the twenty-six children who nearly died had NDEs whereas none of the other children had them. If NDEs are caused by a lack of oxygen to the brain, drugs, hallucinations secondary to coma, or stress and the fear of dying, then the control would have been expected to also have had NDEs, but they did not, indicating that NDEs happen only to the dying.

Morse was determined, he said, to "produce a study that would hold up under the most stringent peer review." He poured over the medical records of each patient, documenting the drugs they took, the anesthesia used on them and the level of oxygen in their blood. His team of med students combed the literature in search of reports of drug use, psychological states or oxygen deprivation that might have produced hallucinations similar to near-death experiences.

When he published his results in the *American Journal of Diseases of Children,* Morse felt he was on solid ground in asserting near-death experiences are not the result of drugs or sleep deprivation, nor are they merely dreams or hallucinations. He was extremely careful to stay on firm scientific ground, labeling them "natural psychological processes associated with dying." While he could not explain what caused NDEs, he could prove that something consistent was going on, something that could not be explained in medical terms.

So what do you suppose happened? If you think his colleagues and the medical community toasted him, and gave him a big fat pat on the back, you are dead wrong. Morse was ridiculed and scorned by other doctors. Soon, prominent physicians questioned whether he could even deliver good patient care.

Skeptics have advanced a number of theories to explain the visions of dying patients. Some attribute them to "anesthetic agents" administered in the hospital, even though Morse found that many of these same people were dying far from a hospital setting. Others consider the visions to be hallucinations produced by narcotics, endorphins or profound oxygen deprivation—none of which, Morse insists, have been shown to correlate with the near death experiences he documented. He believes the medical community rejects his conclusions for a variety of reasons—one being his willingness to talk about death as a positive experience.

He said, "There's a feeling that people come to doctors to keep living, that if death is treated as a result that isn't necessarily negative, then we may not do all we can to avoid it."[43]

---

[43] Several sources were consulted in putting together this anecdote including an article entitled "Spirited Away" appearing in the February 2006 issue of Reader's Digest.

But I don't buy that. You and I know the real reason. These doctors minds are rusted shut. They and many others of the scientific community have much too much invested in believing awareness, mind, and intelligence are contained inside the brain—the result of the sort of rainbow effect we talked about generated by electrons hopping across synapses. To let awareness outside the brain would be to open a huge can of worms for them. But we know it already has been let out by quantum physicists. Our doctor friends need to put that new can of peas in place, rearrange their pyramids, and get themselves up to date.

Okay, Now, How About Possession. Is It Possible?

My research into possession indicates that a great many people, including many medical doctors, believe possession can happen and does happen. Officials of the Roman Catholic Church, for example, still train a number of priests each year to conduct exorcisms, and they officially designate and specify those deemed qualified for the task. Yet exorcism has been strictly controlled by the Church in modern times. According to one source, a twenty-seven page ritual exists which is followed to drive out demons. Moreover, an exorcism isn't something a parish priest can decide on his own to do. Church canon requires an exorcism be performed only upon a direct order "of the bishop, after two careful investigations, based on positive indications that possession is in fact present."

According to the memoirs of Cardinal Jacques Martin [no relation], the former prefect of the pontifical household, Pope John Paul II successfully exorcised a woman in 1982. She was brought to him writhing on the ground. Father Gabriele Amorth told *La Stampa*, an Italian newspaper, that Pope John Paul II successfully conducted three exorcisms during his pontificate. Amorth said, "He carried out these exorcisms because he wanted to give a powerful example. He wanted to give the message that we must once again start exorcising those who are possessed by demons . . . I have seen many strange things [during exorcisms] . . . objects such as nails spat out. The devil told a woman that he would make her spit out a transistor radio and lo and behold she started spitting out bits and pieces of a radio transistor. I have seen levitations, and a force that needed six or eight men to hold the person still. Such things are rare, but they happen."

Interesting, isn't it, that Cotton Mather witnessed one of the Goodwin children levitate, and that the children at Bury St. Edmunds, England, spat out pins and nails—one was a two penny nail, remember?—and that some of the afflicted in Salem coughed up pins as well.

Roman Catholic teachings indicate demons interfere in one of two ways with their victims. They can cause an obsession, in which the demon fills the mind of its victim with evil thoughts. This would seem to be what happened with some of the afflicted in Salem. The second is actual possession in which Satan or one of his minions physically takes over the human body. This may have happened on occasion in Salem such as when Ann Carr Putnam and others were so conflicted they were unable to communicate.

An absolutely fascinating book on this subject was published by Reader's Digest Press in 1976 called *Hostage to the Devil*. It was written by Malachi Martin [also no relation], a former Jesuit Professor at the Pontifical Biblical Institute in Rome, who studied at Oxford and has a doctorate in Semitic languages, archeology, and Oriental history. The book gives extensive background about and relates the full details of five actual exorcisms conducted under the sanction of the Roman Catholic Church. Do not read this book at night if you are alone. Apparently, the depiction of an exorcism related in the popular book and movie, *The Exorcist,* is accurate because that's what the exorcisms Malachi Martin described were like. It's a gross understatement to say that Satan and his buddies are a really, really nasty bunch. You thought Jeffery Dahlmer was sick? He was a Boy Scout in comparison.

Lay Practitioners of Depossession

In recent years, a number of psychiatrists, psychologists, and other mental health practitioners have gotten into the business of what they call "depossession." They'd rather call it depossession than exorcism because they don't necessarily approach it from a religious perspective. They say they rarely encounter Satan and his demons although they tend to agree Satan and his minions exist, and that obsession or possession by them can happen. According Dr. Louise Ireland-Frey, a psychiatrist, "[Satan and demons] do not belong to the human kingdom, being the negative aspect, composed of the 'fallen angels' and their slaves. This is not drawn from a religious source . . . I have been told these things by the dark entities [I have] encountered. A number of them have told us that they are delighted to get us to believe that they exist only when we think of them, speak of them, and 'believe in' them—it makes their work of invading easier! On the other hand, thinking fearfully of them, brooding compulsively, talking often of them certainly does predispose a person to attracting their focused attention."

Certainly, the people of 1692 Salem did a lot of thinking and compulsive brooding over them, and it appears they may have attracted their focused attention as a result. Nevertheless, lay practitioners indicate that in their practices obsession or possession by demons—entities that have never had a human body—is rare. More common are problems stemming from interference by the earthbound spirits of individuals who have died, but are still present among the living.

The approach used to depossess a patient who is afflicted in this way is less confrontational than that of an exorcism by a Catholic priest. In addition, the therapist routinely tries to help the invading spirit find its way into the light.

Let me pause here to say, I can almost hear some of you out there chuckling and a few of you laughing out loud, but I assure you, I am not making this up. In fact, much has been written about this. I conducted a Google search and turned up a web site that offered a dozen different books on the subject. I'm going to relate some of what Dr. Louise Ireland-Frey has to say in her book, *Freeing the Captive: The Emerging Therapy of Spirit Attachment*[44] because her credentials are strong. She's a Phi Beta Kappa graduate of Colorado University, has a master of arts degree from Mount Holyoke College in Massachusetts, and a medical degree from Tulane University.

What Happens After We Die

Dr. Louise Ireland-Frey is a psychiatrist who uses hypnotism to help those who suffer past-life trauma as was the case with Catherine which will be covered in the next chapter. She also uses it to detach earthbound spirits

---
[44] Hampton Roads Publishing, 1999

who may be causing trouble for her patients. She says that when her clients are regressed to a previous life and come to the death experience terminating that lifetime, it's possible to continue the regression past the physical death and on into the after-death state. Similarly, when she contacts earthbound entities—those who may or may not have attached themselves to a living person—she can also ask them to recall the circumstances of their physical death. By the way, Dr. Ireland-Frey uses an intermediary to make this contact. Essentially, she hypnotizes someone, either the patient she is trying to help or a willing assistant, and has the hypnotized individual "channel" the earth-bound entity.

Ireland-Frey goes on to say that under normal circumstances the psycho spiritual part of a person—the mind, the psyche, or soul finds itself floating above the body, still conscious of itself and aware of the people and activities around the dead body. This stage can be brief. The now disembodied consciousness usually feels free and light and relieved, and it senses it can go wherever it seems to be drawn. For instance, it might be drawn through the so-called tunnel and into the light we've heard about. This light is perceived as alive and sentient, a Being of Light who welcomes the personality with understanding, kindness, and love. She says that in fact most people find themselves going to a state that is peaceful and beautiful. As we have noted in the case of NDEs, only an occasional person reports a chilly, lonely or horrifying experience.

There are stages after death which we've already touched on in the discussion of NDEs—the life review, for example, in which the activities, actions, thoughts, and words of the entire life are reviewed and evaluated as to their value and impact on others. The individual sees both his or her successes, weaknesses, and failures, and in this way judges for herself the worth and value of the life just past. It seems to me the world would be a much better place if everyone accepted this model of what happens. So many now believe that when you die, that's it—nothingness—and they live their lives accordingly. Experience for the sake of experience becomes their life goal, rather than achievement, service to others, and the development of character.

But that's another book.

Another stage is one Ireland-Frey calls the "cleansing" which is often described as the feeling of being embraced or surrounded by light. But not all souls go through these stages. As was also touched on, a person who is heavy with negative emotions and undesirable habits such as rage, cruelty, greed and so forth may be too negative to be attracted to the light, and will turn away, perhaps not even perceiving it, and go to a "place"—a vibrational frequency, or "dimension"—that is appropriate to its present nature, i.e., dark and heavy. Ireland-Frey says souls are a little like substances suspended in water, the "heaviest" after death sink to the lowest astral levels, the "lightest" float to the upper levels, and the rest find the appropriate levels in-between. This, she says, is the norm.

But not all follow a normal sequence. Many die not having a clear idea of what to expect after death and find themselves bewildered upon discovering they are still aware. It is as though they are alive, but their body is dead and they cannot reenter it. Rather than going to the light or finding an appropriate vibrational level, they remain on the earth plane where they are able to see and hear living persons but are invisible and inaudible to the living, which they are likely to find very frustrating. Not knowing what to do or where to go, many such disembodied spirits start to wander, either aimlessly, or perhaps to some chosen place or person.

Some wanderers remain in the area of their body—which may now be buried. I have a friend, for example, who says he is sensitive to the presence of the disembodied and will not go near a graveyard. Others may find a home in a house or other building and become the "ghosts" who haunt these places.

The Ghost of Henri's castle

Here's a ghost story you may find interesting. The half French, half-Corsican woman I told you about who was my first wife's friend was married to a French count—Henri was his name. Henri owned a castle in Lorraine. My first wife and I once spent several days there, which was when Henri told me this story.

Henri had inherited this castle and the land and village around it along with his title—after the castle had fallen into disrepair. This was in the early 1980s, and the castle had not been lived in since before World War Two.

Having done well in business, Henri decided to restore the old place. He and his wife spend quite a bit of time there as it was undergoing renovation and were often disturbed by what seemed to be someone down in the basement banging and clanging and screaming in the middle of the night. Finally, they became so annoyed by this, Henri had the workmen tear out a wall that seemed to him might be where the nocturnal uproar was coming from.

A skeleton was behind it.

Henri and his wife had no idea who the skeleton belonged to, but they gave it a Christian burial. Afterward, they were never bothered again by the nocturnal uproar.

Here's what Henri thought about this. Apparently, a man had been bricked up behind the wall while he was still alive—someone didn't like the guy—and he had died there, but had not realized he'd died. The spirit of this dead person could easily have passed through the bricks, but the fellow didn't know this, and had been calling for help ever since. Of course, these were psychic screams, since the ghost had no vocal cords. The middle of the night was the only time the screams for help penetrated the minds of Henri and his wife because that was when all else was quiet, and they were sleeping or near sleep and sensitive to such things.

By the way, time is apparently experienced differently in the spirit dimension of mind or thought. According to Thomas Troward it doesn't exist. So even though the spirit of the dead man had been bricked up for maybe sixty years, he probably didn't experience the passing of those years the way he would have if he'd been alive.

Other Places Wanders Take Up Residence

Let's hope the ghost of Henri's castle headed for the light once it got out from behind that wall. According to Ireland-Frey many wanderers find a place that seems lighter or warmer than the chilly darkness of the earth-bound state in which they have been, and it turns out to be the body or aura of a living person—often without either the living host or the invading spirit being aware of the relationship.

What sort of person is a likely host for an invading spirit?

A person whose aura is weak or "open" is most susceptible. This may be because the individual has been in an accident, or suffered an illness, been under an anesthetic for an operation, or recently suffered an emotional shock such as grief or fear. Children, whose auras are not yet fully protective, are also vulnerable. This would seem to fit the cases in Salem, as well as that of the Goodwin children and the children of Bury St. Edmund. In addition, the Roman Catholic Church states that engaging in occult activities including fortune telling, a seance, Ouija boards and the like can open an invasion path. This recalls to mind the activities the Salem girls may have been involved in such as divining using an egg white dropped into water, and the story already related which turned up on Google.

Degrees of Spirit Attachment

Several degrees of closeness of such attachments have been identified by Ireland-Frey as well as other therapists in her line of work:

The first level is that of temptation of the living person by an aspect of the wanderer—not really an overwhelming compulsion but the thought or idea of doing or saying something that is contrary to the basic personality of the living individual—something out of character. Perhaps this is what was going on except it had progressed beyond the temptation stage, after psalm was sung in the Salem Village church on March 20, 1692, when Abigail William's said to visiting Reverend Lawson, "Now stand up and name your text." This was hardly something an eleven year old girl would normally say in a seventeenth century Puritan church. Or perhaps at the outset of Lawson's sermon when Goodwife Pope one of the afflicted adults—had said, "Now there is enough of that!"

The second level is called "influencing" or "shadowing" when the disembodied entity is affecting the host person mildly or intermittently, as with mood swings, irrational moments, sudden inexplicable fears or depressions.

Third, when the entity is affecting the host's personal feelings and habits more noticeably and frequently, the word "oppression" or "harassing" is used. Dr. Ireland-Frey says someone who is clairvoyant may be able to see the entity attached to the host's aura or within it.

Obsession is next, and here Dr. Ireland-Frey's definition differs slightly from that of the Roman Catholic Church. She says it's a remarkably common condition in which the entity may invade not only the psyche but also the physical body of the host and meld its own personality traits and former bodily feelings with those of the host, often to the confusion and bewilderment of that person. The affected person may become aware of persistent pains, sudden changes in emotions unlike his or her normal feelings, unfamiliar attitudes, or even unnatural traits and talents.

And finally, "possession" is the condition wherein the invading entity takes over the body of the host completely, pushing out the host's own personality (soul) and expressing its own words, feelings, and behaviors through the host's body. Dr. Ireland-Frey says complete possession is rare, and can be spectacular when it happens. Sometimes it may alternate with obsession. A case when a person suddenly goes berserk, for example, may be the result of sudden complete possession. She writes that she has personally seen only one case of complete possession.

It seems to me the Salem afflicted may have experienced some or all of these states at different times throughout the witch hunt of 1692.

The Problem of Evil

I have met many people in the last ten years who are convinced that evil is an illusion, and therefore that Satan and his demons cannot exist. As a result, I believe a couple of paragraphs are called for on this subject.

From what I can determine, there are three major theological models of evil. First is the one the people I've run into subscribe to—the non dualism of eastern thought. Evil is envisioned simply as the other side of a coin. For life there must be death. For growth, decay. For creation, destruction must exist. Consequently, the distinction of evil from good is regarded by non dualism as an illusion. Who can say where one begins and the other ends? This attitude has found its way into Christian and Christian-like sects such as Christian Science and followers of *A Course in Miracles*.[45] It is, however, considered heresy by Christian theologians of the major denominations.

It appears *A Course in Miracles* may contain a lot of good from what people have told me about it, but if it teaches this concept of evil as illusion—that everything is relative—I think it may be whistling past the graveyard. It must be true, as some argue, that even demons and Satan himself have a spark of good deep inside them somewhere since they, like everyone, came from the force we call God. But as for Satan in particular, the spark that's left must be very small indeed. If you don't think so, read Malachi Martin's book, *Hostage to the Devil*.[46]

A second model holds that evil is distinct from good but is nonetheless of God's creation. For God to give us free will, which was essential in order to create us in His image,

---

[45] Foundation for Inner Peace, Second Edition, 1992.
[46] Reader's Digest Press, 1976

God has to allow us the option of making wrong choices. So, at the very least, God "allows" evil to exist. This is the model put forth by Martin Buber, who referred to evil as the yeast in the dough, "the ferment placed in the soul by God without which the human dough does not rise."[47]

The third major model, that embraced by traditional Christianity, might be called "diabolic dualism." Here evil is regarded as being not of God's creation but a ghastly cancer beyond God's control. This model has its pitfalls, but it seems to me to be the only one of the three that deals adequately with the issue of murder and the murderer. God was powerless to stop the Nazis and He was powerless to stop Jeffery Dahmer and other monsters like him. God—or the creative force, or organizing intelligence, or subjective mind, or whatever label you want to put on It, She, Him—can and does through grace [a subject for another book] foster the emergence from bad situations of the best results possible for all concerned. But He, She, It cannot prevent the bad situation from happening in the first place. Anyone who thinks everything is always happening just as it should is in my opinion fooling themselves. I can name many bad things which have happened that do not have any redeeming value—from Katrina, to suicidal maniacs flying airplanes into sky-scrapers, to genocide in Africa, and on and on. For more examples, simply turn on the news.

The Reality of Satan, or Not?

Skeptical readers will surely ask, "How do you expect me to believe there is a Satan when you haven't offered proof?" The truth is I don't expect you to believe. I'm not even sure I believe, but I do hope you will become more

---

[47] *Good and Evil*, Charles Scribner's Sons, New York, 1953

open-minded about the possibility. In fact, I hope you'll arrive where I am, which is, "Well, yeah, maybe so. Maybe there is a Satan, and if there is, then it would seem logical he was behind the Salem fiasco." If you've never experienced Satan firsthand—and I must admit I have not and hope I never do—then it's very difficult for you or me having been raised in the twentieth and twenty-first centuries surrounded on all sides by skeptics—to come to a firm belief that Satan is real. It's like belief in God. Conversion generally requires some kind of actual encounter—a personal experience. Conversion to a belief in Satan is no different. But I can say I know people whose opinion I respect who believe in Satan, and they do so because they've come face to face with him while witnessing an exorcism. One such is the late M. Scott Peck, M.D., author of the runaway best seller, *The Road Less Traveled*.[48]

Scott Peck writes that there is no way he can translate his experience into your experience or my experience. In his book, *People of the Lie*,[49] he said he witnessed and participated in two exorcisms. Toward the end of one, in response to a comment that the spirit must really hate Jesus, the patient, with a full-blown Satanic facial expression, said in a silky, oily voice, "We don't hate Jesus; we just test him." In the middle of the other exorcism, when asked whether the possession was by multiple spirits, the patient with hooded, serpentine eyes answered quietly, almost in a hiss, "They all belong to me." Peck said that the experience of two exorcisms is hardly sufficient for him to have unraveled all the mystery of the spiritual realm. Nor, he says, would the experience of a hundred be sufficient. But he did believe he learned a few things about Satan. He

---

[48] Simon and Schuster, 1978
[49] Simon and Schuster, 1983

says his experience is not sufficient to prove the Judeo-Christian myth and doctrine about Satan, but he didn't learn anything that doesn't support it. In this regard, his experience is the same as Dr. Louise Ireland-Frey and other therapists like her who have supposedly communicated directly with demons, and the man in black himself.

According to this myth and doctrine, in the beginning Satan was God's second-in-command, chief among all His angels, the beautiful and the beloved Lucifer. The service this angel performed on God's behalf was to enhance the spiritual growth of human beings through the use of testing and temptation just as we test our children in school so as to enhance their growth. Satan was primarily a teacher of mankind, which is why he was called Lucifer, which means, "the light bearer." As time went by, however, Satan became so enamored with its adversarial functions that he began to employ them more for his own delight than on God's behalf. This can be seen in the story of Job recounted earlier. Coincidentally, God decided that something more was required than simple testing for the uplifting of mankind. What was required was both an example of Himself and an example to live by. So He sent, Jesus, His only son to live and die as one of us. Satan was superseded by Christ both in function and in God's heart. This did not make Satan happy. Satan was so enamored of himself that he saw it as a personal insult. Puffed up with pride, Satan refused to submit to God's judgment, and rebelled against Him. Satan himself created the situation in which heaven became literally not big enough for the both of them. So Satan was inevitably, by his own doing, cast out into hell, where—once the light bearer—Satan now dwells in darkness as the Father of Lies, nursing continual dreams of revenge against God. And through the angles at his command—who joined Satan in his rebellion and fall—he now wages continual war against God's design.

What Really Happened in Salem?

A major battlefield of this conflict appears to have been Salem in 1692. What better place to stage a fight than in God's very own "city on a hill"?

In Chapter Eleven, I indicated that the strong beliefs held by people in Salem may have been enough to bring about the witchcraft hysteria and to produce convincing symptoms among the afflicted. It's true, I believe, that belief alone may account for much of what happened. It may even have been responsible for the entire debacle. But having reviewed the current literature on Satan, I have to conclude he may actually exist. If he does, he most certainly was behind what happened. For all his faults, Reverend Parris may actually have been right. Maybe the girls playing with the occult did open the door. As he is quoted as having said, "the devil [was] raised among us, and his rage [was] vehement and terrible . . . "

Think about it. If Satan considers himself at war with God and Godliness, then he most certainly would have pounced on Salem as a ideal place to take a stand. Here were people who'd set out to create a shinning example of a Godly community. And what did he cause them to do? Murder twenty-four of their own. But that was just the beginning. Think of the rest of the fallout from what happened. Thomas Hobbes won. The Puritans were left with " . . . no Christ but a light within, and no heaven but a frame of mind."

Even so, the creative force that underlies all reality—

God if you prefer that term—brought the best possible result for all concerned from what was a truly unfortunate situation. Most educated people soon came to reject the idea of an invisible world and the superstitions concerned with it. Science took the high ground for these folks, and as a result, the evolution of humankind in knowledge and technical achievement accelerated like a rocket. It was good for this to have happened. Who, today, would want to live with the ignorance and superstitions of the seventeenth century? A better life is now possible for billions around the world.

But if humankind is to continue to progress, it's time for everyone—including the scientific minded—to realize that a large percentage of us may have thrown the baby out with the bath water. Sure, superstition and mistaken beliefs can kill. They did so in 1692. But the denial of the existence of a spiritual side of reality also kills because it leads to nihilism—the belief that existence is senseless and useless. It kills the individual human spirit. It kills hope and joy, and it could very well stop the evolution of humankind dead in its tracks.

Imagine how much better the world would be for everyone if each one of us realized that someday, after death, he or she would stand in judgment of his or her own life—that each would feel what others felt as a result of the actions, words and deeds chosen in the life just past. Imagine if everyone realized that life is not a one-time affair, but a continuum, and that what a person learns and what is accomplished in this life can have a positive effect in the next.

Imagine if in this world so chock full of terrorism, suicide bombers, and hate that everyone in the world realized Satan and his minions may in fact be real, and fully dedicated to death, and to their struggle to achieve victory over life, freedom and goodness. It might cause a few people to open their eyes and realize it's not a sure thing our civilization, or the planet, will survive. We've come some way in our evolution toward reunification with the light, but we still have far to go before we reach a state when we no longer need this school called Planet Earth. It would be really stupid of us to fall alseep on the job, so to speak, and let the bad guy win.

Chapter Fifteen: What I Really Think About Susannah

Here's what I think. As with most of those hanged, the inscription on Susannah's monument in Amesbury which was quoted in the first chapter is correct. She was, "An honest, hardworking, Christian woman. Accused as a witch, tried and executed at Salem, July 19, 1692. A martyr of superstition."

Perhaps the afflicted accusers were deluded by demons or Satan himself. Or maybe they simply had worked themselves into a frenzy and saw hallucinations and apparitions everywhere because they and their neighbors so firmly believed in their bewitchment and what would happen as a result. Whatever led them to make to their accusations—whether it was hysteria or the devil—Susannah was singled out because she was a smart and capable woman who perhaps should have, in her own best interest, held her tongue more often. She might also have made more of an effort to put others—especially those who were not as intelligent as she—at ease in her presence, which must have been formidable since so many people seem to have been afraid of her. Of course, none of this is grounds for what she was forced to go through. Susannah's life as it turned out was that of a Puritan put to the ultimate test of faith. This was true of all who were hanged. Each refused to lie. They remained steadfast to the end—steadfast to their faith and to their beliefs.

Susannah was apparently familiar with the Bible. She demonstrated this in relating the passage about King Saul, Samuel, and the Witch of Endor. Surely, she and the other accused also were familiar with the story of Job. If so, they must have felt they were being put to a similar test. Perhaps during their incarceration they talked about it among themselves. I hope they did and that it gave them each a measure of consolation—because they passed the test with flying colors, and if there is a heaven, they most certainly were rewarded there.

It must have been the ultimate low point "in the valley of the shadow of death"[50] to have been chained and loaded on a cart and taken to the gallows. Imagine looking up at the rope with a noose on the end and then having a cloth bag pulled over your head. The rope would have been placed around your neck and made tight. Two or three people would have helped you climb the ladder—or lifted you up if your knees were too weak.

I like to think when Susannah fell from that ladder her neck broke instantly, and that she suddenly found her awareness outside of the bag—outside of *her*—looking down at her body dangling at the end of the robe, and at all the people gawking up. Then she would have turned to see a dark tunnel with a bright light at the end. She'd have moved swiftly in the direction of the light. It would have grown larger and nearer until she entered it, and there she would have been bathed in its cleansing peace. This is how doctors Morse, Moody, Kübler-Ross, and others have described it. Family members who had gone before—her mother and father, her husband George—would have welcomed her, and she'd have been home at last after a long and difficult journey through and to the physical plane of reality.

Is that really possible? Or is it only wishful thinking?

After all, doctors as a whole were quick to reject Melvin Morse's research findings on the near death

---

[50] Psalm 23

experiences of children.

There is good reason to believe those nay sayers were wrong. After all, the same bunch also firmly believes thought remains always within the brain—clinging as they do to the old world view. To give you ammunition against them, let me sketch a scientifically plausible explanation for the continuity of life after physical death.

All Is One

Quantum physicists tell us the entire universe is one huge interconnected field that changes when a researcher knows which of two slits a photon goes through. Thomas Troward says thought and life are the same thing and that it is the fabric of the universe. Together these theories indicate there's actually only one mind, and the space this mind occupies is not the cranium of an individual but everywhere. All that is is part of a single whole.

The unity of all explains how I'm able to wake up the second before the alarm goes off. My mind, brain, the clock, everything all of it is seamless. At a deep level, I know what time the clock says, even though I am sound asleep. Accepting this as true will force any old world view person to rearrange a bunch of those cans of peas we've been talking about. If we do enough rearranging and hard thinking, we might even come to understand what a ghost might be. One biochemist, a graduate of the University of Cambridge in England, may be on the right track. His name is Rupert Sheldrake, and his book, *The Rebirth of Nature, The Greening of Science and God,*[51] is fascinating and fully in accord with the notion the universe is an interconnected field.

In the final chapter of Sheldrake's book he notes,

---

[51] Park Street Press; Reprint edition, April 1, 1994

anecdotally, that many children have a mystical sense of connection with the natural world that many lose as they mature.

He quotes a woman, an art teacher, who recounted an experience she had while walking on the Pangbourne Moors at the age of five. She puts into words what many of us may have felt at one time or another but perhaps later dismissed when our "rational" minds again got the upper hand:

> Suddenly I seemed to see the mist as a shimmering gossamer tissue and the harebells, appearing here and there, seemed to shine with a brilliant fire. Somehow I understood that this was the living tissue of life itself, in which all that we call consciousness is embedded, appearing here and there as a shining focus of energy in the more diffused whole. In that moment I knew that I had my special place, as had all other things, animate and so-called inanimate, and that we were all part of this universal tissue which was both fragile yet immensely strong, and utterly good and beneficent.

Sounds like an "all-encompassing organic pattern," which is no doubt why Rupert Sheldrake chose this quotation. You may wish to read his theories in the original, and I encourage you to do so, but it will be worthwhile to summarize some of what he has to say because it may provide a rational explanation concerning ghosts and the existence of an afterlife.

A New Theory of Life

What does this have to do with ghosts and the possibility of an afterlife? While physiologists do their best to explain the functioning of plants and animals in mechanistic terms, explanations of some phenomena are sketchy at best according to Sheldrake. He believes the following can be explained by the existence of what he calls morphic fields: Formation of the structure of organisms, instinctive behavior, learning, and memory.

Sheldrake has set forth the hypothesis that the growth, development and the programmed behavior of organisms are governed by fields which exist much like fields of gravity or electromagnetism and that these fields change and evolve as a species changes and evolves. He calls them "morphic fields," the word "morphic" indicating shape or form. Indeed, these fields contain the collective memory of the entire species.

He writes:

The fields of a given species, such as the giraffe, have evolved; they are inherited by present giraffes from previous giraffes. They contain a kind of collective memory on which each member of the species draws and to which it in turn contributes. The formative activity of the fields is not determined by timeless mathematical laws— although the fields can to some extent be modeled mathematically—but by the actual forms taken up by previous members of the species. The more often a pattern of development is repeated, the more probable it is that it will be followed again. The fields are the means by which the habits of the species are built up, maintained, and inherited.

As indicated above, one of the main elements of the morphic field of a species is that it contains the entire memory of all the members that have gone before. This he maintains can be seen in the development of a human embryo, for example, as it evolves from a fishlike creature through the various stages until it reaches human form. This is how physical characteristics such as the long necks of giraffes are propagated. It is how instincts develop and are passed along. If Sheldrake is right, his theory could form the basis of a scientific explanation for continuation of the existence of an individual after death. If the memories of a species continue, our individual memories must live on in some way after we die as well, whether intact in individual fields, or at minimum as part of the greater field of mankind.

Sheldrake calls his hypothesis formative causation, and it was first proposed in 1981 in his book *A New Science of Life,* and developed further in *The Presence of the Past* (1988). It suggests that self-organizing systems exist at all levels of complexity, including molecules, crystals, cells, tissues, organisms, and societies of organisms such as ants and bees.

Genes Provide the Building Blocks Not the Blueprint

Consideration of the existence of morphic fields provides a compelling explanation of how morphogenesis works. The genes supply the right building blocks of protein and the field provides the blueprint. Sheldrake points out that without a governing [morphogenetic] field scientists are hard pressed to explain something as simple as the shapes of your arms and legs and feet. They say the information is encoded in the genes but are unable to explain where or how. Think about it. Your limbs are made of muscle cells and nerve cells and bone cells and so on. They use the same building materials but have different shapes, just as differently shaped buildings can be constructed with the same type of bricks but with different blueprints.

These fields may also explain a phenomenon of memory which currently has neuroscientists puzzled—where it is located in the brain. One way research on this subject has been conducted is to train an animal to do something and then to cut out parts of its brain in an effort to find where the the memory was stored. Sheldrake writes, "But even after large chunks of their brains have been removed—in some experiments over 60 percent—the hapless animals can often remember what they were trained to do before the operation."

Where Memories Reside

Several theories have been put forth to explain this including backup systems and holograms, but the obvious one according to Sheldrake's hypothesis is that the memory may not be in the brain at all. Scientists have been looking in the wrong place. To quote Sheldrake again, "A search inside your TV set for traces of the programs you watched last week would be doomed to failure for the same reason: The set tunes in to TV transmissions but does not store them." In other words, the brain is a physical link to the memory located in our individual morphic field.

In addition, it appears the brain may not be the only physical link to the memories in a morphic field. Our entire physical body may be linked to our field because it is a projection of that field. That this is so can be seen in the experience of heart transplant recipients, for example, who often report having memories that don't belong to them. One little lady said she started having constant cravings for chicken nuggets and beer after receiving her transplant. The problem was, she'd never before eaten chicken nuggets, and she wasn't a beer drinker. Before, she didn't care for any kind of alcohol. After a recurring dream in which a young man came to her saying he loved her and had given her his heart, she decided to find who her new heart had come from. After a good deal of detective work, she learned it had belonged to a young man, the victim of a motorcycle crash, who'd been found with a box of MacDonald's chicken nuggets and a six pack of beer stuffed inside his motorcycle jacket.[52]

Here's another good one. On January 17, 2006, I took a break from my computer keyboard and writing this book in order to eat lunch. While doing so I watched a series of online video clips at a news web site. One of these reported on a Croatian lumberjack who had received a lifesaving kidney transplant and now is suing the hospital that gave it to him. Apparently, the kidney donor was a 51 year-old-woman. The man's favorite pastime once had been spending time in the local pub carousing with his buddies. Now, because of his new kidney, he believes he has developed a passion for housework and knitting. He thinks this constitutes grounds for suing the hospital because it has made him the laughing stock of his village.

Your Morphogenetic Field and My Morphogenetic Field

Here is a theory I'd like to propose. A person's indivi-

---

[52] Thanks for this anecdote go to Gary E. R. Schwartz and Linda G. S. Russek. *The Living Energy Universe,* Hampton Roads, 1999.

dual morphic field survives death. Philippe's field was what I sensed that night in Marseilles. Susannah Martin's field left her body when her neck snapped, looked down for a few seconds, and then headed to the light. Your field and my field have existed as part of the whole and have been evolving since the first life on earth. Your field and mine are part of the humankind field and of all life, but each are also separate fields. Perhaps they became differentiated at the point in evolution when we became aware of ourselves. Your individual field has continued evolving. It has come into physical reality many times in a long succession of bodies, and in many different incarnations. For my friend in Marseilles, the most recent happened to have been as the incarnation I came to know as Philippe Sirot. Eventually, he will be born again with a new physical body. All Philippe's memories will come with him, whether or not he consciously recalls them, and he will most likely be troubled in the new go-round with a number of issues to resolve, given his suicide and the dangling love affair with Joel he left behind.

I realize this may be hard for some readers to believe. Because most of us do not have memories of past lives, it seems logical to assume that this is our first and only visit to planet Earth. But stop and think. Most of us do not remember much, if anything, of what happened to us before the age of four, yet those years surely existed, and what happened then can have an important effect on us in terms of how we relate to the world. Psychologists and psychiatrists will attest to this.

The same is true of past-life experiences. They can be important in determining who we are, what likes and dislikes we may be born with, our temperament, our talents, our phobias. They may determine our sexual preferences. We arrive on the scene in each incarnation with our full past life memory intact albeit unconscious. It is part of the mechanics of how we evolution.

An Update on Reincarnation

Much has come to light about reincarnation in the past twenty or thirty years. So much that today an open-minded individual would have difficulty refuting it if he would only take some time to dispassionately review the evidence. For example, Ian Stevenson, Carlson Professor of Psychiatry and Director of the Division of Personality Studies at the Health Sciences Center of the University of Virginia, has collected over 2,600 reported cases of past-life memories of which 65 detailed reports have been published. Specific information was matched with the former identity, including family, residence, and manner of death. Check out the bibliography in the back of this book. Read one or two of Stevenson's books. You may come to realize life is a continuum rather than a one night stand, and this will have an effect on how you go about your daily life and relate to the world. Had Philippe known this, for example, I doubt he would have taken his own life because he would have been aware he'd have to face a similar situation again, and again, until he got it right—not unlike the movie *Groundhog Day*. This may be how we evolve. It may be part of the mechanism of evolution in general, working hand in hand with survival of the fittest.

Psychiatrists and Reincarnation

In researching reincarnation, I've found that libraries are well stocked on the subject. Since becoming interested, I have met and come to know two different people who make their livings by helping others remember past lives and then to release buried memories that are holding their patients back. In some cases, thousands of years have passed since a debilitating incident took place. I've visited the School of Metaphysics in Missouri and watched trained readers of the Akashic records report on past lives of workshop attendees. Additionally, I've read four books written by different past life therapists and edited a fifth. Rather than relate what is contained in those, however, I will give you a quick summary of a case reported in the 1988 book, *Many Lives, Many Masters.*[53] I've chosen this because the author, Brian L. Weiss, M.D., cannot be accused by anyone of being a Looney Tune. He is a Phi Beta Kappa, magna cum laude graduate of Columbia University who received his medical degree from Yale, interned at New York's Bellevue Medical Center, and went on to become chief resident of the department of psychiatry at the Yale University School of Medicine. At the time of the case covered in his book, he was head of the department of psychiatry at Mount Sinai Medical Center in Miami Beach.

Weiss is a medical doctor and a scientist who has published widely in professional journals. Ethnically Jewish, he was a skeptic who had no interest in reincarnation. He knew most in his field do not believe in such things and waited six years before giving in to the feeling that he had an obligation to share what he had learned. He had much more to lose than to gain by telling the story of the woman called Catherine (not her real name) who came to him in 1980 seeking help for her anxiety, panic attacks and phobias. Read his book. I'll hit only a few highlights.

---

[53] Fireside, 1988

The Case of Catherine

For eighteen months, Weiss used conventional therapy, which means he and Catherine talked about and analyzed her life and her relationships. When nothing worked, he tried hypnosis in an effort to find out what she might be repressing that would account for her neuroses. Forgotten events in her childhood, in fact, were revealed that seemed to be at the root of several of her problems. As is customary in this type of therapy, she was instructed to remember them after she had been brought out of the hypnotic state. Dr. Weiss discussed what had been uncovered in an effort to dispel her anxieties. But as days went by, her symptoms remained as severe as ever.

He tried hypnotism again. This time he regressed her back to the age of two, but she recalled nothing that shed new light on her problems. He gave her firm instructions, "Go back to the time from which your symptoms arise." Nothing had prepared him for what happened next. She slipped into a past life that took place almost 4,000 years ago. Weiss was astounded as she described herself in detail, her surroundings and others in that life, including specific episodes, and in later sessions entire lifetimes, that seemed to be at the root of her problems.

Weiss continued using hypnosis in an effort to rid Catherine of her neuroses. In weekly sessions that spanned several months, she recalled and recounted in detail the highlights of twelve previous lifetimes, including the moment of death in each. People who played a role in one lifetime often reappeared as someone else in another, including Dr. Weiss himself, who had been her teacher some 3500 years ago.

Catherine had not had a happy existence over the last forty centuries. The overwhelming number of memories from her past lives were unhappy and proved to be the roots of her present day symptoms. Bringing them into her consciousness and talking about them enabled her to recover. Considering the number and intensity of her neuroses, psychotherapy would normally have lasted years before she was cured according to Dr. Weiss. In fact, her symptoms disappeared within months. She became happier and more at peace than she had ever been.

Weiss is an experienced psychotherapist who has dealt with thousands of patients. He is convinced that Catherine was not faking. She was unsophisticated and of average intelligence, a young woman who made her living as a laboratory technician. He thinks it quite impossible she could have pulled off such an elaborate hoax and kept it up every week for months. Think about it. She was a physically attractive twenty-eight year old woman of average intelligence. She had a high school diploma and some vocational training. Could she have faked her neuroses? Could she have faked gradual improvement from one visit to the next, all the way to a state of being completely free of them? Dr. Weiss does not think so. Also, and this is where the plot thickens, she conveyed information about Weiss's father and an infant son, both of whom had died. Weiss is convinced she could not have known anything about them through normal channels.

Life Between Lives

This message from the other side leads to what some may find the most amazing aspect of her story—the spaces between past lives. Once, after having been murdered, she floated out of her body and was reborn very quickly. At the end of her next life, she described an experience remarkably similar to that related by thousands who have been clinically dead and have come back to life. She rose out of her body, felt at peace, and was aware of an energy-giving light. It was at this time in this session that spirit entities spoke through her to Dr. Weiss for the first time. In a loud, husky voice and without hesitation Catherine said, "Our task is to learn, to become Godlike through knowledge. We know so little. You are here to be my teacher. I have so much to learn. By knowledge we approach God, and then we can rest. Then we come back and help others."

Catherine was able to recall her past lives after she was brought out of a hypnotic state, but not the conversations Dr. Weiss had through her with several different spirit entities. These "masters," as he came to call them, spoke through her primarily for his benefit and only indirectly for hers. I will not go into detail as you may wish to read his book. Essentially, they told him we incarnate into the physical world to learn what cannot be learned on the nonphysical planes. There, whatever is felt or imagined instantly appears real or greatly magnified. The slightest ill will becomes rage. The smallest feeling of affection turns to all encompassing love. Imagine a demon, and a thought form of it will suddenly materialize. Picture a lovely sunset viewed from a secluded beach, and you will find you are there. Because of this we need the thickness of matter. You see, matter slows things down so we can work things out. Earth is a school, and the most important lessons we come here to learn have to do with charity, hope, faith and love, as well as to learn to trust and not to have fear.

We Arrive Now at the End of Our Journey

In light of the theories of quantum mechanics, scientifically-demonstrated psychic phenomena, Ian Stevenson's research on reincarnation, Thomas Troward's theory of life and thought, and Sheldrake's of morphogenetic fields, perhaps there is a scientific basis for believing in life after death and in continuation and growth of the soul over many lifetimes. If this is the case, my wish came true for Susannah and the others.

And you know what? Perhaps Susannah has returned to earth once or twice since that life in seventeenth century New England. It seems possible to me now. I wonder what her mission was and what lessons she wanted to learn.

Perhaps she wanted to learn humility and when to hold her tongue. Perhaps her mission was to bring a boy up to be a man who believed women could do anything men could do, to instill in that boy an inherent skepticism that would keep him from blindly accepting what people in authority say, and rather, to submit to an internal compass what is said by Church leaders, people in positions of authority in government or science, and in practically any discipline for that matter.

Perhaps it was to establish as a role model for him a woman who had been falsely convicted of witchcraft and to sow seeds that would lead him to write a book that would result in opening minds to a new world view.

Perhaps Susannah came back as my mom, Evelyn Stadelman Martin.

Who knows? Stranger things have happened.

APPENDIX

COTTON MATHER, MEMORABLE PROVIDENCES, RELATING TO WITCHCRAFTS AND POSSESSIONS (1689)

Mather published in 1689 a bestselling book detailing an episode of supposed witchcraft a year earlier involving an Irish washerwoman named Goody Glover. Mather's account, describing the symptoms of witchcraft, was widely read and discussed throughout Puritan New England. The book was in the meager library of Samuel Parris, the Salem minister in whose house began the tragic events of 1692.

Memorable Providences, Relating to Witchcrafts and Possessions. A Faithful Account of many Wonderful and Surprising Things, that have befallen several Bewitched and Possessed Persons in New-England. Particularly, A Narrative of the marvellous Trouble and Releef Experienced by a pious Family in Boston, very lately and sadly molested with Evil Spirits.

Whereunto is added, a Discourse delivered unto a Congregation in Boston, on the Occasion of that Illustrious Providence. As also a Discourse delivered unto the same Congregation; on the occasion of an horrible Self-Murder Committed in the Town. With an Appendix, in vindication of a Chapter in a late Book of Remarkable Providence, from the Columnies of a Quaker at Pen-silvania.

Written by Cotton Mather, Minister of the Gospel, and Recommended by the Ministers of Boston, and Charleston. Printed at Boston in N. England by ;R.P. 1689. Sold by Joseph Brunning, at his Shop at the Corner of the Prison-Lane next the Exchange.

To the Honorable Wait Winthrop Esq;

Sr.
By the special Disposal and Providence of the Almighty God, there now comes abroad into the world a little History of several very astonishing Witchcrafts and Possessions, which partly my own Ocular Observation, and partly my undoubted Information, hath enabled me to offer unto the publick Notice of my Neighbours. It must be the Subject, and not the Manner or the Author of this Writing, that has made any people desire its Publication; For there are such obvious Defects in Both, as would render me very unreasonable, if I should wish about This or Any Composure of mine, O That it were printed in a book! But tho there want not Faults in this Discourse, to give me Discontent enough, my Displeasure at them will be recompensed by the Satisfaction I take in my Dedication of it; which I now no less properly than cheerfully make unto Your Self; whom I reckon among the Best of my Friends, and the Ablest of my readers. Your Knowledge has Qualified You to make those Reflections on the following Relations, which few can Think, and tis not fit that all should See. How far the Platonic Notions of Demons which were, it may be, much more espoused by those primitive Christians and Scholars that we call

The Fathers, than they see countenanced in the ensuing Narratives, are to be allowed by a serious man, your Scriptural Divinity, join'd with Your most Rational Philosphy, will help You to Judge at an uncommon rate. Had I on the Occasion before me handled the Doctrin of Demons, or launced forth into Speculations about magical Mysteries, I might have made some Ostentation, that I have read something and thought a little in my time; but it would neither have been Convenient for me, nor Profitable for those plain Folkes, whose Edification I have all along aimed at. I have therefore here but briefly touch't every thing with an American Pen; a Pen which your Desert likewise has further Entitled You to the utmost Expressions of Respectand Honor from. Though I have no Commission, yet I am sure I shall meet with no Crimination, if I here publickly wish You all manner of Happiness, in the Name of the great Multitudes whom you have laid under everlasting Obligations. Wherefore in the name of the many hundred Sick people, whom your charitable and skilful Hands have most freely dispens'd your no less generous than secret Medicines to; and in the name of Your whole Countrey, which hath long had cause to believe that you will succeed Your Honourable Father and Grandfather in successful Endeavours for our Welfare; I say, In their Name, I now do wish you all the Prosperity of them that love Jerusalem. And whereas it hath been sometimes observed, That the Genius of an Author is commonly Discovered in the Dedicatory Epistle, I shall be content if this Dedicatory Epistle of mine, have now discovered me to be,

(Sir) Your sincere and very humble Servant,

Mather.

The Introduction

It was once the Mistake of one gone to the Congregation of the Dead, concerning the Survivers, if one went unto them from the dead, they will repent. The blessed God hath made some to come from the Damned, for the Conviction (may it also be for the Conversion) of us that are yet alive. The Devils themselves are by Compulsion come to confute the Atheism and Sadducism, and to reporve the Madness of ungodly men. Those condemned prisoners of our Atmosphere have not really sent Letthers of Thanks from Hell, to those that are on Earth, promoting of their Interest, yet they have been forced, as of old, To confess that Jesus was the Holy one of God, so of late, to declare that Sin and Vice are the things which they are delighted in. But should one of those hideous Wights appear visibly with fiery chains upon him, and utter audibly his roarings and his warnings in one of our Congregations, it would not produce new Hearts in those whom the Scriptures hadled in our Ministry do not effect. However, it becomes the Embassadors of the L. Jesus to leave no stroke untouch't that may conduce to bring men from the power of Satan unto God; and for this cause it, that I have permitted the ensuing Histories to be published. They contain Things of undoubted Certainty, and they suggest Things of Importance unconceivably. Indeed they are only one Head of Collections which in my little time of Observation I have made of Memorable Providences, with Reflections thereupon, to be reserved among other effects of my Diversion from my more state and more weary Studies. But I can with a Contentment beyond meer Patience give those rescinded Sheets unto the Stationer, when I see what pains Mr. Baxtrer, Mr. Glanvil, Dr. More, and several other Great Names have taken to publish Histories of Witchcrafts and Possdessions unto the world. I said, Let me also run after them; and this with the more Alacrity because, I have tidings ready. Go then, my little Book, as a Lackey, to the more elaborate Essays of those learned men. Go tell Mankind, that there are Devils and Witches; and that tho those night-birds least appear where the Day-light of the Gospel comes, yet New-Engl. has had Exemples of their Existence and Operation; and that no only the Wigwams of Indians, where the pagan Powaws often raise their masters, in the shapes of Bears and Snakes and Fires, but the House of Christians, wh ere our God has had his constant Worship, have undergone the Annoyance of Evil spirits. Go tell the world, What Prays can do beyond all Devils and Witches, and What it is that these Monsters love to do; and through the Demons in the Audience of several standers-by threatned much disgrace to thy Author, if he let thee come abroad, yet venture That, and in this way seek a just Revenge on Them for the Disturbance they have given to such as have called on the Name of God.

Witchcrafts and Possessions.

The First Exemple.

Section I. There dwells at this time, in the south part of Boston, a sober and pious man, whose Name is John Goodwin, whose Trade is that of a Mason, and whose Wife (to which a Good Report gives a share with him in all the Characters of Vertue) has made him the Father of six (now living) Children. Of these Children, all but the Eldest, who works with his Father at his Calling, and the Youngest, who lives yet upon the Breast of its mother, have laboured under the direful effects of a (no less palpable than) stupendous Witchcraft. Indeed that exempted Son had also, as was thought, some lighter touches of it, in unaccountable stabbs and pains now and then upon him; as indeed every person in the Family at some time or other had, except the godly Father, and the suckiii,, Infant, who never felt any impressions of it. But these Four Children mentioned, were handled in so sad and stran(re a manner, as has given matter of Discourse and Wonder to all the Countrey, and of History not unworthy to be considered by more than all the serious or the curious Readers in this New-English World.

Sect. II. The four Children (whereof the Eldest was about Thirteen, and the youngest was perhaps about a third part so many years of age') had enjoyed a Religious Education, and answered it with a very towardly Ingenuity.' They had an observable Affection unto Divine and

Sacred things; and those of them that were capable of it, seem'd to have such a Resentment, of their eternal Concernments as is not altogether usual. Their Parents also kept them to a continual Employnient, which did more than deliver them from the Temptations of Idleness, and as young as they were, they took a delight in it) it may be as much as they should have done. In a word, Such was the whole Temper and Carriage of the Children, that there cannot easily be any thing more unreasonable, than to imagine that a Design to Dissemble could cause them to fall into any of their odd Fits; though there should not have happened, as there did, a thousand Things, wherein it was perfectly impossible for any Dissimulation of theirs to produce what scores of spectators were amazed at.

Sect. III. About Midsummer, in the year 1688, the Eldest of these Children, who is a Daughter, saw cause to examine their Washerwoman, upon their missing of some Linnen ' which twas fear'd she had stollen from them; and of what use this linnen might bee to serve the Witchcraft intended, the Theef's Tempter knows! This Laundress was the Daughter of an ignorant and a scandalous old Woman in the Neighbourhood; whose miserable Husband before he died, had sometimes complained of her, that she was undoubtedly a Witch, and that whenever his Head was laid, she would quickly arrive unto the punishments due to such an one. This Woman in her daughters Defence bestow'd very bad Language upon the Girl that put her to the Question; immediately upon which, the poor child became variously indisposed in her health, an visited with strange Fits, beyond those that attend an Epilepsy or a Catalepsy, or those thatthey call The Diseases of Astonishment.

Sect. IV. It was not long before one of her Sisters, an two of her Brothers, were seized, in.Order one after another with Affects' like those that molested her. Within a fe weeks, they were all four tortured every where in a manner s very grievous, that it would have broke an heart of stone t have seen their Agonies. Skilful Physicians were consulted for their Help, and particularly our worthy and prudent Friend Dr. Thomas Oakes,' who found Iiimself so affrontcd by the Dist'empers of the children, that he concluded nothing but an hellish Witchcraft could be the Original of these Maladies. And that which yet more confirmed such Apprehension was, That for one good while, the children were tormented just in the same part of their bodies all at the same time together; and tho they saw and heard not one anothers complaints, tho likewise their pains and sprains were swift like Lightening, yet when (suppose) the Neck, or the Hand, or the Back of one was Rack't, so it was at that instant with t'other too.

Sect. V. The variety of their tortures increased continually; and tho about Nine or Ten at Night they alwaies had a Release from their miseries, and ate and slept all night for the most part indifferently well, yet in the day time they were handled with so many sorts of Ails, that it would require of us almost as much time to Relate them all, as it did of them to Endure them. Sometimes they would be Deaf, sometimes

Dumb, and sometimes Blind, and often, all this at once. One while their Tongues would be drawn down their Throats; another-while they would be pull'd out upon their Chins, to a prodigious length. They would have their Mouths opened unto such a Wideness, that their Jaws went out of joint; and anon they would clap together again with a Force like that of a strong Spring-Lock. The same would happen to their Shoulder-Blades, and their Elbows, and Hand-wrists, and several of their joints. They would at times ly in a benummed condition and be drawn together as those that are ty'd Neck and Heels;' and presently be stretched out, yea, drawn Backwards, to such a degree that it was fear'd the very skin of their Bellies would have crack'd. They would make most pitteous out-cries, that they were cut with Knives, and struck with Blows that they could not bear. Their Necks would be broken, so that their Neck-bone would seem dissolved unto them that felt after it; and yet on the sudden, it would become, again so stiff that there was no stirring of their Heads; yea, their Heads would be twisted almost round; and if main Force at any time obstructed a dangerous motion which they seem'd to be upon, they would roar exceedingly. Thus they lay some weeks most pittiful Spectacles; and this while as a further Demonstration of Witchcraft in these horrid Effects, when I went to Prayer by one of them, that was very desireous to hear what I said, the Child utterly lost her Hearing till our Prayer was over.

Sect. VI. It was a Religious Family that these Afflictions happened unto; and none but a Religious Contrivance to obtain Releef, would have been welcome to them. Many superstitious proposals were made unto them, by persons that were I know not who, nor what, with Arguments fetch't from I know not how much Necessity and Experience; but the distressed Parents rejected all such counsils, with a gracious Resolution, to oppose Devils with no other weapons but Prayers and Tears, unto Him that has the Chaining of them; and to try first whether Graces were not the best things to encounter Witchcrafts with. Accordingly they requested the four Miliisters of Boston, with the Minister of Chai-Istown,to keep a Day of Prayer at their thus haunted house; which they did in the Company of some devout people there. Immediately upon this Day, the youngest of the four children was delivered, and never felt any trouble as afore. But there was yet a greater Effect of these our Applications unto our God!

Sect. VII. The Report of the Calamities of the Family for which we were thus concerned arrived now unto the ears of the Magistrates, who presently and prudent y apply'd themselves, with a just vigour, to enquire into the story. The Father of the Children complained of his Neighbour, the suspected ill woman, whose name was Glover; and she being sent for by the Justices, gave such a wretched Account of her self, that they saw cause to commit her unto the Gaolers Custody. Goodwin had no proof that could have done her any Hurt; but the Hag had not power to deny her interest in the Enchantment of the Children; and I when she was asked, Whether she believed there was a God? her Answer was too blasphemous and horrible for any Pen of mine to mention. An Experiment was made, Whether she could recite the Lords

Prayer; and it was found, that tho clause after clause was most carefully repeated unto her, yet when she said it after them that prompted her, she could not Possibly avoid making Nonsense of it, with some ridiculous Depravations. This Experip ment I had the curiosity since to see made upon two more, and it had the same Event. Upon Commitment of this extrordinary Woman, all the Children had some present ease,; until one (related unto her) accidentally meeting one or two of them, entertained them with her Blessing, that is, Railing; upon which Three of them fell ill again, as they were before.

Sect. VIII. It was not long before the Witch thus in the Trap, was brought upon her Tryal; at which, thro' the Efficacy of a Charm, I suppose, used upon her, by one or some of her Cruel the Court could receive Answers from her in one but the Irish, which was her Native Language; altho she under-stood the English very well, and had accustomed her whole Family to none but that Language in her former Conversation; and therefore the Communication between the Bench and the Bar,' was now cheefly convey'd by two honest and faithful men that were interpreters. It was long before she could with any direct Answers plead unto her Indictment and; when she did plead, it was with Confession rather than Denial of her Guilt. Order was given to search the old womans house, from whence there were brought into the Court, several small Images, or Puppets, or Babies, made of Raggs, and stuff't with Goat's hair, and other such Ingredients. When these were produced, the vile Woman acknowledged, that her way to torment the Objects of her malice, was by wetting of her Finger with her Spittle, and streaking of those little Images. The abused Children were then present, and the Woman still kept stooping and shrinking as one that was almost prest to Death with a mighty Weight upon her. But one of the Images being brought unto her, immediately she started up after an odd manner, and took it into her hand; but she had no sooner taken it, than one of the Children fell into sad Fits, before the whole Assembly. This the Judges bad their just Apprehensions at; and carefully causing the Repetition of the Experiment, found again the same event of it. They asked her, Whether she had any to stand by her: She replied, She had; and looking very pertly in the Air, she added, No, He's gone. And she then confessed, that she had One, who was her Prince, with whom she maintained, I know not what Communion. For which cause, the night after, she was heard expostulating with a Devil, for his thus deserting her; telling him that Because he had served her so basely and falsly, she had confessed all. However to make all clear, The Court appointed five or six Physicians one evening to examine her very strictly, whether she were not craz'd in her Intellectuals, and had not procured to her self by Folly and Madness the Reputation of a Witch. Diverse hours did they spend with her; and in all that while no Discourse came from her, but what was pertinent and agreeable: particularly, when they asked her, What she thought would become of her soul? she reply'd "You ask me, a very solemn Question, and I cannot well tell what to say to it." She own'd her self a Roman Catholick; and could recite her Pater Noster in Latin very readily; but there was one Clause or two alwaies too hard for her, whereof she said,

" She could not repeat it, if she might have all the world." In the up-shot, the Doctors returned her Compos Mentis; and Sentence of Death was pass'd upon her.

Sect. IX. Diverse dayes were passed between her being Arraigned and Condemned. In this time one of her Neighbours had been giving in her Testimony of what another of her Neighbours had upon her Death related concerning her. It seems one Howen about Six years before, had been cruell bewitched to Death; but before she died, she called one Hughes unto her, Telling her that she laid her Death to the charge of Glover; That she had seen Glover sometimes come down her Chimney; That she should remember this, for within this Six years she might have Occasion to declare it. This Hughes now preparing her Testimony, immediately one of her children, a fine boy, well grown towards Youth, was taken ill, just in the same woful and surprising manner that Goodwins children were. One night particularly, The Boy said he saw a Black thing with a Blue Cap in the Room, Tormenting of him; and he complained most bitterly of a Hand put into the Bed, to pull out his Bowels. The next day the mother of the boy went unto Glover, in the Prison, and asked her, Why she tortured her poor lad at such a wicked rate? This Witch replied, that she did it because of wrong done to her self and her daughter. Hughes denied (as well she might) that she had done her any wrong. "Well then," sayes Glover, "Let me see your child and he shall be well again." Glover went on, and told her of her own accord, " I was at your house last night." Sayes Hughes, "In what shape?" Sayes Glover, "As a black thing with a blue Cap." Saye's Hughes, "What did you do there?" SayesGIover,"with my hand in the Bed I tryed to pull out the boyes Bowels, but I could not." They parted; but the next day Hughes appearing at Court, had her Boy with her; and Glover passing by the Boy, expressed her good wishes for him; tho' I suppose, his Parent had no design of any mighty Respect unto the Hag, by having him with her there. But the Boy had no more Indispositions after the Condemnation of the Woman

Sect. X. While the miserable old Woman was under Condemnation, I did my self twice give a visit unto her. She never denyed the guilt of the Witchcraft charg'd upon her; but she confessed very little about the Circumstances of her Confederacies with the Devils; only, she said, That she us'd to be at meetings, which her Prince and Four more were present at. As for those Four, She told who they were; and for her Prince, her account plainly was, that he was the Devil. She entertained me with nothing but Irish ', which Language I had not Learning enough to understand without an Interpreter; only one time, when I was representing unto her That and How her Prince had cheated her, as her self would quickly find; she reply'd, I think in English, and with passion ioo, "If it be so, I am sorry for that!" I offer'd many Questions unto her, unto which, after long silence, she told me, She would fain give me a full Answer, but they would not give her leave. It was demanded, "They! Who is that They ? " and she return'd, that They were her Spirits, or her Saints, (for they say, the same Word in Irish signifies both). And at another time, she included her two Mistresses, as she call'd them in that They, but when it was enquired, Who those two were, she fell into, a Rage, and would be no more urged. I Sett before her the Necessity and Equity of her breaking her Covenant with Hell, and giving her self to the Lord Jesus Christ, by an everlasting Covenant; To which her Answer was, that I spoke a very Reasonable thing, but she could not do it. I asked her whether she would consent or desire to be pray'd for; To that she said, If Prayer would do her any good, shee could pray for her self. And when it was again propounded, she said, She could not unless her spirits (or angels) would give her leave. However, against her will I pray'd with her, which if it were a Fault it was in excess of Pitty. When I had done, shee thank'd me with many good Words; but I was no sooner out of her sight , than she took a stone, a long and slender stone, and with her Finger and Spittle fell to tormenting it; though whom or what she meant, I had the mercy never to understand.

Sect. XI. When this Witch was going to her Execution, she said, the Children should not be relieved by her Death, for others had a hand in it as well as she; and she named one among the rest, whom it might have been thought Natural Affection would have advised the Concealing of. It came to pass accordingly, That the Three children continued in their Furnace as before, and it grew rather Seven times hotter than it was. All their former Ails pursued them still, with an addition of (tis not easy to tell how many) more, but such as gave more sensible Demonstrations of an Enchantment growing very far towards a Possession by Evil spirits.

Sect. XII. The Children in their Fits would still cry out upon They and Them as the Authors of all their Harm; but who that They and Them were, they were not able to declare. At last, the Boy obtain'd at some times a sight of some shapes in the room. There were Three or Four of 'em, the Names of which the child would pretend at certain seasons to tell; only the Name of One, who was counted a Sager Rag than the rest, he still so stammered at, that he was put upon some Periphrasis in describing her. A Blow at the place where the Boy beheld the Spectre was alwaies felt by the Boy himself in the part of his Body that answered what might be stricken at; and this tho his Back were turn'd; which was once and again so exactly tried, that there could be no Collusion in the Business. But as a Blow at the Apparition alwaies hurt him, so it alwaies help't him too; for after the Agonies, which a Push or Stab of That had put him to, were over, (as in a minute or 2 they would be) the Boy would have a respite from his Fits a considerable while ' and the Hobgoblins disappear. It is very credibly reported that a wound was this way given to an Obnoxious woman in the town, whose name I will not expose: for we should be tender in such Relations lest we wrong the Reputation of the Innocent by stories not enough enquired into.

Sect. XIII. The Fits of the Children yet more arriv'd unto such Motions as were beyond the Efficacy of any natural Distemper in the World. They would bark at one another like Dogs, and again purr like

so many Cats. They would sometimes complain,, that they were in a
Red-hot Oven, sweating and panting at the same time unreasonably:
Anon they would say, Cold water was thrown upon them, at which
they would shiver very much. They would cry out of dismal Blowes
with great Cudgels laid upon them; and tho' we saw no cudgels nor
blowes, yet we could see the Marks left by them in Red Streaks upon
their bodies afterward. And one of them would be roasted on an
invisible Spit, run into his Mouth, and out at his Foot, he lying, and
rolling, and groaning as if it had been so in the most sensible manner
in the world; and then he would shriek, that Knives were cutting of
him. Sometimes also he would have his head so forcibly, tho not
visibly, nail'd unto the Floor, that it was as much as a strong man
could do to pull it up. One while they would all be so Limber, that it
was judg'd every Bone of them could be bent. Another while they
would be so stiff, that not a joint of them could be stir'd. They would
sometimes be as though they were mad, and then they would climb
over high Fences, beyond the Imagination of them that look'd after
them. Yea, They would fly like Geese; and be carried with an
incredible Swiftness thro the air, having but just their Toes now and
then upon the ground, and their Arms waved like the W'ings of a Bird.
One of them, in the House of a kind Neighbour and Gentleman (Mr.
Willis) flew the length of the Room, anout 20 foot, and flew just into
an Infants high armed Chair; (as tis affirmed) none seeing her feet all
the way touch the floor.

Sect. XIV. Many wayes did the Devils take to make the children do
mischief both to themselves and others; but thro the singular
Providence of God, they always fail'd in the attempts. For they could
never essay the doing of any harm, unless there were some-body at
hand that might prevent it; and seldome without first shrieking out,
"They say, I must do such a thing!" Diverse times they went to strike
furious Blowes at their tenderest and dearest friends, or to fling them
down staires when they had them at the Top, but the warnings from the
mouths of the children themselves, would still anticipate what the
Devils did intend. They diverse times were very near Burning, or
Drowning of themselves, but the Children themselves by their own
pitiiful and seasonable cries for Help, still procured their Deliverance:
Which made me to Consider, Whether the Little, ones had not their
Angels, in the plain sense of Our Saviours Intimation. Sometimes,
When they were tying their own Neck-clothes, their compelled hands
miserably strangled themselves, till perhaps, the standers-by gave some
Relief unto them. But if any small Mischief happen'd to be done where
they were. as the Tearing or Dirtying of a Garment, the Falling of a
C'up, the breaking of a Glass or the like; they would rejoice extremely,
and fall into a pleasure and Laughter very extraordinary. All which
things cornpar'd with the Temper of the Children, when they are
themselves, may suggest some very peculiar Thoughts unto us.

Sect. XV. They were not in a constant Torture for some Weeks, but
were a little quiet, unless upon some incidental provocations; upon
which the Devils would handle them like Tigres, and wound them in a

manner very horrible. Particularly, Upon the least Reproof of their Parents for any unfit thing they said or did, most grievous woful Heart-breaking Agonies would they fall into. If any useful thing were to be done to them, or by them, they would have all sortsof Troubles fall upon them. It would sometimes cost one of them an Hour or Two to be undrest in the evenin , or drest in the morning. For if any one went to unty a string, or undo a Button about them, or the contrary ' ; they would be twisted into such postures as made the thing impossible. And at Whiles, they would be so managed in their Beds, that no Bed-clothes could for an hour or two be laid upon them; nor could they go to wash their Hands, without having them clasp't so odly together, there was no doing of it. But when their Friends were near tired with Waiting, anon they might do what they would unto them. Whatever Work they were bid to do, they would be so snap't in the member which was to do it, that they with grief still desisted from it. If one ordered them to Rub a clean Table, they were able to do it without any disturbance; if to rub a dirty Table, presently they would with many Torrnents be made uncapable. And sometimes, tho but seldome, they were kept from eating their meals, by having their Teeth sett when they carried any thing unto their Mouthes.

Sect. XVI. But nothing in the World would so discompose them as a Religious Exercise. If there were anv Discourse of God, or Christ, or any of the things which are not seen qnd are eternal, they would be cast into intolerable Anguishes. Once, those two Worthy Ministers Mr. Fisk' and Mr. Thatcher,2 bestowing some gracious Counsils on the Boy, whom they there found at a Neighbours house, he immediately lost his Hearing, so that he heard not one word, but just the last word of all they said. Much more, All Praying to God, and Reading of His word, would occasion a very terrible Vexation to them: they would then stop their own Ears with their own Hands; and roar, and shriek; and holla, to drown the Voice of the Devotion. Yea, if any one in the Room took up a Bible to look into it, tho the Children could see nothing of it, as being in a croud of Spectators, or having their Faces another way, yet would they be in wonderful Miseries, till the Bible were laid aside. In short, No good thing must then be endured near those Children, Which (while they are themselves) do love every good thing in a measure that proclaims in them the Fear of God.

Sect. XVII. My Employments were such, that I could not visit this afflicted Family so often as I would; Where-fore, that I might show them what kindness I could, as also that I might have a full opportunity to observe the extraordinary Circumstances of the Children, and that I might be furnished with Evidence and Argument as a Critical Eye-Witness to confute the Saducism of this debauched Age; I took the Eldest of them home to my House. The young Woman continued well at our house, for diverse dayes, and apply'd her self to such Actions not only of Industry, but of Piety, as she had been no stranger to. But on the Twentieth of November in the Fore-noon, she cry'd out, "Ah, They have found me out! I thought it would be so!" and immediately she fell into her fits again. I shall now confine my

Story cheefly to Her, from whose Case the Reader may shape some Conjecture at the Accidents of the Rest.

Sect. XVIII. Variety of Tortures now siez'd upon the Girl; in which besides the forementioned Ails returning upon her, she often would cough up a Ball as big as a small Egg, into the side of her Wind-pipe, that would near choak her, till by Stroking and by Drinking it was carried down again. At the beginning of her Fits usually she kept odly Looking up the Chimney, but could not say what she saw. When I bad her Cry to the Lord Jesus for Help, her Teeth were instantly sett; upon which I added, "Yet, child, Look unto Him," and then her Eyes were presently pulled into her head, so farr, that one might have fear'd she should never have us'd them more. When I prayed in the Room, first her Arms were with a strong, tho not seen Force clap't upon her ears; and when her hands were with violence pull'd away, she crted out, " They make such a noise, I cannot hear a word!" She likewise complain'd, that Goody Glover's Chain was upon her- Leg, and when she essay'd to go, her postures were exactly sluch as the chained Witch had before she died. But the manner still was, that her Tortures in a small while would pass over, and Frolick succeed; in which she would continue many hours, nay, whole days, talking perhaps never wickedly, but alwaies wittily, beyond her self; and at certain provocations, her Tortures would renew upon her, till we had left off to give them. But she frequently told us, that if she might but steal, or be drunk, she should be well immediately.

Sect. XIX. In her ludicrous Fits, one while she would be for Flying; and she would be carried hither and thither, tho not long from the ground, yet so long as to exceed the ordinary power of Nature in our Opinion of it: another-while she would be for Diving, and use the Actions of it towards the Floor, on which, if we had not held her, she would have throwrn her self. Being at this exercise she told us, That They said, stie must go down to the Bottom of our Well, for there was Plate there, and They said, They would bring her safely up again. This did she tell us, tho she had never heard of any Plate there! and we ourselves who had newly bought the house, hardly knew of any; but the former Owner of the House just then coming in, told us there had been Plate for many Years at the Bottom of the Well. She had once a great mind to have eaten a roasted Apple, but whenever she attempted to eat it, her Teeth would be sett, and sometimes, if she went to take it up her Arm would be made so stiff, that she could not possibly bring heir hand to her Mouth: at last she said, " Now They say, I shall eat it, if I eat it quickly "; and she nimbly eat it all up. Moreover, There was one very singular passion that frequently attended her. An Invisible Chain would be clapt about her, and shee, in much pain and Fear, cry out, When They began to put it on. Once I did with my own hand knock it; off as it began to be fastned about her. But ordinarily) Wlien 'it was on, shee'd be pull'd out of her seat with such violence towards the Fire, that it has been as much as one or two of us could do to keep her out. Her Eyes were not brought to be perpendicular to her feet, when she rose out of her Seat, as the Mechanism of a Humane' Body requires in them that rise, but she was one dragg'd wholly by other Hands: and once, When I gave a stamp on the Hearth, just between her and the Fire, she scream'd out, (tho I think she saw me not) that I Jarr'd the Chain, and hurt her Back.

Sect. XX. While she was in her Frolicks I was willing to try, Whether she could read or no; and I found, not only That If she went to read the Bible her Eyes would be strangely twisted and blinded, and her Neck presently broken, butalso that if any one else did read the Bible in the Room, tho it were wholly out of her sight, and without the least voice or noise of it, she would be cast into very terrible Agonies. Yet once Falling into her Maladies a little time after she bad read the 59th Psalm, I said unto the standers by, "Poor child! she can't now read the Psalm she readd a little while ago," she listened her self unto something that none of us could hear and made us be silent for some few Seconds of a minute. Whereupon she said, " But I can read it, they say I shall! " So I show'd her the Psalm, and she readd it all over to us. Then said 1, "Child, say Amen to it:" but that she could not do. I added, 'Read the next: " but no where else in the Bible could she read a word. I brought her a Quakers Book; and That she could quietly read whole pages of; only the Name of God and Christ she still skip't over, being unable to pronounce it, except sometimes with stammering a minute or two or more upon it. When we urged her to tell what the word was that she missed, shee'd say, "I must not speak it; They say I must not, you know what it is, it's G and 0 and D; " so shee'd spell the Name unto us. I brought her again one that I thought was a Good Book; and presently she was handled with intolerable Torments. But when I show'd her a JestBook, as, The Oxford Jests, or the Cambridge Jests, she could read them without any Disturbance ' and have witty Descants upon them too. I entertained her with a Book that pretends to prove, That there are no Witches; and that she could read very well, only the Name Devils, and Witches, could not be uttered by her without extraordinary Difficulty. I produced a Book to her that proves, That there are Witches, and that she had not power to read. When I readd in the Room the Story of Ann Cole,' in my Fathers Remarkable Providences, and came to the Exclamation which the Narrative saies the Demons made upon her, " Ah she runs to the Rock!" it cast her into inexpressible Agonies; and shee'd fall into them whenever I had the Expression of, "Running to the Rock)" afterwards. A popish Book also she could endure very well; but it would kill her to look into any Book, that (in my Opinion) it might have bin profitable and edifying for her to be reading of. These Experiments were often enough repeated, and still with the same Success, before Witnesses not a few. The good Books that were found so mortal to her were cheefly such as lay ever at hand in the Room. One was the Guid to Heaven from the Word, which I had given her. Another of them was Mr. Willard's little (but precious) Treatise of Justification. Diverse Books published by my Father I also tried upon her; partictilarly, his Mystery of Christ; and another small Book of his about Faith and Repentance, and the day of Judgement. Once being very merrily talking by a Table that had this last Book upon it, she just opened the Book, and was immediately struck backwards as dead upon the floor. I hope I have not spoil'd the credit of the Books, By telling how much the Devils hated them. I shall therefore add, That my Grandfather Cottons Catechism called Milk for Babes, and The Assemblies Catechism, would bring hideous Convulsions on the Child if she look't into them; tho she had once learn't them with all the love that could be.

Sect. XXI. I was not unsensible that this Girls Capacity or incapacity to read, was no Test for Truth to be determined by, and therefore I did not proceed much further in this fanciful Business, not knowing What snares the Devils might lay for us in the Tryals. A few further Tryals, I confess, I did make; but what the event of 'em was, I shall not relate, because I would not offend. But that which most made me to wonder was, That one bringing to her a certain Prayer-Book, she not only could Read it very well, but also did read a large part of it over, and calling it Her Bible, she took in it a delight and put on it a Respect more than Ordinary. If she were going into her tortures, at the offer of this Book, she, would come out of her fits and read; and her Attendents were almost under a Temptation to use it as a Charm, to make and keep her quiet. Only, When she came to the Lords Prayer, (now and then occurring in this Book) she would have her eyes put out, so that she must turn over a new leaf, and then she could read again. Whereas also there are Scriptures in that Book, she could read them there, but if I shew'd her the very same Scriptures in the Bible, she should sooner Dy than read them. And she was likewise made unable to read the Psalms in an ancient meeter, which this prayer-book had in the same volumne with it. There were, I think I may say, no less than Multitudes of Witnesses to this odd thing; and I should not have been a faithful and honest Historian, if I had withheld from the World this part of my History: But I make no Reflections on it. Those inconsiderable men that are provoked at it (if any shall be of so little Sense as to be provoked) must be angry at the Devils, and not at me; their Malice, and not my Writing, deserves the Blame of any Aspersion which a true History may seem to cast on a Book that some have enough manifested their Concernment for.

Sect. XXII. There was another most unaccountable Circumstance which now attended her; and until she came to our House, I think, she never had Experience of it. Ever now and then, an Invisible Horse would be brought unto her, by those whom she only called, "them," and, "Her Company": upon the Approach of Which, her eyes would be still closed up; for (said she) "They say, I am a Tell-Tale, and therefore they will not let me see them." Upon this would she give a Spring as one mounting an Horse, and Settling her self in a RidingPosture-she would in her Chair be agitated as one sometimes Ambleing, sometimes Trotting, and sometimes Galloping very furiously. In these motions we could not perceive that she was stirred by the stress of her feet, upon the ground; for often she touch't it not; but she mostly continued in her Chair, though sometimes in her hard Trott we doubted she would have been tossed over the Back of it. Once being angry at his Dulness, When she said, she would cut off his head if she had a knife, I gave her my Sheath, wherewith she suddenly gave her self a stroke on the Neck, but complained, it would not cut. When she had rode a minute or two or three, shee'd pretend to be at a Rendezvous with Them, that were Her Company; there shee'd maintain a Discourse with them, and asking many Questions concerning her self, (for we gave her none of ours) shee'd Listen much, and Received Answers from them that indeed none but her self perceived. Then would she return and inform us, how They did intend to handle her for a day or two afterwards, besides some other things that she enquired of them. Her Horse would sometimes throw her, with much Violence; but she would mount again; and one of the Standers-by once imagining them that were Her Company, to be before her (for she call'd unto them to stay for her) he struck with his Cane in the Air where he thought they were, and tho her eyes were wholly shutt, yet she cry'd out, that he struck her. Her Fantastic Journeyes were mostly performed in her Chair without removing from it; but sometimes would she ride from her Chair, and be carried odly on the Floor, from one part of the Room to another, in the postures of a Riding Woman. If any of us asked her, Who her Company were? She generally replyed, I don't know. But If we were instant in our Demand, she would with some witty Flout or other turn it off. Once I said, "Child, if you can't tell their Names, pray tell me what Clothes they have on;" and the Words were no sooner out of my mouth, but she was laid for dead upon the Floor.

Sect. XXIII. One of the Spectators once ask'd her, Whether she could not ride up stairs; unto which her Answer was, That she believe'd she could, for her Horse could do very notable things. Accordingly, when her Horse came to her again, to our Admiration she Rode (that is, was tossed as one that rode) up the stairs: there then stood open the Study of one belonging to the Family, into which entring, she stood immediately upon her Feet, and cry'd out, "They are gone; they are gone! They say, that they cannot,-God won't let 'em come here! " She also added a Reason for it, which the Owner of the Study thought more kind than true. And she presently and perfectly came to her self, so that her whole Discourse and Carriage was altered unto the greatest measure of Sobriety, and she satt Reading of the Bible and Good Books, for a good part of the Afternoon. Her Affairs calling her anon to go down again, the Daemons were in a quarter of a minute as bad upon her as before, and her Horse was Waiting for her. I understanding of it, immediately would have her up to the study of the young man where she had been at ease before; meerly to try Whether there had not been a Fallacy in what had newly happened: but she was now so twisted and writhen, that it gave me much trouble to get her into my Arms, and much more to drag her up the stairs. She was pulled out of my hands, and when I recovered my Hold, she was thrust so hard upon me, that I had almost fallen backwards, and her own breast was sore afterwards, by their Compressions to detain her; she seem'd heavier indeed than three of her self. With incredible Forcing (tho she kept Screaming, "They say I must not go in!") at length we pull'd her in; where she was no sooner come, but she could stand on her Feet, and with an altered tone, could thank me, saying, "now I am well." At first shee'd be somewhat faint, and say, She felt something go out of her; but in a minute or two, she could attend any Devotion or Business as well as ever in her Life; and both spoke and did as became a person of good Discretion. I was loth to make a Charm of the Room; yet some strangers that came to visit us, the Week after, desiring to see the Experiment made, I permitted more than two or three Repetitions of it; and it still succeded as I have declared. Once when I was assisting 'em in carrying of her up, she was torn out of all our hands; and to my self, she cry'd out, "Mr. M., One of them is going to push you down the stairs, have a care." I remember not that I felt any Thrust or Blow; but I think I was unaccountably made to step down backward two or three stairs, and within a few hours she told me by whom it was.

Sect. XXIV. One of those that had bin concerned for her Welfare, had newly implored the great God that the young woman might be able to declare whom she apprehended her self troubled by. Presently upon this her Horse returned, only it pestered her with such ugly paces, that she fell out with her Company, and threatned now to tell all, for their so abusing her. I was going abroad, and she said unto them that were about her, "Mr. M. is gone abroad, my horse won't come back, till he come home; and then I believe" (said she softly,) "Ishall tell him all." I staid abroad an hour or two,andthen Returning, When I was just come to my Gate, before I had given the least Sign or Noise of my being there, she said, "My Horse is come!" and intimated, that I was at the Door. When I came in, I found her mounted after her fashion, upon her Aerial Steed; which carried her Fancy to the Journeys end. There (or rather then) she maintained a considerable Discourse with Her Company, Listening very attentively when she had propounded any Question, and receiving the Answers with impressions made upon her mind. She said; " Well what do you say? How many Fits more am I to have?-pray, can ye tell how long it shall be before you are hang'd for what you have done?-You are filthy Witches to my knowledge, I shall see some of you go after your sister; You would have killd me; but you can't, I don't fear you.-You would have thrown Mr Mather down stairs, but you could not.-Well! How shall I be To morrow? I Pray, What do you think of Tomorrow?Fare ye well.-You have brought me such an ugly Horse, I am angry at you; I could find in my heart to tell all." So she began her homeward-paces; but when she had gone a little way, (that is a little while) she said, 'O I have forgot one Question, I must go back again; " and back she rides. She had that day been diverse times warning us, that they had been contriving to do some harm to 'my Wife, by a Fall or a Blow, or the like; and when she came out of her mysterious Journeys, she would still be careful concerning Her. Accordingly she now calls to her Company again, "Hark you, One thing more before we part! What hurt is it you will do to Mrs. Mather? will you do her any hurt? "Here she list'ned some time; and then clapping her hands, cry'd out, " 0, I am glad on't, they can do Mrs. Mather no hurt: they try, but they say they can't." So she returns and at once, Dismissing her Horse, and opening her eyes, she call'd me to her, "Now Sir," (said she) 'I'll tell you all. I have learn'd who they are that are the cause of my trouble, there's three of them," (and she named who) " if they were out of the way, I should bewell. They say, they can tell now how long I shall be troubled, But they won't. Only they seem to think, their power will be broke this Week. They seem also to say, that I shall be very ill To morow, but they are themselves terribly afraid of to morrow; They fear, that to morrow we shall be delivered. They say too, that they can't hurt Mrs. Mather, which I am glad of. But they said, they would kill me to night, if I went to bed before ten a clock, if I told a word." And other things did she say, not now to be recited.

Sect. XXV. The Day following, which was, I think, about the twenty seventh of November, Mr. Morton of Charlestown, and Mr. Allen, Mr. Moody, Mr. Willard, and my self, of Boston, with some devout Neighbours, kept another Day of Prayer, at John Goodwin's house; and we had all the Children present with us there. The children were miserably tortured, while we laboured in our Prayers; but our good God was nigh unto us, in what we call'd upon Him for. From this day the power of the Enemy was broken; and the children, though Assaults after this were made upon them, yet were not so cruelly handled as before. The Liberty of the Children encreased daily more and more, and their Vexation abated by degrees; till within a little while they arrived to Perfect Ease, which for some weeks or months they cheerfully enjoyed. Thus Good it is for us to draw near to God.

Sect. XXVI. Within a day or two after the Fast, the young Woman had two remarkable Attempts made upon her, by her invisible Adversaries. Once, they were Dragging her into the Oven that was then heating, while there was none in the Room to help her. She clap't her hands on the Mantletree' to save her self; but they were beaten off; and she had been burned, if at her Out-cryes one had not come in from abr6ad for her Relief. Another time, they putt an unseen Rope with a cruel Noose about her Neck, Whereby she was choaked, until she was black in the Face; and though it was taken off before it had kill'd her, yet there were the red Marks of it, and of a Finger and a Thumb near it, remaining to be seen for a while afterwards.

Sect. XXVII. This was the last Molestation that they gave her for a While; and she dwelt at my house the rest of the Winter, having by an obliging and vertuous Conversation, made her self enough Welcome to the Family. But within about a Fortnight, she was visited with two dayes of as Extraordinary Obsessions as any we had been the Spectators of. I thought it convenient for me to entertain my Congregation with a Sermon upon the memorable Providences which these Children had been concerned in. When I had begun to study my Sermon, her Tormentors 'again seiz'd upon her; and all Fryday and Saturday, did they manage her with a special Design, as was plain, to disturb me in what I was about. In the worst of her extravacancies formerly, she was more dutiful to my self, than I had reason to Expect, but now her whole carriage to me was with a Sauciness that I had not been us'd to be treated with. She would knock at my Study Door, affirming, That some below would be glad to see me; when there was none that ask't for me. She would callto me with multiplyed Impertinencies, and throw small things at me wherewith she could not give me any hurt. . Shee'd Hector me at a strange rate for the work I was at, and threaten me with I know not what mischief for it. She got a History that I had Written of this Witchcraft, and tho she had before this readd it over and over, yet now she could not read (I believe) one entire Sentence of it; but she made of it the most ridiculous Travesty in the World, with such a Patness and excess of Fancy, to supply the sense that she put upon it, as I was amazed at. And she particularly told me,That I should quickly come to disgrace by that History.

Sect. XXVIII. But there were many other Wonders beheld by us before these two dayes were out. Few tortures attended her, but such as were provoked; her Frolicks being the things that had most possession of her. I was in Latin telling some young Gentlemen of the Colledge, That if I should bid her Look to God, her Eyes would be put out, upon which her eyes were presently served so. I was in some surprize, When I saw that her Troublers understood Latin, and it made me willing to try a little more of their Capacity. We continually found, that if an English Bible were in any part of the Room seriously look'd into, though she saw and heard nothing of it, she would immediately be in very dismal Agonies. We now made a Tryal more than once or twice, of the Greek New Testament, and the Hebrew Old Testament; and We still found, That if one should go to read in it never so secretly and silently, it would procure her that Anguish, Which there was no enduring of. But I thought, at length, I fell upon one inferior Language which the Daemons did not seem so well to understand.

Sect. XXIX. Devotion was now, as formerly, the terriblest of all the provocations that could be given her. I could by no means bring her to own, That she desired the mercies of God, and the prayers of good men. I would have obtained a Sign of such a Desire, by her Lifting up of her hand; but she stirr'd it not: I then lifted up her hand my self, and though the standers-by thought a more insignificant thing could not be propounded, I said, " Child, If you desire those things, let your hand fall, when I take mine away: " I took my hand away, and liers continued strangely and stifiy stretched out, so that for some time, she could not take it down. During these two dayes we had Prayers oftener in our Family than at other times; and this was her usual Behavior at them. The man that prayed, usually began with Reading the Word of Cod; which once as he was going to do, she call'd to him, "Read of Mary Magdelen, out of whom the Lord cast seven Devils." During the time of Reading, she would be laid as one fast asleep; but when Prayer was begun, the Devils would still throw her on the Floor, at the feet of him that prayed. There would she lye and Whistle and sing and roar, to drown the voice of the Prayer; but that being a little too audible for Them, they would shutt close her Mouth and her cars, and yet make such odd noises in her Threat as that she her self could not hear our Cries to God for her. Shee'd also fetch very terrible Blowes with her Fist, and Kicks with her Foot at the man that prayed; but still (for he had bid that none should hinder her) hei, Fist and Foot would alwaies recoil, when they came within a few hairs breadths of him just as if Rebounding against a Wall; so that she touch'd him not, but then would beg hard of other people to strike him, and particularly she entreated them to take the Tongs and smite him; Which not being done, she cryed out of him, "He has wounded me in the Head." But before Prayer was out, she would be laid for Dead, wholly sensless and (unless to a severe Trial) Breathless; with her Belly swelled like a Drum, and sometimes with croaking Noises in it; thus would she ly, most exactly with the stiffness and posture of one that had been two Days laid out for Dead. Once lying thus, as he that was praying was alluding to the words of the Canaanitess, and saying, "Lord, have mercy on a Daughter vexed with a Devil; " there came a big, but low voice from her, saying, "There's Two or Three of them " (or us!) and the standers-by were under that Apprehension, as that they cannot relate whether her mouth mov'd in speaking of it. When Prayer was ended, she would Revive in a minute or two, and continue as Frolicksome as before. She thus continued until Saturday towards the Evening; when, after this man had been at Prayer, I charged all my Family to admit of no Diversion by her Frolicks, from such exercises as it was proper to begin the Sabbath with. They took the Counsel; and tho she essayed, with as witty and as nimble and as various an Application to each of them successively as ever I saw, to make them laugh, yet they kept close to their good Books which then called for their Attention. When she saw that, immediately she fell asleep; and in two or three hours, she waked perfectly her self; weeping bitterly to remember (for as one come out of a dream she could remember) what had befallen her.

Sect. XXX. After this, we had no more such entertainments. The Demons it may be would once or twice in a Week trouble her for a few minutes with perhaps a twisting and a twinkling of her eyes, or a certain Cough which did seem to be more than ordinary. Moreover, Both she at my house, and her Sist,,,r at home, at the time which they call Christmas, were by the Daemons made very drunk, though they had no strong Drink (as we are fully sure) to make them so. When she began to feel her self thus drunk, she complain'd, "O they say they will have me to keep Christmas with them! They will disgrace me when they can do nothing else! " And immediately the Ridiculous Behaviours of one drunk were with a wonderful exactness represented in her Speaking, and Reeling, and Spewing, and anon Sleeping, till she was well again. But the Vexations of the Children otherwise abated continually. They first came to be alwaies Quiet, unless upon Provocations. Then they got Liberty to work, but not to read: then further on, to read, but not aloud, at last they were wholly delivered; and for many Weeks remained so.

Sect. XXXI. I was not unsensible, that it might be an easie thing to be too bold, and go too far, in making of Experiments: Nor was I so unphilosophical as not to discern many opportunityes of Giving and Solving many Problemes which the pneumatic Discipline' is concerned in. I confess I have Learn't much more than I sought, and I have bin informed of some things relating to the invisible World, which as I did not think it lawful to ask, so I do not think it proper to tell; yet I will give a Touch upon one Problem commonly Discoursed of; that is, Whether the Devils know our Thoughts, or no? I will not give the Reader my Opinion of it, but only my Experiment. That they do not, was conjectured from this: We could cheat them when we spoke one thing, and mean't another. This was found when the Children were to be undressed. The Devils would still in wayes beyond the Force of any Imposture, wonderfully twist the part that was to be undress't, so that there was no coming at it. But, if we said, untye his neckcloth, and the parties bidden, at the same time, understood our intent to be, unty his Shooe! The Neckcloth, and not the shooe, has been made strangely inaccessible. But on the other side, That they do, may be conjectured from This. I called the young Woman at my House by her Name, intending to mention unto her some Religious Expedient whereby she might, as I thought, much relieve her self; presently her Neck was broke, and I continued watching my Opportunity to say what I designed. I could not get her to come out of her Fit, until I had laid aside my purpose of speaking what I thought, and then she reviv'd immediately. Moreover a young Gentleman visiting of me at my Study to ask my advice about curing the Atheism and Blasphemy which he complained his Thoughts were more than ordinarily then infested with; after some Discourse I carried him down to see this Girl who was then molested with her unseen Fiends; but when he came, she treated him very coursly and rudely, asking him What he came to the house for? and seemed very ang' at his beingthere, urging him to be gone with a very impetuous Importunity. Perhaps all Devils are not alike sagacious.

Sect. XXXII, The Last Fit that the young Woman had, was very peculiar. The Daemons having once again seiz'd her, they made her pretend to be Dying; and Dying truly we fear'd at last she was: She lay, she tossed, she pull'd just like one Dying, and urged hard for some one to dy with her, seeming loth to dy alone. She argued concerning Death, in strains that quite amazed us; and concluded, That though she was loth to dy, yet if God said she must, she must; adding something about the state of the Countrey, which we wondred at. Anon, the Fit went over; and as I guessed it would be, it was the last Fit she had at our House. But all my Library never afforded me any Commentary on those Paragraphs of the Gospels, which speak of Demoniacs, equal to that which the passions of this Child have given me.

Sect. XXXIII. This is the Story of Goodwins Children, a Story all made up of Wonders! I have related nothing but what I judge to be true. I was my self an Eye-witness to a large part of what I tell; and I hope my neighbours have long thought, That I have otherwise learned Christ, than to ly unto the World. Yea, there is, I believe, scarce any one particular, in this Narrative, which more than one credible Witness will not be ready to make Oath unto. The things of most Concernment in it were before many Critical Observersand the Whole happened in the Metropolis of the English America, unto a religious and industrious Family which was visited by all sorts of Persons, that had a mind to satisfy themselves. I do now likewise publish the History,

While the thing is yet fresh and New; and I challenge all men to detect so much as one designed Falshood, yea, or so much as one important Mistake, from the Egg to the Apple of it. I have Writ as plainly as becomes an Historian, as truly as becomes a Christian, tho perhaps not so profitably as becamea Divine. But I am resolv'd after this, never to use but just one grain of patience with any man that shall go to impose upon me a Denial of Devils, or of Witches. I shall count that man Ignorant who shall suspect, but I shall count him down-right Impudent if he Assert the Non-Existence of things which we have had such palpable. Convictions of. I am sure he cannot be a Civil, (and some will question whether he can be an honest man) that shall go to,deride the Being of things which a whole Countrey has now beheld an house of pious people suffering not a few Vexations by. But if the Sadducee, or the Atheist, have no right Impressions by these Memorable Providences made upon his mind; yet I hope those that know what it is to be sober will not repent any pains that they may have taken in perusing what Records of these Witchcrafts and Possessions, I thus leave unto Posterity.'

The Salem witchcraft papers, Volume 2 : verbatim transcripts of the legal documents of the Salem witchcraft outbreak of 1692
Susannah Martin Executed July 19, 1692

(Warrant for Arrest of Susannah Martin)

To: To The Marshall of the County of Essex or his Lawfull deputie or to the Constable
of Amesburry.

You are in their Majests names hereby required forthwith or as soon as may be to apprehend and bring (before us) Susanna Martin of Amesbury in the County of Essex Widdow at the house of Lt Nathaniell Ingersalls in Salem Village, in order to her Examination Relateing to high Suspition of Sundry acts of Witchcraft donne or Committed by her upon the Bodys of Mary Walcot Abigail Williams Ann putnam and Marcy Lewis of Salem Village or farmes

Where by great hurt and dammage hath benne donne to the bodys of Said persons according to Compl't of Capt Jonathan Walcot & Serg't Thomas putnam in behalfe of their Majests this day Exhibited before us for themselfes and also for Severall of theire Neighbours and here of You are not to faile at your perills. Dated Salem Aprile 30th 1692

*John. Hathorne [*unclear:*] Assists

*Jonathan Corwin

(Reverse) according this warrant I have apprehended susanna Martin widdow of Amsbery and have brought or caused hir to be brought to the place appointed for his examination

me *Orlando Bagly: Constable of Amsbery

-550-

salem village this 2:th may 1692

(Reverse) Susanna Martin Warrant

(*Essex County Archives, Salem -- Witchcraft Vol. 1 Page 57*)

(Mittimus for Susannah Martin, Lydia Dustin, Dorcas Hoar, and Sarah Morey)
To: To. the Keeper of theire Majests Goale
in Boston

You are in theire Majests names hereby required to take into, your care and safe Custody the Bodys of Susanah Martin of Amesbury

Widdow, Lydia Dastin of Reding Wi[ddow], Dorcas Hoare of Beverly
widdow and Sarah Murrill also of Beverly who all stand Charged with
high Suspition of Sundry acts of Witchcraft donne or Committed by
them upon the Bodys of Mary Walcot Marcy Lewis Abigail Williams
Ann putnam Elizabeth Hubbert and Susannah Sheldon and Goody
Viber of Salem Village or farmes whereby great hurt and dammage hath
beene donne to the bodys [of] said persons according to Complaint of
Capt Jonathan Walcot and Serj't Thomas putnam of Salem Village
Yeoman Exhibited Salem April the 30th. 1692: Whome you are to
secure in order to theire further Examination or Tryall and hereof you
are not to faile

Dated Salem Village May 2d. 1692
*John Hathorne [*unclear*:] Assists

*Jonathan. Corwin

(*Essex County Archives, Salem -- Witchcraft Vol. 1 Page 62*)

(Examination of Susannah Martin)

The Examination of Susan: Martin. 2. May 1692

As soon as she came in Many had fits.

Do you know this Woman

Abig: Williams saith it is Goody Martin she hath hurt me often.
Others by fits were hindered from speaking. Eliz: Hubbard said she
hath not been hurt by her. John Indian said he hath not seen her
----
-551-
Mercy Lewes pointed to her & fell into a little fit. Ann Putman threw
her Glove in a fit at her The examinant laught.

What do you laugh at it?

Well I may at such folly.

Is this folly? The hurt of these persons.

I never hurt man woman or child.

Mercy Lewes cryed out she hath hurt me a great many times, & pulls
me down

Then Martin laught againe

Mary Walcot saith this woman hath hurt me a great many times.

Sus: Sheldon also accused her of afflicting her.

What do you say to this?

I have no hand in Witchcraft.

What did you do? Did not you give your consent?

No, never in my life.

What ails this people?

I do not know.

But w't do you think?

I do not desire to spend my judgm't upon it.

Do not you think they are Bewitcht?

No. I do not think they are

Tell me your thoughts about them.

Why my thoughts are my own, when they are in, but when they are out they are anothers.

You said their Master -- who do you think is their Master?

If they be dealing in the black art, you may know as well as I.

Well what have you done towards this?

Nothing.

Why it is you, or your appearance.

I cannot help it.

That may be your Master.

I desire to lead my self according to the word of God.

Is this according to Gods word?

If I were such. a person I would tell you the truth.

How comes your appearance just now to hurt these.

How do I know?

Are not you willing to tell the Truth?

I cannot tell: He that appeared in sams shape a glorifyed saint can appear in any ones shape.

Do you beleive these do not say true?

They may lye for ought I know

May not you lye?

I dare not tell a lye if it would save my life.

Then you will speak the Truth.

I have spake nothing else, I would do them any good.

I do not think you have such affections for them, whom just now you insinuated had the Devill for their Master.

Eliz: Hubbard was afflicted & then the Marshal w'o was by her said she pincht her hand.

Severall of the afflicted cryed out they [saw] her upon the beam.

Pray God discover you, if you be guilty.

Amen Amen A false tongue will never make a guilty person.

You have been a long time coming to the Court to day, you can come fast enough in the night.said Mercy Lewes.

No, sweet heart, said the examinat, And then Mercy Lewes, & all, or many of the rest, were afflicted

John Indian fell into a violent fit, & said it was that woman, she bites, she bites, and then she was biting her lips

Have you not compassion for these afflicted?

No, I have none

Some cryed out there was the black man with her, & Goody Bibber who had not accused her before confirmed it:

Abig: William upon trial could not come near her -- Nor Goody Bibber. Nor Mary Walcot. John Indian cryed he would Kill her if he came near her, but he was flung down in his approach to her

What is the reason these cannot come near you?

I cannot tell. It may be the Devil bears me more malice than an other

Do not you see how God evidently discovers you?

No, not a bit for that.

All the congregation think so.

Let them think w't. they will.

What is the reason these cannot come near you?

I do not know but they can if they will, or else if you please, I will come to them.

What is the black man whispering to you?

There was none whispered to me

(Reverse) The Examination of Susannah Martin

(*Essex County Archives, Salem -- Witchcraft Vol. 1 Page 59*)

-553-

(Examination of Susannah Martin -- Second Version)

The Examination of Susannah Martin. 2. May. 1692

As soon as she came into the meeting-house many fell into fits

Hath this Woman hurt you?

Abig: Williams said it is Goody Martin, she hath hurt me often Others by fits were hindered from speaking.

Eliz: Hubbard said she had not hurt her. John Indian said he never saw her Mercy Lewes pointed at her & fell into a fit. Ann Putman threw her Glove in a fit at her

What do you laught at it?

Well I may at such folly.

Is this folly, to see these so hurt?

I never hurt man, woman or child.

Mercy Lewes cryed out, she hath hurt me a great many times &
plucks me down.

Then Martin laught againe

Mary Walcot said this woman hath hurt her a great many times

Susannah Sheldon also accused her of hurting her

What do you say to this?

I have no hand in Witchcraft.

What did you do? Did you consent these should be hurt?

No never in my life.

What ails these people?

I do not know.

But what do you think ails them?

I do not desire to spend my judgment upon it

Do you think they are Bewitcht?

No I do not think they are.

Well tell us your thoughts about them?

My thoughts are mine own when they are in, but when they are out
they are an others

You said their Master -- Who do you think is their Master?

If they be dealing in the black art, you may know as well as I.

What have you done towards the hurt of these?

I have done nothing

Why it is you, or your appearance

I cannot help it

That may be your Master that hurt them

I desire to lead my life according to the word of God

Is this according to the word of God?

If I were such a person I would tell you the Truth

How comes your appearance just now to hurt these?

How do I know?

Are you not willing to tell the Truth?

I cannot tell: He that appeared in sams::shape can appear in any ones shape.

Do you beleive these afflicted persons do not say true?

they may lye for ought I know.

May not you lye?

I dare not tell a lye if it would save my life

Then you will not speak the truth will you?

I have spoken nothing else. I would do them any good.

I do not think that you have such affections for these whom just now you insinuated had the Devil for their Master

The marshall said she pincht her hands & Eliz: Hubbard was immediately afflicted.

Severall of the afflicted cryed out they saw her upon the Beam.

Pray God discover you if you be guilty.

Amen, Amen. A false tongue will never make a guilty person.

You have been a long time coming to day said Mercy Lewes, you can come fast enough in the night

No sweet heart --

And then said Mercy, & all the afflicted beside almost were afflicted

John Indian fell into a fit, & cryed it was that woman, she bites, she bites. And then said Martin was biting her lips.

Have not you compassion on these afflicted --

No I have none

They cryed out there was the black man along with her, & Goody Bibber confirmed it

Abig: Williams went towards her, but could not come near her. nor Goody Bibber tho she had not accused her before: also Mary Walcot could not come near her. John Indian said he would kill her, if he came near her, but he fell down before he could touch her

What is the reason these cannot come near you?

I cannot tell it may be the Devil bears me more malice than an other.

Do you not see God evidently discovering you?

No, not a bit for that.

All the congregation besides think so.

-555-

Let them think what they will.

What is the reason these cannot come to you?

I do not know but they can if they will or else if you please

I will come to them.

What was that the black man whisperd to you?

There was none whispered to me.

(*Essex County Archives, Salem -- Witchcraft Vol. 1 Page 59*)

(Indictment v. Susannah Martin, No. 1)

Anno Regis et Reginae Willm et Mariae . nunc Angliae &c Quarto Essex ss.

The Jurors for our Sovereigne Lord & Lady the King and Queen prsents That Susanna Martin of Amsbury in the County of Essex widdow the Second Day of may in the forth year of the Reigne of our Sovereigne Lord and Lady William and Mary by the Grace of God of England Scottland: France and Ireland King and Queen: Defenders of the faith &. divers other Dayes and Times as well before as after certaine Detestable arts, called witchcrafts & Sorceries wickedly and feloniously hath used Practised & Exercised at and within the

Townership of Salem in the County of Essex aforesaid in upon and ag't one Mary Wallcott of Salem Village Single woman, by which Said wicked arts the s'd. Mary walcott the Second day of May in the forth year afores'd: and at Divers other Dayes & times as well before as after was, and is Tortored Afflicted Pined wasted and Tormented as also for Sundry other acts of witchcraft by Said Susanah Martin committed and Done before and Since that time ag't the Peace of our Sovereigne Lord & Lady william and Mary King and Queen of England theire Crowne and Dignity and ag't: the forme of the Statute in that case made & Provided.

Sarah Vibber Sworn

Mary Wolcutt Sworn

[M]r Sam'll Parris. Sworn

Elizabeth Hubbard

Marcy Lewis

(Reverse) Bil a Vera

(*Essex County Archives, Salem -- Witchcraft Vol. 1 Page 58*)

-556-

(Indictment v. Susannah Martin, No. 2.)

Anno Regis et Reginae Willm et Mariae : nunc Angliae &c Quarto Essex ss

The Jurors for our Sovereigne Lord & Lady the King and Queen: prsents That Susanah Martin of Amsbury in the County of Essex widdow the Second day of may in the forth Year of the Reigne of our Sovereigne Lord & Lady william and Mary by the Grace of God of England Scottland France & Ireland King and Queen Defenders of the faith &c: and divers other Dayes & times as well before as after. certaine Detestable Arts called witchcrafts and Sorceries wickedly: and felloniously hath used Practised & Exercised at and within the Towneship of Salem in the County of Essex aforesd: in and upon and ag't: one Marcy Lewis: of Salem Villiage Singlewoman by which said wicked arts the: Said Marcy Lewis. the said second day of may in the forth year aforesaid and at Divers other dayes and times as well before as after was and is Tortured: Afflicted Pined wasted and Torminted as also for Sundrey other acts of witchcraft by said Suzanah Martin Committed and done before and since that time ag't the Peace of our Sovereigne Lord. and Lady William & Mary King & Queen of

England there Crowne and Dignity. and ag't the forme of the Statute in that case made and Provided.

Witnesses

Marcy Lewis

Mr. Samll: Parris Sworn

Anne Puttman Sworn

Sarah Biber Sworne

Elizabeth Hubbard

Mary Wallcott Sworne in Court June 2d. 92.

(Reverse) S. Martin No. 2 In[d]ictm't

(*Essex County Archives, Salem -- Witchcraft Vol. 1 Page 58*)

**The Wonders of the Invisible World, by Cotton Mather, 1693 ;
from Narratives of the Witchcraft Cases, 1648-1706**

III. The Tryal of Susanna Martin,130 At the Court of Oyer and Terminer, Held by Adjournment at Salem, June 29, 1692.

I. Susanna Martin, pleading Not Guilty to the Indictment of Witchcraft brought in against her, there were produced the evidences of many persons very sensibly and grievously Bewitched; who all complaned of the prisoner at the Bar, as the person whom they Believed the cause of their Miseries. And now, as well as in the other Trials, there was an extraordinary endeavour by Witchcrafts, with Cruel and Frequent Fits, to hinder the poor sufferers from giving in their complaints; which the Court was forced with much patience to obtain, by much waiting and watching for it.

II. There was now also an Account given, of what passed at her first examination before the Magistrates. The cast of her eye then striking the Afflicted People to the ground, whether they saw that Cast or no; there were these among other passages between the Magistrates and the Examinate.

(See transcripts of examination on prior pages)

III. The Court accounted themselves Alarum'd by these things, to Enquire further into the Conversation of the Prisoner; and see what there might occur, to render these Accusations further credible. Whereupon, John Allen, of Salisbury, testify'd, That he refusing, because of the weakness of his Oxen, to Cart some Staves, at the request of this Martin, she was displeased at it; and said, "It had been as good that he had; for his Oxen should never do him much more Service." Whereupon this Deponent said, "Dost thou threaten me, thou old Witch? I'l throw thee into the Brook": Which to avoid, she flew over the Bridge, and escaped. But, as he was going home, one of his Oxen Tired, so that he was forced to Unyoke him, that he might get him home. He then put his Oxen, with many more, upon Salisbury Beach, where Cattle did use to get Flesh. In a few days, all the Oxen upon the Beach were found by their Tracks, to have run unto the mouth of

----

-231-
Merrimack-River, and not returned; but the next day they were found come ashore upon Plum-Island. They that sought them used all imaginable gentleness, but they would still run away with a violence that seemed wholly Diabolical, till they came near the mouth of Merrimack-River; when they ran right into the Sea, swimming as far as they could be seen. One of them then swam back again, with a swiftness amazing to the Beholders, who stood ready to receive him, and help up his Tired Carcass: But the Beast ran furiously up into the Island, and from thence, through the Marishes, up into Newbury Town,

and so up into the Woods; and there after a while found near Amesbury. So that, of Fourteen good Oxen, there was only this saved: the rest were all cast up, some in one place, and some in another, Drowned.

IV. John Atkinson Testify'd, That he Exchanged a Cow with a Son of Susanna Martins, whereat she muttered, and was unwilling he should have it. Going to Receive this Cow, tho' he Hamstring'd her, and Halter'd her, she of a Tame Creature grew so mad, that they could scarce get her along. She broke all the Ropes that were fastned unto her, and though she were Ty'd fast unto a Tree, yet she made her Escape, and gave them such further Trouble, as they could ascribe to no cause but Witchcraft.

V. Bernard Peache testify'd, That being in Bed on a Lords-day Night, he heard a scrabbling at the Window, whereat he then saw Susanna Martin come in, and jump down upon the Floor. She took hold of this Deponents Feet, and drawing his Body up into an Heap, she lay upon him near Two Hours; in all which time he could neither speak nor stirr. At length, when he could begin to move, he laid hold on her Hand, and pulling it up to his mouth, he bit three of her Fingers, as he judged, unto the Bone. Whereupon she went from the Chamber, down the Stairs, out at the Door. This Deponent there-upon called unto the people of the House, to advise them of what passed; and he himself did follow her. The people saw her not; but there being a Bucket at the Left-hand of the Door, there was a drop of Blood found on it; and several more drops of Blood upon the Snow newly fallen abroad. There was likewise the print of her two Feet just without the Threshold; but no more sign of any Footing further off.

-232-

At another time this Deponent was desired by the Prisoner, to come unto an Husking of Corn, at her House; and she said, If he did not come, it were better that he did! He went not; but the Night following, Susanna Martin, as he judged, and another came towards him. One of them said, "Here he is!" but he having a Quarter-staff, made a Blow at them. The Roof of the Barn broke his Blow; but following them to the Window, he made another Blow at them, and struck them down; yet they got up, and got out, and he saw no more of them.

About this time, there was a Rumour about the Town, that Martin had a Broken Head; but the Deponent could say nothing to that.

The said Peache also testify'd the Bewitching of Cattle to Death, upon Martin's Discontents.

VI. Robert Downer testifyed, That this Prisoner being some years ago prosecuted at Court for a Witch,131 he then said unto her, He believed she was a Witch. Whereat she being dissatisfied, said, That some Shee-Devil would Shortly fetch him away! Which words were heard by others, as well as himself. The Night following, as he lay in his Bed, there came in at the Window the likeness of a Cat, which Flew upon him, took fast hold of his Throat, lay on him a considerable while, and almost killed him. At length he remembred what Susanna Martin had threatned the Day before; and with much striving he cryed out, "Avoid, thou Shee-Devil! In the Name of God the Father, the Son, and the Holy Ghost, Avoid!" Whereupon it left him, leap'd on the Floor, and Flew out at the Window.

And there also came in several Testimonies, that before ever Downer spoke a word of this Accident, Susanna Martin and her Family had related, How this Downer had been Handled!

VII. John Kembal testifyed, that Susanna Martin, upon a Causeless Disgust, had threatned him, about a certain Cow of his, That she should never do him any more Good: and it

----

came to pass accordingly. For soon after the Cow was found stark Dead on the dry Ground, without any Distemper to be discerned upon her. Upon which he was followed with a strange Death upon more of his Cattle, whereof he lost in One Spring to the value of Thirty Pounds. But the said John Kembal had a further Testimony to give in against the Prisoner which was truly admirable.

Being desirous to furnish himself with a Dog, he applied himself to buy one of this Martin, who had a Bitch with Whelps in her House. But she not letting him have his Choice, he said, he would supply himself then at one Blezdels. Having mark'd a puppy which he lik'd at Blezdels, he met George Martin, the Husband of the prisoner, going by, who asked him, Whether he would not have one of his Wives Puppies? and he answered, No. The same Day, one Edmund Eliot, being at Martins House, heard George Martin relate, where this Kembal had been, and what he had said. Whereupon Susanna Martin replyed, "If I live, I'll give him Puppies enough!" Within a few Dayes after, this Kembal coming out of the Woods, there arose a little Black Cloud in the N.W. and Kembal immediately felt a Force upon him, which made him not able to avoid running upon the stumps of Trees, that were before him, albeit he had a broad, plain Cart way, before him; but tho' he had his Ax also on his Shoulder to endanger him in his Falls, he could not forbear going out of his way to tumble over them. When he came below the Meeting-House, there appeared unto him a little thing like a Puppy, of a Darkish Colour; and it shot backwards and forwards between his Legs. He had the Courage to use all possible Endeavours of Cutting it with his Ax; but he could not Hit it; the Puppy gave a jump from him, and went, as to him it seem'd, into the Ground. Going a little further, there appeared unto him a Black Puppy, somewhat bigger than the first, but as Black as a Cole. Its motions were quicker than those of his Ax; it Flew at his Belly, and away; then at his Throat; so, over his Shoulder one way, and then over his Shoulder another way. His heart now began to fail him, and he thought the Dog would have Tore his Throat out. But he recovered himself, and called upon God in his Distress; and Naming the Name of Jesus Christ, it Vanished away at once. The Deponent Spoke

---

-234-

not one Word of these Accidents, for fear of affrighting his wife. But the next Morning, Edmond Eliot going into Martins House, this woman asked him where Kembal was? He Replyed, At home, a bed, for ought he knew. She returned, "They say, he was frighted last Night." Eliot asked, "With what?" She answered, "With Puppies." Eliot asked, Where she heard of it, for he had heard nothing of it? She rejoined, "About the Town." Altho' Kembal had mentioned the Matter to no Creature Living.

VIII. William Brown testify'd, that Heaven having blessed him with a most Pious and prudent wife, this wife of his one day mett with Susanna Martin; but when she approch'd just unto her, Martin vanished out of sight, and left her extremely affrighted. After which time, the said Martin often appear'd unto her, giving her no little trouble; and when she did come, she was visited with Birds that sorely peck't and Prick'd her; and sometimes a Bunch, like a pullets egg, would Rise in her throat, ready to Choak her, till she cry'd out, "Witch, you shan't choak me!" While this good Woman was in this Extremity, the Church appointed a Day of Prayer, on her behalf; whereupon her Trouble ceas'd; she saw not Martin as formerly; and the Church, instead of their Fast, gave Thanks for her Deliverance. But a considerable while after, she being Summoned to give in some Evidence at the Court, against this Martin, quickly thereupon this Martin came behind her, while she was milking her Cow, and said unto her, "For thy defaming me at Court, I'l make thee the miserablest Creature in the World." Soon after which, she fell into a strange kind of Distemper, and became horribly Frantick, and uncapable of any Reasonable Action; the Physicians declaring, that her Distemper was preternatural, and that some Devil had certainly Bewitched her; and in that Condition she now remained.

IX. Sarah Atkinson testify'd, That Susanna Martin came from Amesbury to their House at Newbury, in an extraordinary Season, when it was not fit for any one to Travel. She came (as she said unto Atkinson) all that long way on Foot. She brag'd and show'd how dry she was; nor could it be perceived that so much as the Soles of her Shoes were wet. Atkinson was amazed at it; and professed, that she should her self have

---

-235-

been wet up to the knees, if she had then came so far; but Martin reply'd, She scorn'd to be Drabbled! It was noted, that this Testimony upon her Trial cast her in a very singular Confusion.

X. John Pressy testify'd, That being one Evening very unaccountably Bewildred, near a field of Martins, and several times, as one under an Enchantment, returning to the place he had left, at length he saw a marvellous Light, about the Bigness of an Half-Bushel, near two Rod out of the way. He went, and struck at it with a Stick, and laid it on with all his might. He gave it near forty blows; and felt it a palpable substance. But going from it, his Heels were struck up, and he was laid with his Back on the Ground, Sliding, as he thought, into a Pit; from whence he recover'd, by taking hold on the Bush; altho' afterwards he could find no such Pit in the place. Having, after his Recovery, gone five or six Rod, he saw Susanna Martin standing on his Left-hand, as the Light had done before; but they changed no words with one another. He could scarce find his House in his Return; but at length he got home, extreamly affrighted. The next day, it was upon Enquiry understood, that Martin was in a miserable condition by pains and hurts that were upon her.

It was further testify'd by this Deponent, That after he had given in some Evidence against Susanna Martin, many years ago, she gave him foul words about it; and said, He should never prosper more; particularly, That he should never have more than two Cows; that tho' he were never so likely to have more, yet he should never have them. And that from that very Day to this, namely for Twenty Years together, he could never exceed that Number; but some strange thing or other still prevented his having of any more.

XI. Jervis Ring testifyed, that about seven years ago, he was oftentimes and grievously Oppressed in the Night, but saw not who Troubled him, until at last he, Lying perfectly Awake, plainly saw Susanna Martin approach him. She came to him, and forceably Bit him by the Finger; so that the Print of the Bite is now so long after to be seen upon him.

XII. But besides all of these Evidences, there was a most wonderful Account of one Joseph Ring, produced on this Occasion.

-236-

This man has been strangely carried about by Dæmons, from one Witch-Meeting to another, for near two years together; and for one Quarter of this Time, they have made him and kept him Dumb, tho' he is now again able to speak. There was one T. H.132 who having, as tis judged, a Design of engaging this Joseph Ring in a Snare of Devillism, contrived a wile, to bring this Ring two Shillings in Debt unto him.

Afterwards, this poor man would be visited with unknown shapes, and this T. H. sometimes among them; which would force him away with them, unto unknown Places, where he saw meetings, Feastings, Dancings; and after his Return, wherein they hurried him along thro' the Air, he gave Demonstrations to the Neighbours, that he had indeed been so transported. When he was brought unto these Hellish meetings, one of the First things they still133 did unto him, was to give him a knock on the Back, whereupon he was ever as if Bound with Chains, uncapable of Stirring out of the place, till they should Release him. He related, that there often came to him a man, who presented him a Book, whereto he would have him set his Hand; promising to him, that he should then have even what he would; and presenting him with all the Delectable Things, persons, and places, that he could imagine. But he refusing to subscribe, the business would end with dreadful Shapes, Noises and Screeches, which almost scared him out of his witts. Once with the Book, there was a Pen offered him, and an Inkhorn with Liquor in it, that seemed like Blood: but he never toucht it.

This man did now affirm, that he saw the Prisoner at several of those Hellish Randezvouzes.

Note, This Woman was one of the most Impudent, Scurrilous, wicked creatures in the world; and she did now throughout her whole Trial discover herself to be such an one. Yet when she was asked, what she had to say for her self? her Cheef Plea was, That she had Led a most virtuous and Holy Life!

[130] Of Amesbury. She too had been long accused. For the trial records see *Records of Salem Witchcraft*, I. 193-233. She was executed on July 19.

[131] In 1669. She was then bound over to the Superior Court, but was discharged without trial. (Hutchinson, *History of Massachusetts*, II., ch. I., as published from an earlier draft, with notes by W. F. Poole, in *N. E. Hist. and Gen. Register*, XXIV.)

[132] Thomas Hardy, of Great Island, near Portsmouth. See *Records*, I. 216.

[133] Always.

-237-

BIBLIOGRAPHY

Armstrong, Karen (1993), *A History of God*, Alfred A. Knopf, Inc., New York

Bohm, David (1980), *Wholeness and the Implicate Order*, Rutledge & Kegan, London

Butler, W. E. (1990), *Lords of Light*, Destiny books, Rochester, Vermont

Campbell, Joseph with Bill Moyers (1988), *The Power of Myth*, Doubleday, New York

Campbell, Joseph (1971), *The Portable Jung*, Viking Press, New York

Chopra, Deepak (1993), *Ageless Body, Timeless Mind*, Harmony Books, Crown, New York

Conner, Sibella (1994), "The Dark Side of Near Death," *Richmond Times-Dispatch*, September 4, 1994, pages G1 and G4.

Dass, Ram (1978), *Journey of Awakening*, Bantam New Age Books, New York

Eadie, Betty J. (1992), *Embraced By The Light*, Gold Leaf Press, Placerville, California

Goldberg, Philip (1983), *The Intuitive Edge*, Jeremy P. Tarcher, Inc., Los Angeles

Gould, Stephen Jay (1980), *The Panda's Thumb*, W. W. Norton & Company, New York

Herrigel, Eugen (1953), *Zen in the Art of Archery*, Panteon Books, Random House, New York

Hill, Napoleon (1960), *Think and Grow Rich*, Fawcett Crest, New York

Howe, Quincy, Jr. (1974), *Reincarnation for the Christian*, The Westminster Press, Philadelphia

Karpinski, Gloria D. (1990), *Where Two Worlds Touch*, Ballantine, New York

Keyes, Ken Jr. (1975), *Handbook to Higher Consciousness,* Fifth Edition, Love Line Books, Coos Bay, Oregon

Kubler-Ross, Elisabeth (1991), *On Life After Death,* Celestial Arts, Berkeley, California

Ireland-Frey, Louise (1999), *Freeing the Captives,* Hampton Roads, Charlottesville, VA

Modi, Shakuntala, M.D., (1998), *Remarkable Healings,* Hampton Roads, Charlottesville, VA

Monroe, Robert A. (1985), *Far Journeys,* Souvenir Press, Ltd., London

Moody, Raymond A., M. D., (1988), *The Light Beyond,* Bantam, New York

Morse, Melvin, M.D. (with Paul Perry), (1990), *Closer to the Light,* Ballantine Books, New York

Newton, Michael. Ph.D., (1994), *Journey of Souls,*Llewellyn, St. Paul, Minnesota

Parker, DeWitt H. (1928), *Schopenhauer Selections,* Charles Scribners Sons, New York

Peck, M. Scott (1978), *The Road Less Traveled,* Simon and Schuster, New York

Peck, M. Scott (1993), *Further Along The Road Less Traveled,* Simon and Schuster, New York

Peck, M. Scott (1998), *People of the Lie,* 2nd Edition, Touchstone, New York

Peat, F. David (1991), *The Philosopher's Stone,* Bantam, New York

Sheehy, Gail (1976), *Passages: Predictable Crises of Adult Life,* Dutton, New York

Sheldrake, Rupert (1991), *The Rebirth of Nature, The Greening of Science and God,* Bantam, New York

Smith, Huston (1986), *The Religions of Man*, HarperCollins, New York

Smith, E. Lester, (1975), *Intelligence Came First*, Theosophical Publishing House, Wheaton, Illinois.

Spindrift Papers, *Exploring Prayer and Healing Through the Experimental Test*, Volume I 1975-1993, Spindrift, Inc., Ft. Lauderdale, Florida

Stevens, Jose and Lena S. Stevens (1988), *Secrets of Shamanism*, Avon Books, New York

Stevenson, Ian (1997), *Where Reincarnation and Biology Intersect*, Praeger Publishing.

Stevenson, Ian (1974), *Twenty Cases Suggestive of Reincarnation*, University Press of Virginia, Charlottesville

Troward, Thomas, and Allen, James (2002), *How to Master Life: Two Ground-Breaking Works by Past Masters*, "The Edinburgh Lectures on Mental Science" and "As a Man Thinketh," Oaklea Press, Richmond.

Wade, Nicholas (1995), "Double Helixes, Chickens and Eggs," *New York Times Magazine*, January 29, 1995

Watts, Alan (1966), *The Book*, Vintage Books, Random House, New York

Weiss, Brian L., M.D. (1988), *Many Lives, Many Masters*, Simon & Schuster, New York

Whitton, Joel L., M.D., Ph.D., (1986), *Life Between Life*, Warner Books, New York

Zukav, Gary (1979), *The Dancing Wu Li Masters*, Bantam, New York

INDEX

Stephen Hawley Martin is the only two-time winner of the *Writer's Digest* Book Award for Fiction, and he has also won the top prize for fiction from *Independent Publisher.* Before becoming a full-time writer of books, he was a principal of one of America's leading ad firms, The Martin Agency. A native of Richmond, he lives in central Virginia with his wife and three school-age children.